T0305146

Entrepreneurship and the Creation of Small Firms

Empirical Studies of New Ventures

Edited by

Carin Holmquist

Professor and holder of Family Stefan Persson Chair in Entrepreneurship, Stockholm School of Economics, Sweden

Johan Wiklund

Kauffman eProfessor and Associate Professor of Entrepreneurship, Syracuse University, USA and Professor, Jönköping International Business School, Sweden

Edward Elgar
Cheltenham, UK • Northampton, MA, USA

Published by
Edward Elgar Publishing Limited
The Lypiatts
15 Lansdown Road
Cheltenham
Glos GL50 2JA
UK

Edward Elgar Publishing, Inc.
William Pratt House
9 Dewey Court
Northampton
Massachusetts 01060
USA

A catalogue record for this book
is available from the British Library

Library of Congress Control Number: 2009936745

ISBN 978 1 84844 041 8

Printed and bound by MPG Books Group, UK

Contents

Contributors

Carin Holmquist holds the Family Stefan Persson Chair in Entrepreneurship and Business Creation at the Stockholm School of Economics. Carin received her doctorate and MBA from Umeå University (Sweden) where she previously worked as associate professor and professor in entrepreneurship. Her research focuses on women's entrepreneurship, international entrepreneurship and organization of entrepreneurship.

Johan Wiklund is Kauffman eProfessor at Whitman School of Management, Syracuse University, USA; Professor of Entrepreneurship at Jönköping International Business School, Sweden; and Professor Two at Nordland Research Institute, Norway. His research interests include: entrepreneurial failure; small business growth; the decision to be self-employed; new venture creation; and corporate entrepreneurship. He is considered a leading authority in entrepreneurship research and has conducted research for several governments and the OECD. Wiklund is Editorial Board member of *Journal of Management Studies, Strategic Entrepreneurship Journal, Journal of Business Venturing, Family Business Review, International Entrepreneurship and Management Journal* and *Entrepreneurship Theory and Practice* and has published in the *Strategic Management Journal, Journal of Management, Journal of Management Studies, Journal of Business Venturing, Entrepreneurship Theory and Practice*, among other journals.

Roger Svensson is a senior research fellow at The Research Institute of Industrial Economics (IFN) in Stockholm and Associate Professor in Economics at Mälardalen University. Roger received his Ph.D. in economics from Uppsala University. His fields of research cover patents and intellectual property rights, technology transfer and innovations, entrepreneurship, service sectors and procurement. His research focuses mainly on empirical economics.

Karl Wennberg is a PhD candidate at the Center for Entrepreneurship, Stockholm School of Economics. His research deals with entrepreneurship and decision making under uncertainty. Specifically, his dissertation focuses on how behavioral decision making affect processes of entrepreneurial exit.

Sari Roininen is a researcher at Luleå University of Technology (Sweden), where she also received her doctorate in business administration and economics within the research field of eentrepreneurship. Her research is in the field of new venture creation processes; she investigates academic spin-offs and generic ventures in order to explain the complexity of different establishment processes. The effects of networking activities on new and young ventures' entrepreneurial behavior and firm performance has been a recent research area of interest.

Håkan Ylinenpää is professor (chair) in Entrepreneurship and head of division of Entrepreneurship and Industrial organization at Luleå University of Technology, Sweden. Research interest is focused on entrepreneurial innovation activities and strategies, especially in small and medium-sized enterprises, innovation system research, and knowledge management, and preferably involves research in close collaboration with practise and/or policy-makers in regional, national or international programs and projects. His scientific production involves numerous scientific journal articles, books/book chapters, and conference papers.

Frédéric Delmar is a professor in entrepreneurship at EMLYON Business School. He is also affiliated to the Research Institute of Industrial Economics, Stockholm Sweden. Frédéric received his PhD from Stockholm School of Economics. His main research interest lies in the early development of new ventures as well as organizational growth. He finds the behavioral aspects of entrepreneurship to be particularly interesting. His work has been published in a number of journals like *Management Science, Strategic Management Journal, Strategic Organization, Journal of Business Venturing, Entrepreneurship Theory and Practice*, and books.

Karin Hellerstedt is a PhD student at Jönköping International Business School in Sweden. Her research interest is new venture teams and knowledge intensive entrepreneurship. She has extensive experience in working with micro-data and match employer employee datasets. In her thesis she relies on such data and constructs team level variables, which enables her to study the structure and development of new venture teams. She also has several years experience of teaching entrepreneurship courses at bachelor and master levels.

Christian Czernich is co-founder and managing partner of carpima Invest, an M&A advisory and investment firm in Vienna, Austria. Before founding carpima Invest, he spent several years in investment banking and private equity, among others in Unicredit Group. Christian has conducted research on the determinants of survival of entrepreneurial projects in Swedish multinationals, investment decisions of venture capital firms in Silicon Valley, as well as on the emergence of new business ideas during the dot-com boom and bust. His research interest focus on the emergence and differential survival of new (business) ideas, corporate entrepreneurship, and venture capital and private equity firms. Christian holds a PhD from the Stockholm School of Economics and a MSc. from the University of Innsbruck, Austria.

Ivo Zander is the Anders Wall Professor of Entrepreneurship at Uppsala University. Before moving into the area of entrepreneurship, he conducted research on regional agglomerations and the internationalization of research and development in multinational corporations. His current research interests include corporate entrepreneurship, strategies for entrepreneurial firms, art entrepreneurship, and the entrepreneurial dynamics of accelerated internationalization. He teaches entrepreneurship and various aspects of growing and managing the international firm, including internationalization and innovation and entrepreneurship in the established multinational corporation.

Anders Landberg is a researcher at the Center for Entrepreneurship and Business Creation, Stockholm School of Economics. His research focuses on entrepreneurs' perceptions of the start-up process as well as their coping activities to realize their venture ideas. Anders specifically investigates entrepreneurs' perceptions of resistance to their venture creation activities and how their energetic resources influence both perceptions and coping under stress.

Svante Andersson is Professor in Business Administration at the School of Business and Engineering, Halmstad University, Sweden. Andersson received his doctorate from Linköping University (Sweden). He has been a visiting researcher at AGSM, University of New South Wales, Sydney, Australia and The University of the Sunshine Coast, Australia. His research is in the field of international entrepreneurship and firms' growth. He investigates how different factors affect firms' internationalization and growth. Especially, has the influence of managers and entrepreneurs been focused upon.

Preface

Is European research in the area of entrepreneurship lagging behind the US? After all, bibliometric studies, citations and leading awards in this field of research seem to be dominated by scholars from the US. According to the editors of *Entrepreneurship and the Creation of Small Firms: Empirical Studies of New Ventures* this view is not only too simplistic but also inadequate. Rather, the explanation can be attributed differences in research traditions, both when it comes to publications, the way work is organized and language used. Using Sweden as their case, this book provides insights to these differences and stress that a number of important research contributions in this field do in fact emanate from outside the US. In particular, Swedish research was more oriented towards rigorous empirical, long-term and policy-oriented research. That confronts with research conducted in the US, focusing on shorter articles published in leading international scientific journals. Still, Swedish and European research has also rapidly adapted the US norm. At centre stage in this book are seven contributions by 11 Swedish researchers, spanning advanced methodologies that range from econometric analyses of extensive data sets to case studies and more qualitative approaches. The variety in research issues addressed is similarly impressive, including performance of new ventures, human capital and explanation to internationalization, to mention a few. Hence, this book provides solid evidence that a highly competitive and policy-relevant research tradition also exist in Europe.

Carin Holmquist holds the Family Stefan Persson Chair in Entrepreneurship and Business Creation at the Stockholm School of Economics, while Johan Wiklund is Kauffman eProfessor at Whitman School of Management, Syracuse University. This book is a product of FSF's (Foundation for Small Business Research) research program The Dynamics of Entrepreneurship which the editors have chaired together.

1. Introduction

Carin Holmquist and Johan Wiklund

The reader of back issues of international entrepreneurship journals could easily get the impression that North America totally dominated the field early on and that research from the rest of the world is gradually catching up with an increased number of publications now originating from other countries. To some extent, this image is correct. Birch's study, from the early 1980s, of how small firms generated the majority of new jobs in the US paired with the rise of technology-based new firms such as Microsoft and Apple during the same time, indeed spurred entrepreneurship research in North America. It also led to an insight that the world was transitioning from a big business to an entrepreneurship economy. In official documents this change was acknowledged much later by the EU in the Lisbon declaration of the late 1990s.

Such an image is however too simplistic and uni-dimensional. Entrepreneurship research has a longstanding tradition also outside of the US. Sweden was a very early entrant into entrepreneurship. Dick Ramström introduced small business research at Umeå University in the beginning of the 1970s, inspired by early work done in the UK. This soon became the dominant focus of management research at this institution. Many of the current entrepreneurship professors in Sweden have their research training and wrote their dissertations here. The vast majority of this research was written in Swedish, which of course severely limited readership. Publication in domestic languages has remained a limitation to research dissemination for many European countries. It is only in recent years that English language publication in international journals has become the norm for disseminating results. A drawback is of course that despite large amounts of high quality research, much of it remains unknown to a wider audience.

As Swedish researchers increasingly entered the international research scene during the 1990s, they did so from a strong position, which led to many achievements. Since then, Swedish academics have been editors for leading journals (*Entrepreneurship and Regional Development*, *Entrepreneurship Theory and Practice*, *Small Business Economics*), have hosted major conferences (ICSB in 1996, Babson in 2001), have won multiple best paper and best dissertation awards at the Babson and Academy of Management conferences, have written some of the best cited works in all the major journals, and the Swede Bengt Johannisson is one of the only two non-English speaking recipients of the FSF-Nutek International Award for Entrepreneurship and Small Business Research. Collectively, these accomplishments show that Swedish entrepreneurship research has a high standing and substantial impact on the international scene. This is further emphasized by the move of Swedish entrepreneurship academics to universities in foreign countries.

The quality of Swedish data is well known and respected in the international entrepreneurship research community. There are however equally important traits that make Swedish entrepreneurship research unique. One such trait is the close interaction between researchers and practical research, from the policy level to the level of individual entrepreneurs. This tradition of problem-driven research, common also in other social sciences in Sweden, has led to real changes in the empirical context based on research. Another unique trait is that different, even conflicting, scientific positions are not only accepted, but acknowledged. Traditionally entrepreneurship researchers in Sweden have debated, communicated and even cooperated crossing barriers posed by different scientific approaches. We will return to these issues in the concluding chapter.

This is the setting for this book on start-up and growth, showcasing Swedish contemporary research on the subject. This book is one of the outcomes of a program that we lead within FSF and we gratefully acknowledge the support of FSF and the help of members of the FSF Scientific Forum, some as authors and some as reviewers (each chapter was reviewed by two persons). In this introduction we present the context of Swedish entrepreneurship research as a general background to the remainder of the chapters.

The Swedish Entrepreneurship Context

As noted above, Swedish entrepreneurship research started in the 1970s with a focus on small business management issues. This empirical focus is reflective of the economic situation of Sweden at that time. Starting in the 1870s, Sweden experienced a century of outstanding economic growth, transcending from one of the poorest countries in Europe to the most prosperous country in the world. Swedish companies were early entrants into the international and global scenes. With increasing globalization, Swedish companies became global conglomerates successively moving sales, production, R&D and management (in that order) abroad. The Swedish economy was, and still is, characterized by a small number of very large, globally leading companies that have been essential in the country's wealth creation. There are a few mid-sized companies and a large number of small firms. The research that started on small business could be seen a complement to the extensive research that was already carried out with a focus on the large multinationals, the Uppsala School being one famous example.

As economic growth slowed down, it became clear that there were structural problems in the Swedish economy. Relevant to entrepreneurship research, it was evident that the rate of renewal of the economy was low. There were relatively few start-ups of new firms and the vast majority of the multinationals were founded over 100 years ago. The large public sector has also been depicted as a reason for the sluggish transformation of the economy and the few start-ups in Sweden. As the low rate of renewal has been perceived as a problem, research on start-ups and corporate entrepreneurship has come to complement the former strong focus on small business management.

Globalization and Mainstreaming of Swedish Entrepreneurship Research

Not only has there been a change in focus of Swedish entrepreneurship research, but also it is driven by real changes in the Swedish economy. Just as global societal changes have affected the economy and patterns of entrepreneurial processes, these changes have had direct effects on the nature of Swedish entrepreneurship research. This internationalization is facilitated by the rapid changes in information and communication technology and by the increased mobility of academics. Research is today global and mainstream research in virtually any field is conducted in an environment where international publication is the norm. This has led to a context where publications in top-ranked journals and citation impact the most important markers of good research. It has resulted in a change in dissemination of research, from books and reports to the shorter article format, each article often confined to discussing one or two issues from larger research programs. As a consequence, the number of articles being published and the number of journals show an almost exponential increase.

Standardization in terms of language is also evident. Few citations refer to work not published in English – language choice has become a marker for quality in research. Bibliographic research (Danell 2001) has shown that the way internationalization of research is accomplished has also led to a strong Anglo-American dominance in publishing, citation etc. Sometimes to a degree near US (and UK) 'colonization' of the rest of the world, i.e. researchers from other countries are adapting to and following the norms of the American research context instead of forming specific, say Swedish or European norms. The citation and publications patterns clearly indicate an extremely strong US domination – this is also evident in the fact that the annual meetings of the US Academy of Management have become a dominant arena for the global research community in the wide field of management. Notably however, entrepreneurship research has not reached the state of being a 'global village' where research from different countries and regions is fully integrated. Citation analyses show that there is regional clustering in terms of research topics and individuals involved in the research (Schildt, Zahra & Sillanpää 2006, Reader & Watkins 2006).

There are however, also very strong positive aspects of this globalization of research. First, it encourages and makes communication of research possible – the use of a common language and common forms, such as articles, facilitates discussion. Second, it provides critical mass in specialized research areas. For entrepreneurship, the number of researchers with a specific specialization in one country is often too small to provide a good research environment. Third, internationalization stresses the necessity of sound and good research practices through competition for publication and citations. Fourth, it creates an arena where the different research field can build legitimacy for themselves.

The main problem with this development is the relative one-sidedness of influence where other traditions than the mainstream 'speak quietly' and tend to wither away. There are fewer European outlets, journals and conferences, and we do not see much of cross-fertilization between research traditions. For instance citations to European journals are less common among US researchers (Danell 2001). There is a bias in it that empirical data that is not US or international tend to become marginalized (Holmquist & Sundin 1997). Most importantly, the stream of ideas, publications etc are mainly one-way, i.e. the US research is leading and the rest of the world is following – replicating and/or building on it. This is detrimental to the diversity of research where constant exchange and discussion is vital. Another sign of this US dominance is the cross-country mobility of researchers, where more researchers are going to North America compared to the number of researchers going to Europe. Researcher mobility, over borders, is increasing and many excellent researchers from Sweden choose to move abroad.

Another potential problem is that specific and unique empirical traits are marginalized and treated as having marginal scientific importance. The remedy for this tendency is attention to the empirical setting studied. Currently, there is a gap in entrepreneurship research, a gap created by the decreased focus on problem-driven research.[1] Zahra (2007) argues that all use

---

[1] There is growing awareness of this lack of problem-driven research, for instance the August 2007 issue of *Academy of Management Journal* (AMJ) has a forum on 'Research with Relevance to Practice'

of theory should be anchored in the object of our studies – the phenomenon of entrepreneurship – i.e. theories should consider the context it is applied to. Cross-cultural, comparative and global research programs are also helpful. GEM is an excellent example of this; their results show the multifaceted empirical context of entrepreneurship over the world.

The Current Nature of Swedish Entrepreneurship Research

So, where does the national history and current international mainstreaming leave contemporary Swedish entrepreneurship research? Some previous attempts have been made to characterize this research (e.g., Landström & Johannisson, 2001), but these authors failed to discern any clear patterns. Here, we wish to emphasize the characteristics that we feel have rendered Swedish entrepreneurship research a strong international position and that are also present among the chapters included in this book. We would argue that more than anything, Swedish research is characterized by very strong empirical work. There are several reasons for this. First, access to data is great in Sweden. Swedish authorities collect extensive data on firms and individuals and much of this information is public. Response rates to questionnaires are also notably high. In addition to generally providing for high data quality, this facilitates repeated surveying of samples because of low attrition as well as long questionnaires and inclusion of sensitive questions. Companies are also open to having researchers on site conducting case studies and collecting qualitative data. In sum, it is easy to access high quality data in Sweden regardless of the means used for collection them. Second, building on the Germanic tradition, doctoral dissertations are important independent research works. Swedish doctoral dissertations are published books and PhD students spend several years to complete their thesis. Often they devote more than five years to their PhDs, where most of that time is spent on the actual dissertation. This allows for extensive empirical work and reliance on more time consuming data collection methods than in many other countries. Third, Sweden does not have a tenure system. Therefore, after completing the dissertation, Swedish academics are not under intense pressure for publishing a stream of papers. There are of course drawbacks to the lack of time pressure during and after the dissertation, but one major advantage is that it allows for substantial empirical work and time consuming methods, such as panel studies and longitudinal real-time case studies.

Another defining characteristic is the interest in the relevance of research, in particular as it relates to policy implications.[2] Sweden spends substantial resources on public policy measures and many policy agencies are also major funders of entrepreneurship research. Thus, there is a close relationship between public policy and entrepreneurship research. The earliest studies were done in very close collaboration with entrepreneurs and communities. With the focus on publication, this collaborative research tradition has weakened but it is still strong. Swedish entrepreneurship researchers are heavily involved in formulating policies and forming opinion in Swedish society at all levels.

In their review of Swedish entrepreneurship research, Landström & Johannisson (2001) were unable to isolate any dominating theory or research question. This still holds today. It is not relevant to talk about any typical Swedish 'School'. On the contrary, Swedish research is integrated into the international mainstream. The contributions to this book show the breadth of approaches and research questions that form Swedish entrepreneurship research today.

In sum, we would argue that currently Sweden is characterized by: (a) continued attention to quality of empirical work and extensive empirical work, generally leading to high quality research; (b) a multitude of approaches to studying entrepreneurship, many of which are novel, and could be inspiring for others; (c) a great concern for the relevance and practical implications of the research; and (d) a global outlook, quickly integrating research from the US, Europe and elsewhere.

It is our firm belief that Swedish entrepreneurship research can contribute much more. It is highly relevant to showcase contemporary Swedish research on start-up and growth because of the unique position of our research community. We have excellent empirical data, we are well connected to the empirical setting we study leading to relevant research questions, we are global in our outlook and at the same time, part of the mainstream research that we build on our more classical European traditions.

Included Chapters

The broad brush that we have used to paint a picture of Swedish entrepreneurship research and its development, forms a backdrop to the chapters included in this book, to which we now turn. The authors and chapters included represent what we consider modern representatives of

---

[2] One could argue that there are so many new and small businesses that turning to policy makers and encouraging them to change policies has greater impact and is more relevant that developing advice and implications for entrepreneurs.

contemporary Swedish entrepreneurship scholars. While firmly rooted in the Swedish tradition, these authors are active and publish in the international research arena.

A central tenant of modern conceptualizations of entrepreneurship is that entrepreneurial opportunities can be exploited within many different organizational contexts (Shane & Venkataraman, 2000). For example, an employee who comes up with a new idea may decide to exploit that idea within his or her current employment or may instead choose to strike out and start his or her own business. The antecedents and consequences of organizational mode chosen for commercializing entrepreneurial opportunities are poorly understood. To a large extent, this is because virtually no research has been conducted on the topic, which is a major shortcoming in the field. In his chapter 'New start-up firms among Swedish patent holders', Roger Svensson examines this important issue. Sampling patents, Svensson surveyed the patent holders of all patents granted to individuals and firms with fewer than 1000 employees during a single year. In this chapter, he is able to establish the organizational context in which the invention originates as well as the context in which it is being exploited. Svensson finds a strong relationship between the organizational mode of the invention and that chosen for exploitation. He also finds that exploitation mode has implications for the financial performance of the invention. It appears that performance improves if the inventor is not responsible for the commercialization, suggesting that the skill sets needed for opportunity discovery are likely to differ from those valuable to opportunity exploitation. In sum, the chapter shows the importance of separating opportunity discovery from exploitation in entrepreneurship research.

In his chapter 'Entrepreneurial human capital: A real options perspective', Karl Wennberg starts with one of Svensson's conclusions – the notion that the skills needed for opportunity discovery are likely different from those needed for opportunity exploitation and then focuses on the latter. Wennberg isolates general human capital variables such as education and human capital variables specific to the task of running a business and hypothesizes how they influence entry into and exit from entrepreneurship. Further, real options theory suggests that investment decisions are influenced by the level of uncertainty and the irreversibility of a specific investment. Using this logic, Wennberg suggests that given that a person has discovered an entrepreneurial opportunity, such real option considerations influence if he or she pursues the opportunity and starts a business. Wennberg then moves on to test these hypotheses on a thirteen year long panel of all inhabitants in Sweden. Finding support for the human capital as well as the real options logic, one of the important conclusions to be drawn from this research is that a better understanding of the decision to enter into entrepreneurship can be gained from simultaneously considering the nature of the individual and the opportunity. Using human capital theory and real options logic, Wennberg develops a clever way of jointly studying the two using secondary data.

In Sweden and elsewhere, there is a strong interest in promoting the commercialization of university knowledge, using the start-up of knowledge-intensive firms as a vehicle. Students and faculty are encouraged to start their own businesses. Extensive support schemes have been put in place specifically targeting these kinds of businesses. The chapter 'New ventures' entry strategies: A comparison of academic and non-academic business start-ups' by Roininen and Ylinenpää, uses six in-depth case studies to ask the question if start-up and early growth processes differ between businesses originating from universities started by students or faculty, and businesses started outside of this environment. The answer to the question is an unconditional yes. Roininen and Ylinenpää find similarities within each set of firms and differences between the two sets. The university spin-offs are built around new knowledge and need to create a market for their products where none existed. This requires extensive resources and networks. The firms started outside of this environment originate in the perception of a market gap that needs to be filled, leading to faster and less resource demanding exploitation strategies. An important contribution of this chapter is the contextualization of the start-up process, which leads to insights about how different they may be. There are substantial policy implications of this chapter, in particular, regarding how university spin-offs could be supported.

Like Wennberg's chapter, the chapter 'How human capital affects self-employment among the science and technology labor force' by Johan Wiklund, Frederic Delmar and Karin Hellerstedt, utilizes a large longitudinal data set and human capital theory. Like Roininen and Ylinenpää's chapter, it deals with knowledge-intensive entrepreneurship. Viewing the entry into self-employment as an occupational choice, these authors analyze the propensity of the highly educated science and technology labor force to switch to self-employment. They find that the opportunity cost of self-employment works as a strong deterrent. Labor market experience and current wages work against the probability of becoming self-employed. They conclude that those individuals, with the highest probability of discovering valuable opportunities, may also have the highest opportunity cost for entering self-employment and are less likely to engage in entrepreneurship unless they perceive the value of the opportunity to be substantial.

We noted earlier that modern conceptualizations of entrepreneurship agree that such activities can take place in any organizational context. In the corporate context, the challenges are quite different than in start-ups. While the entrepreneurs of start-ups need to convince customers, suppliers, employees and so on, about the legitimacy of the new organization and overcome their liabilities of newness, corporate entrepreneurs have to convince superiors that they should invest in their new business concepts. This is not an easy task because new initiatives break with the established ways of operating. Christian Czernich and Ivo Zander, in their chapter 'The framing of new business concepts in established organizations: An exploratory investigation', examine the strategies that corporate entrepreneurs use to receive support for their new initiatives. More specifically, they examine how the corporate entrepreneurs 'frame' new concepts. Examining 49 new business concepts within 18 firms, they find that most corporate entrepreneurs frame new business concepts as means of generating new opportunities rather than avoiding threats and they focus on novelty rather than similarity with previous projects. Interestingly though, they did not find any framing strategy, which was more successful than the other in generating internal support. The authors conclude that corporate entrepreneurs do not frame new business concepts in ways the literature has identified as most successful or effective. Further, the relationship between framing and success appears more complex than assumed.

The psychological approach to entrepreneurship is broadening, extending beyond cognitions into emotions. Not least, there is a growing interest in entrepreneurial passion. In line with these contemporary developments, Landberg, in his chapter 'Refueling or running dry: Entrepreneurs' energetic resources and the start-up process', introduces the concept of energetic resources. This concept is akin to passion and perseverance as energetic resources provides entrepreneurs with the energy to cope with goal disruptive events. Thus, Landberg provides a novel lens through which it is possible to understand why entrepreneurs interrupt or persevere with their start-up attempts. Following closely, four nascent entrepreneurs for one and a half years, Landberg carefully analyzes how they cope with over twenty goal disruptions. A main conclusion is that, whether entrepreneurs replenish or deplete their energetic resources depends on the overall life situations of the entrepreneurs rather than on issues specific to the business.

Research on internationalization has a long and strong tradition in Sweden (cf. above). This research deals almost exclusively with the internationalization of established firms. Svante Andersson's chapter, 'International entrepreneurship and the theory of effectuation', provides a counter-balance to this research with its focus on the so-called 'born globals' i.e., new ventures that are already international from the outset. Andersson uses Sarasvathy's (2001) distinction between causal and effectual logic in decision making to unveil how decision making is conducted in a born global firm. Interviews were conducted with key decision makers over a series of years. The results show that the effectuation dominated in the case studied, i.e., the firm leveraged contingencies, relied on strategic alliances, and sought to control rather than predict the future.

In the final chapter, we discuss and draw the wider implications of the research presented in this volume as well as Swedish entrepreneurship research in general. We conclude by discussing where the entrepreneurship field is moving and the role of Swedish entrepreneurship research in this development.

REFERENCES

Danell, R (2001) 'Internationalization and Homogenization: A Bibliometric Study of International Management Research'. Doctoral theses at the Department of Socoiology, Umeå University, No 22, 2001.

Holmquist, C. & Sundin, E. (1997) *In search of excellence eller Att falla i farstun för det utländska* (In search of excellence or Blinded by the Foreign). Nordic Management Research Conference Bodö. Awarded 2nd best paper.

Landström, H. and Johannisson, B. (2001). Theoretical foundations of Swedish entrepreneurship and small-business research. *Scandinavian Journal of Managment*, 17:225-248.

Reader D. & Watkins D. (2006). The social and collaborative nature of entrepreneurship scholarship: A co-citation and perceptual analysis. *Entrepreneurship Theory and Practice* 30(3): 417-441.

Sarasvathy, S.D., 2001. Causation and effectuation: toward a theoretical shift from economic inevitability to entrepreneurial contingency. *Academy of Management Review* 26 (2), 243–263.

Schildt, H. A., Zahra, S. A., & Sillanpaa, A. (2006). Scholarly communities in entrepreneurship research: A co-citation analysis. *Entrepreneurship: Theory and Practice, 30(3):* 399-415.

Shane, S., Venkataraman, S., 2000. The promise of entrepreneurship as a field of research. *Academy of Management Review* 25(1):217-226.

Zahra, S. (2007). Contextualizing theory building in entrepreneurship research. *Journal of Business Venturing* 22: 443 – 452.

2. New Start-Up Firms among Swedish Patent Holders

Roger Svensson

1. INTRODUCTION

The purpose of this chapter is to describe and analyze *how* patents are commercialized and what implications this choice has on commercialization performance. Specific emphasis will be on patents, which are commercialized in new start-up firms. However, throughout the chapter, the new firm alternative will be compared with the other possible modes of commercialization, i.e. patents that are sold, licensed, or commercialized in existing firms, where the inventor is either owner or employed. Four aspects of new start-up firms and other modes of commercialization are described and analyzed below:

1) Which owners/inventors commercialize their patents?
2) Which owners/inventors start-up new firms and which ones use other modes of commercialization?
3) How is the mode choice related to the performance of commercialization in profit-terms?
4) How is the mode of commercialization related to the renewal and the value of patents?

In the empirical analysis, a unique dataset of Swedish patents granted to medium-sized and small firms as well as individuals is used. The dataset is based on a survey where the response rate is 80 percent. Patents rather than inventions are chosen here as the unit of observation, since the former are much easier to identify and follow. Detailed information about individual patents is available in the dataset; for example, if, when and how the patent is commercialized, performance in profit-terms of the commercialization as well as the renewal scheme of patents. Further, variables measure the place where the invention behind the patent was created, financing during the R&D and commercialization phases, and if the new product replaced an old one in the firm. Such a detailed database on the commercialization process of patents does not exist anywhere else.

In an international comparison, Sweden is characterized by a relatively high number of patents per capita (EU, 2001). There is also a relative lack of private venture capital invested in early and small projects – especially compared to the U.S. Instead, government financing is more common (Braunerhjelm, 1999). Otherwise, much of the analysis in the present chapter should be applicable for patents in other countries as well.

The chapter is organized as follows: Basic theory about patents and commercialization is discussed in section 2. The database and sample selection are described in section 3. The commercialization choice and the mode of commercialization are analyzed in section 4. These modes are related to performance of commercialization in section 5. How the mode of commercialization affects renewal of patents is analyzed in section 6, and the final section describes the conclusion of the study.

2. BASIC THEORY

According to the basic theory, a patent holder wants to maximize the expected profit from his patent – either through commercializing the patent or through keeping the patent by strategic reasons. In the case of commercialization, there are two main choices: 1) to develop the patent by himself/herself, either in his/her existing firm or through setting up a new firm; or 2) to let somebody else commercialize the patent, either through a licensing or an acquisition contract. The expected profit from developing the patent himself/herself will be a function of expected further developing costs, expected set-up costs for starting production, and the expected profits from production. Lack of financial resources is one of the largest problems during the R&D-phase. In the later commercialization phase, several complementary resources are needed, e.g., financing, marketing and manufacturing capabilities. One obvious factor that reduces the costs of development and production is when the patentee already has an existing firm which produces and distributes goods or services (Gans and Stern, 2003; Norbäck and Persson, 2008).

The expected profit from selling or licensing the patent is the difference between the expected fixed and/or variable incomes from the acquisition or licensing contract and the search and transaction costs of finding an external firm. Since patents are unique products, patentees and external firms have different information about the patent, causing adverse selection problems (Anton and Yao, 1994). This will increase the search and transaction costs of finding interesting projects and evaluating the technical and commercial potential for external firms. Therefore, market imperfections are likely to exist in the market for acquisition and licensing of patents with the consequence that very few patents are licensed and acquired. The only alternative for many patentees who want to commercialize their patents is then to commercialize in their existing firms or to start new ones.

Gans *et al.* (2002) argue theoretically that the involvement of private venture capitalists or business angels will reduce the search and transaction costs of finding an external firm. The reason is that such actors not only provide financing and knowledge, but also have networks with external manufacturing firms. The authors show empirically that the probability of a licensing or an acquisition contract increases when private venture capitalists are involved.

One characteristic of knowledge is that it is often 'tacit' and not always possible to codify. In the case of patents, this means that the inventor knows more about the invention than what he/she can write down or include in the patent application (Rosenberg, 1990; Pavitt, 1991). Hence, commercialization of patents often requires the involvement of the inventor, since he/she has specific technological knowledge about the patent. However, this involvement creates moral hazard problems. Therefore, it is important to give inventors incentives to work hard when patents are licensed or acquired.

The optimal commercialization decision will also depend on whether the patent holder has previous related patents. The probability of a defensive strategy, where the patent protects other related patents, increases when the patentee holds related patents.

The problems related to asymmetrical information will not only cause problems to match patentees and external manufacturing firms, but there will also be a lack of external financing. External financiers face the same problems of adverse selection as external manufacturing firms do (Kaplan and Strömberg, 2001). It might also be problematic for external financiers to control if inventors are working in their own, or in the external financier's, interests. Thus in the case of financing, moral hazard problems might also arise. To overcome market failures and the gap between inventors and external financiers, different countries have applied various strategies (Braunerhjelm, 1999; Bottazzi *et al.*, 2004). In the United States, the government has facilitated private market solutions and the growth of private venture capital (PVC) firms (Gompers and Lerner 2001). In Sweden, the government has intervened by offering financial assistance and loans to inventors and small and medium-sized technology-based firms.

3. DATABASE AND SAMPLE SELECTION

A detailed database on individual Swedish patents is used to follow the commercialization process[1]. Patents granted in 1998 were chosen for the current database.[2] In 1998, 2760 patents were granted in Sweden. 776 of these were granted to foreign firms, 902 to large Swedish firms with more than 1000 employees, and 1082 to Swedish individuals and firms with less than 1000 employees. Information about inventors, applying firms and their addresses for each patent was bought from the Swedish Patent and Registration Office (PRV). Based on this, a questionnaire was sent out to the inventors in 2003.[3]

In a pilot survey carried out in 2002, it turned out that large Swedish firms refused to provide information on individual patents. Furthermore, it is impossible to persuade foreign firms to fill in questionnaires about patents. These firms are mostly large multinational firms. Therefore, the population consists of 1082 patents granted to Swedish individuals and firms with less than 1000 employees. This sample selection is not a problem, as long as the conclusions drawn refer to small and medium-sized firms and individuals.

In the questionnaire, we asked the inventors about the work place where the invention was created, if and when the patent was commercialized, which kind of commercialization mode was chosen, as well as the performance of the commercialization, etc. As many as 867 of the inventors filled in and returned the questionnaire, i.e., the response rate was 80% (867 out of 1082).[4] This response rate is very high, considering inventors or applying firms usually regard information about inventions and patents to be secret. Non-responses primarily depend on the addresses from PRV being out of date and to a smaller degree on inventors refusing to reply. The term commerciali-

---

[1] All inventions do not result in patents. However, since an invention, which does not result in a patent, is not registered anywhere, there are two problems in empirically analyzing the invention rather than the patent. First, it is impossible to find these new ideas, products and developments among all firms and individuals. On the other hand, all patents are registered. Second, even if the 'inventions' are found, it is difficult to judge whether they are sufficient improvements to be called inventions. Only the national and international patent offices make such judgements. Therefore, the choice of the patent rather than the invention is the only alternative for an empirical study of the commercialization process.

[2] In a previous pilot study (Svensson, 2002), the commercialization started within five years after the application year for most patents. According to Pakes (1986), most of the uncertainty of the value of the patent is resolved during the first three-four years after the patent application. The year the patent is granted is used here as the sample criteria, but patents filed in a specific year might have been preferable. The choice of patents granted in a specific year is, however, not a problem in the statistical estimations.

[3] Each patent always has at least one inventor and often also an applying firm. The inventors or the applying firm can be the owner of the patent, but the inventors can also indirectly be owners of the patent, via the applying firm. Sometimes the inventors are only employed in the applying firm, which owns the patent. If the patent had more than one inventor, the questionnaire was sent to one inventor only.

[4] 85% of the patents were applied for between 1994 and 1997.

zation here means that the owners of the patent have introduced an innovation in an existing or in a new firm, licensed or sold the patent.

Kind of firm where the invention was created	Number of patents			Percent Commercialized
	Commercialization			
	Yes	No	Total	
Medium-sized firms (101-1000 employees)	77	39	116	66 %
Small firms (11-100 employees)	137	64	201	68 %
Micro companies (2-10 employees)	105	37	142	74 %
Inventors (1-4 inventors)	207	201	408	51 %
Total	526	341	867	61 %

Table 2.1 Commercialization of patents across firm sizes, number of patents and percent

4. COMMERCIALIZATION AND MODE CHOICE

The firm size distribution of the 867 patents and the commercialization rates are described in Table 2.1. As many as 408 patents (47%) were granted to individual inventors, and 116, 201, and 142 patents were granted to medium-sized firms (101-1000 employees), small firms (11-100 employees) and micro companies (2-10 employees) respectively.[5] In 2003, the end year of observation, commercialization had been started for 526 of these patents (61%). The commercialization rate of the firm groups is between 66% and 74%, whereas the rate of the individuals is not higher than 51%. A contingent-table test suggests there to be a significant difference in the commercialization rate between firms and individuals. The chi-square value is 30.6 (with 3 d.f.), significant at the one-percent level.

In Figure 2.1, the share of commercialized patents and the hazard function for the sample are shown. The patent application year is set to 0. The curve of commercialized patents increases steeply at the beginning and reaches almost

---

[5] The group of individual inventors includes private persons, self-employed inventors as well as two-three inventors, who are organized in trading companies or private firms without employees.

50% after 3 years.[6] Thereafter it levels away at about 60 %, indicating that if a patent is commercialized, this is most likely to happen during the first 4-5 years after application. Accordingly, the hazard function, which measures the conditional probability of a patent being commercialized, is the highest during the first three years after the application year.[7]

Share/probability

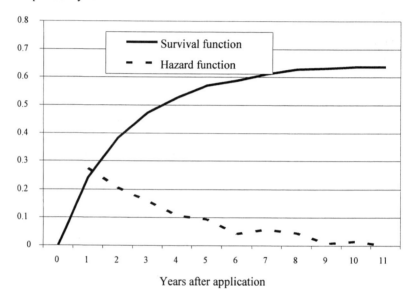

Years after application

Figure 2.1 Survival and hazard functions for commercialization

In Svensson (2007a), survival models are used to estimate which explanatory factors are important for the commercialization choice. It was concluded that firms commercialize faster and to a greater extent, than individual inventors. This is not surprising as firms have more resources and capabilities than individual inventors. Another conclusion was that the more government financing the inventors received during the R&D-phase, the longer it took until commercialization was initiated. Patents financed by the government were also more likely never to be commercialized. The explanation for this

---

[6] The share of commercialized patents is estimated through the Life-table method (actuarial method) and equals: 1 minus the survival function. The survival function shows how large a share of the patents which is still not commercialized after a specific time point (= survives).

[7] The hazard function shows the conditional probability of a patent being commercialized in a specific time period given that it has 'survived' (has not been commercialized) until the beginning of this period.

behaviour could be found in either the loan terms, where the inventors could avoid repayment if the patent was never commercialized, or in a negative selection of projects.

Five different modes of commercialization are used throughout this chapter.

- Commercialization in a new firm, the inventor is owner (and works).
- Commercialization in the existing firm, the inventor is owner (and works).
- Commercialization in the existing firm, the inventor is employed.
- Licensing the patent to an external firm.
- Selling the patent to an external firm.

Mode	Internal / external commercialization	Responsible for commercialization	Inventor ownership	Inventors' income
New firm	Internal	Inventor	Yes	Profit + wage
Existing firm, owner	Internal	Inventor	Yes	Profit + wage
Existing firm employed	Internal	Entrepreneur	No	Wage
Licensing	External	Entrepreneur	Yes	Royalty (+ consultancy)
Selling	External	Entrepreneur	No	Fixed payment (+consultancy)

Table 2.2 Characteristics of commercialization modes

The general characteristics of the different modes are summarized in Table 2.2.[8] The new firm alternative means that the firm was started up by the inventors with the purpose to commercialize the specific patent in question.

In the second group, the inventors are also owners of the patent, and most of these firms have earlier been started by the inventors. Thus, these inventors are also firm creators. In the first two groups, the patent is commercialized

---

[8] There may be exceptions to these general rules in the table.

Firm size	Commercialization mode – first choice					Total
	Acquired	Licensing	Existing firm employed	Existing firm owner	New firm	
Medium-sized firms	0	0	73	4	0	77
Small firms	2	2	67	66	0	137
Micro companies	4	7	16	77	1	105
Inventors	13	37	2	85	70	207
Total	19	46	158	232	71	526

Firm size	Commercialization mode – second choice					Total
	Acquired	Licensing	Existing firm employed	Existing firm owner	New firm	
Medium-sized firms	4	0	0	0	1	5
Small firms	8	0	0	0	1	9
Micro companies	5	6	0	0	2	13
Inventors	20	0	0	0	0	20
Total	37	6	0	0	4	47

Table 2.3 Commercialization mode across firm types, number of patents

internally *and* inventors are responsible for the commercialization. The third group, where inventors are employed by an entrepreneur is a hybrid. It is true that the patent is commercialized in the firm, where it was created, but inventors are not responsible for the commercialization. The last two groups (selling and licensing) imply that the patent is commercialized outside the original firm where the invention was created and inventors are not responsible for the commercialization. Licensing means that royalty payment, based on the external firm's turnover, is involved.

In Table 2.3, it is shown how the patents were commercialized across firm groups. Most patents were commercialized in the same firm (the existing firm) where the invention was created. It is also obvious that the inventor's ownership in existing firms is related to the firm size. The larger the firm, the higher is the probability that the inventor is only employed and not the owner, and vice versa. A new firm – based on the patent – was started up in 71 cases, 46 patents were licensed and only 19 were sold. Medium-sized firms never used external commercialization (licensing or selling) as a first choice. The smaller the firm, the higher is the probability that the patent is sold or licensed. New firms are almost exclusively started by individual inventors.

However, the owner can later decide to change the mode of commercialization. As can be seen in the lower part of Table 2.3, this occurs for 47 patents – most of them were originally commercialized in the existing firm. But now the pattern is quite different, external commercialization dominates – especially selling the patent. In total, 56 patents were sold and 52 were licensed. 75 patents were commercialized in new firms, which is 14% of all commercialized patents. This percentage could be compared with statistics on American patents, where around 10% of all patents are commercialized in new firms (AUTM, 1998).

Share of patents

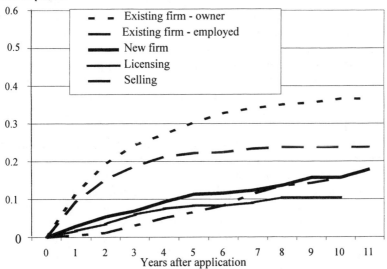

Figure 2.2 Survival functions across commercialization modes

Figure 2.2 shows the commercialization pattern for the five different modes. Although the final shares can be calculated from Table 2.2, the curves show how fast the commercialization starts. Not surprisingly, commercialization in existing firms where the inventors are employees is the mode that occurs closest to the application year. Its survival function already levels away after three years. Most of these firms are small or medium-sized and have at least some resources necessary for commercialization. If the firm owner wants to commercialize, then he/she starts right after the application. The curve for commercialization in existing firms, where inventors are owners, levels away in a similar way, but not the survival function for new firms. New firms are mostly closely held companies or firms with no employees. Consequently, they have less resources and commercialization starts later for larger or incumbent firms. An interesting difference appears between the curves of licensed and sold patents. The curve for sold patents lies below the one for licensed patents in the beginning, but after six years it catches the latter and passes, indicating that acquisition contracts occur later than licensing contracts. This was also observed in the lower part of Table 2.2, where selling the patent was a second-choice commercialization mode.

The choice of commercialization mode across external financing is described in Table 2.4. Patents with soft government financing in the R&D-phase are sold or licensed (external commercialization) to the same degree (7-10%) as those without such financing. However, only 39% (56 out of 142) of the government financed patents are commercialized in existing or new firms (internal commercialization) compared to 56% (405 out of 725) of the patents without this financing. Svensson (2007a) shows in a survival model that patents with soft government loans are commercialized to a lower degree. This depends on the terms of the loans. If the borrower gets income from the commercialization, he/she must repay the loan as a share of project turnover, but if he/she closes down the project or fails, then the loan is written off.

Thus, there are few incentives for borrowers to take further risks with commercialization. However, the terms for repayment in the case of selling or licensing the patent are more generous. The borrower only needs to repay 35 % of income.

An interesting observation can be made for private venture capital. Patents financed by business angels and private venture capital firms are sold or licensed to more than 15% (7 out of 48) compared to 7% (58 out of 819) for patents without private venture capital. This would be an indication that private venture capitalists reduce the search and transaction costs to find an external firm to get a licensing or acquisition contract with. An important difference between private and government financiers is that private financiers do not only provide financing, but also competence and networks with manufacturing firms.

By estimating survival models with competitive risks it is shown that new firms are started by patent owners, who have no previous firm (Svensson, 2008). Women are more likely to commercialize their patents in a new firm and new firms are more frequent as commercialization mode if the patentee has more similar patents. In contrast to the descriptive statistics above, the estimations do not support the view that patent owners who receive financing from private venture capital firms / business angels in the R&D-phase, sell or license their patents to a higher degree. Other results from the estimations are that firms prefer to commercialize in their existing firm and very seldom license or sell their patents (Svensson, 2008). In line with these statistics, soft government financing decreases the probability that the patentee commercializes the patent in his own firm, but has no impact on the choice to sell or license the patent. Finally, if the inventor is also the owner of the patent, then the probability that he/she sells or license the patent increases.

External financing		Commercialization mode – first choice					Commer cialized patents	All pa- tents
		External		Internal				
		Sel- ling	Licen- sing	Existing firm		New firm		
				Emp- loyed	Ow- ner			
Govern- ment financing	Yes	3	10	1	35	20	69	142
	No	16	36	157	197	51	457	725
Total		19	46	158	232	71	530	867
Private venture capital	Yes	3	4	5	9	7	28	48
	No	16	42	153	223	64	498	819
Total		19	46	158	232	71	526	867

Table 2.4 Commercialization mode across external financing, number of patents

5. PERFORMANCE OF COMMERCIALIZATION

In this section, the performance of the commercialization in profit-terms is analyzed. This measure will be related to the mode of commercialization and the activity of inventors. Schumpeter (1934), the father of the entrepreneur-ship theory, claimed that the stages of invention and innovation (commer-cialization) were clearly separated. According to this view, the inventor invents and another person or firm – the entrepreneur – introduces the product to the market. The first interesting question is whether Schumpeter was right that invention and innovation take place in independent units. If the answer is yes, then the performance would be worse if the inventor also acts as an entrepreneur and brings his own product to the market. It is not unlikely that somebody else than the inventor should be responsible for the commercialization as the invention and innovation stages require different skills.

The second question concerns whether entrepreneurs, who involve the inventor in the commercialization process, are more successful than those entrepreneurs who do not. As was mentioned in section 2, inventions often need to be adapted to market conditions during commercialization. Such adaptation relies on the inventor's private technical knowledge of the invention. A large part of the knowledge is not possible to codify, and is thus tacit (Rosenberg, 1990; Pavitt, 1991). By involving the inventor, the entrepreneur can reduce uncertainty in entrepreneurial activities. In addition, the entrepreneur also reduces the risks of being exposed to increased competition from follow-up innovations by the inventor, or from other firms to whom the inventor may find it profitable to license an invention.

In the database, there is one measure on profitability of commerciali-zation. At the end point of observation (year 2003), the inventors were asked to estimate whether the commercialized invention would yield profit, attain break-even or result in a loss. If they did not know, the reply was registered as a missing value (uncertain outcome).[9] In Table 2.5, performance of commercialization in profit terms is described across modes. Patents commercialized in new firms have the worst performance. Existing firms, where the inventor is employed has the best performance, but this mode is strongly correlated to medium-sized and small-sized firms in the sample. The difference between the two groups of existing firms, where inventors are employed and owners, is striking.

Dividing the modes into two groups: 1) somebody else than the inventor is responsible for the commercialization (selling, licensing the patent or commercialization in an existing firm where the inventor is employed); and 2) the inventor commercializes in his own firm (existing or new firm where the inventor is owner) shows that the former group has a better performance. A contingent table test based on the subtotals gives the chi-square-value 28.70, significant at the 1 %-level.

In Braunerhjelm and Svensson (2007), performance is described across activity of inventors during the commercialization. Surprisingly, there is no evidence that activity of inventors has any impact on the performance. Thus,

---

[9] For a vast majority of the patents, the commercialization had reached such a stage that there was no uncertainty at all about the performance. The missing values could also be treated as a fourth, uncertain, outcome.

based on descriptive statistics, it seems like Schumpeters' view, that the stages of invention and innovation should be separate activities, is correct.

Previous studies, which have analyzed performance and values of patents, have focused on the renewal scheme of patents (Griliches 1990). The assumption has then been that more valuable patents are renewed for longer time periods than less valuable ones. An advantage with the profit measure used in our study is that it actually shows if the patent has been commercialized and if the commercialized patent was profitable or not for the owner. The renewal studies do not say anything about whether the patent has been commercialized and whether any innovation has been introduced into the market. A drawback of the performance measure used in this section is that it does not take account of the fact that non-commercialized patents may also be profitable for the owner; for example defensive patents. Therefore, the mode choice will also be related to the renewal scheme in the next section.

Commercialization mode (first choice)	Performance				Total
	Profit	Break-even	Loss	Missing value	
Selling	10	3	6	0	19
Licensing	21	7	13	5	46
Existing firm, inventor is employed	104	30	15	9	158
Subtotal inventor NOT responsible	*135*	*40*	*34*	*14*	*223*
Existing firm, inventor is owner	100	45	64	23	232
New firm	11	9	32	19	71
Subtotal inventor responsible	*111*	*54*	*96*	*42*	*303*
Total	246	94	130	56	526
Chi-square (3 d.f.) = 28.70 *** (based on subtotals)					

Table 2.5 Performance across mode of commercialization, number of patents

In a statistical model with a discrete dependent variable, Braunerhjelm and Svensson (2007) test how different modes of commercialization and inventor activity influence the profit level of commercialized patents. The estimations show that the performance is superior when somebody else than the inventor is responsible for the commercialization, i.e. the patent is sold or licensed or the inventor is employed by an entrepreneur, compared to the alternative when the inventor commercializes in his own existing or new firm. In the former case, the probability of a successful commercialization is 23%-units higher than in the latter case. This is in line with Schumpeter's view that invention and innovation should be separate stages. However, another result is that activity of inventors during the commercialization is important for the performance. This is especially interesting to observe when the inventor is not responsible for the commercialization (the patent is licensed, sold or when the inventor is employed by an entrepreneur and not owner). The explanation would be that the inventor is important for further adaptation of the innovation and to reduce uncertainty. In this sense, the results contradict Schumpeter's view that invention and innovation are separate stages. The overall interpretation of the estimations is that inventors are more successful as transmitters of knowledge than as firm creators or entrepreneurs.

If commercialization within the own firm is inferior, why do not all inventors let somebody else being responsible for the commercialization? Firstly, many studies have shown that individual inventors often are over-optimistic about their own inventions and capabilities (de Meza and Southey 1996; Fraser and Greene, 2006). Secondly, as mentioned in section 2, the market for licensing and acquisition of patents is imperfect. This means that too few patents are sold/licensed and too many inventors commercialize patents in their own firms.

6. RENEWAL OF PATENTS

Swedish patents have a statutory period of twenty years and the owners must pay an annual renewal fee to keep their patents in force. If the renewal fee is not paid even for one year, then the patent expires forever. The renewal fees are increasing with time. In the patent literature, the renewal of patents (see e.g. Pakes 1986; Schankerman and Pakes 1986; Griliches, 1990) has been the standard measure of patent values. Griliches argues that the percentage of renewed patents indicates how large a share of the patents has a positive economic value after different numbers of years. The models in Pakes (1986) and Schankerman and Pakes (1986) are based on the assumption that more valuable patents are renewed for longer periods than less valuable patents. The main conclusions of these studies are that most patents have a low value and that it depreciates fast, and only a few have a significant high value. In other words, the value distribution of patents is severely skewed to the right.

The renewal measure has the advantage that it also takes into account the fact that non-commercialized patents may be profitable to keep for the owners. However, as already stated in the previous section, there are some problems with the renewal measure. The renewal of patents does not say anything about whether the patent has been commercialized and whether any innovation has been introduced into the market. There is also an identification problem, where it is almost impossible for the observer to know whether the renewed patent has a low or a high value. There is another interesting aspect of previous renewal studies: The renewal scheme have seldom been related to explanatory factors.

One obvious hypothesis to test is how the commercialization decision influences the renewal scheme and thereby the value of patents and how different modes of commercialization affect the renewal decision. For example, are patents commercialized in new firms renewed for longer time periods than patents using other modes? On average, commercialized patents should obviously be more valuable than those that are not commercialized, because the main reason for most inventors to apply for a patent is simply to defend the invention from imitations when the innovation is introduced in the market. There are also defensive reasons to applying for a patent; for example, to deter competitors from using the invention, or to protect other closely related inventions/patents, i.e. in the latter case the patent serves as a shadow patent.

In the literature it is hard to find any hypothesis on how the commercialization mode would influence the renewal scheme. Most patents need further development before the product is ready for the market. It is the inventors who often have this specific technological knowledge which is needed. Thus, the inventors have tacit knowledge which can neither be codified nor transmitted to the external firm. Based on this fact, Dechenaux *et al.* (2007) claim that acquired and licensed patents should include both variables and fixed fees – otherwise either the inventors or the external firm have few incentives to make an effort during the commercialization. The variables fees give incentives for the inventors to work hard and the fixed fees give incentives for the external firm to undertake further investments in the project.

In the database, we have not asked the external firm how successful the commercialization was when the patent was acquired or licensed. We only know how successful the original owners of the patent were in profit-terms, based on which mode they had chosen. This was analyzed in the previous section, where selling or licensing the patent were the most successful modes. However, it is possible to indirectly measure if the licensing or acquisition was successful for the external firm. Analyzing the renewal schemes after patents have been acquired or licensed gives indications about success. If licensed or acquired patents are not renewed to the same extent as other commercialized patents, then one would conclude that this mode was not successful with respect to commercialization.

Commercialized patents are compared to renewed patents in Table 2.6. As expected, the renewed patents (71%) have been commercialized to a higher degree than the dead ones (48%). The chi-square value below the table shows that there is a strong correlation between commercialized and renewed patents. However, 35% of the patents that have been commercialized have already expired. This is either due to the products having a short lifecycle or the commercialization having failed. In Table 2.6, it can also be observed that 42% of the non-commercialized patents are still valid. Many of these patents might be defensive patents, with the purpose of defending other patents, but then the owner should have more similar granted patents. Among the commercialized patents in our database, 46% of the owners have at least one more similar patent. Among the non-commercialized patents, this percentage is only 33%. If the patent was not commercialized, the Inventor was also asked: why? Among the 341 non-commercialized patents, only 15 inventors answered that the patent served as a shadow-patent was one of the reasons for it not having been commercialized.[10] Thus, I conclude that keeping patents for strategic reasons is not common among individuals and small firms. This strategy is more frequent among large multinational firms.

Patents still alive 2004	Commercialized patents latest in 2003			Percent Commer- cialized
	Yes	No	Total	
Yes	340	142	482	71 %
No	186	199	385	48 %
Total	526	341	867	61 %
Percent still alive	65 %	42 %	56 %	

Note: Chi-square-value is 44.32, significant at the 1 percent level for 1 d.f.

Table 2.6 Commercialized patents and patents still alive in 2004, number of patents and percent

In can also be shown that patents which are still valid have a higher share of successful outcome in profit-terms as compared to expired patents, but the

---

[10] The most frequent reasons here were: 1) problems with financing (115 patents); 2) problems with marketing (75 patents); 3) problems in finding a manufacturing firm/licensor (74 patents); and 4) the product is not yet ready for commercialization (62 patents). Note that inventors may have mentioned more than one reason why the patent was not commercialized.

probability increases as the life of the expired patent becomes longer. There are however many exceptions. For example, some patents, which expired after only 1-5 years, were profitable, while many patents which were still renewed and commercialized have been losses for the owners. Therefore, the assumption that more valuable patents are renewed for longer periods is somewhat shaky in the renewal studies. However, the longer the commercialized patents have been renewed, the higher is the probability of a profitable commercialization. Those still valid are the most successful ones.

In Figure 2.3, the survival and hazard functions for the whole sample of patents are estimated by the Life-table method (actuarial method). Since patents are not in the risk set of expiring until they have been granted, the start year is set to either 1997 or 1998 depending on whether the grant date occurs before or after the renewal (application) date. Year 1 is then the first possible year when the patent can expire. The survival function falls from the

Share / probability

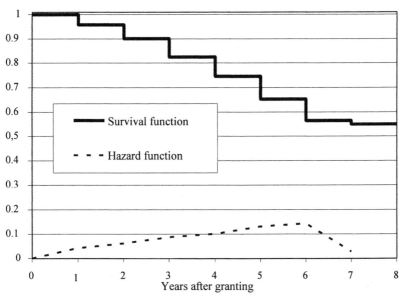

Figure 2.3 Survival and Hazard functions for the renewal of patents

beginning and more steeply for each year. The corresponding hazard functions have an increasing trend.[11] It would also be interesting to estimate

---

[11]The survival and hazard functions are not so reliable for the seventh year, since there is no year 7 for those patents with a start year of 1998.

survival and hazard functions with respect to commercialization and commercialization modes, but these are time-dependent variables and are instead
included in the Cox estimations.

In Table 2.7, the renewal scheme is shown across modes of commercialization. For each mode, the numbers of patents that are still alive in 2004,
have expired or have changed mode are shown. As many as 43% of the sold
patents have expired compared to 35% for licensed patents and 30-35% for
patents commercialized in existing or new firms. By looking closer at the
expired patents, it turns out that sold patents survive less than three years after
they have been acquired. The other groups of patents survive around four
years or more after they have been commercialized. Thus, sold patents are
renewed to a lower degree and shorter time periods than the other modes.
However, here I have not taken account of other factors, which may influence
the renewal decision.

Mode (both first and second choice)	Changed mode	Still alive In 2004	Expired	Total	% expired	Years until expired*
Acquired patents	0	32	24	56	43 %	2.8
Licensed patents	6	28	18	52	35 %	3.9
Existing firm, employed	9	102	47	158	30 %	5.6
Existing firm, owner	28	133	71	232	31 %	5.3
New firm	4	45	26	75	35 %	4.3

Note: * Measured from the commercialization date.

*Table 2.7 Renewal of patents across commercialization modes, number of
patents, percents and years*

Using Cox survival models, Svensson (2007b) estimates how the commercialization and mode choices influence the renewal scheme. This is the
first study ever which includes the commercialization decision when
analyzing patent renewal schemes. The estimations show that commercialized

patents have a 48% lower hazard (conditional probability) of expiring than those which are not commercialized. When looking at different modes, it turns out that acquired/licensed patents with fixed and variable fees and those commercialized in existing and new firms all have a significantly lower hazard than non-commercialized patents, i.e. these commercialized patents survive longer periods. The hazard is lowered between 48-57% for these modes. Patents commercialized in new firms do not differ significantly from licensed patents or patents commercialized in existing firms. However, the most interesting result is that acquired/licensed patents with only fixed or variable fees do not lower the hazard. In fact, the probability of renewal for those patents is almost as low as if the patent was not commercialized at all. This result indicates that there is moral hazard and adverse selection problems when acquired/licensed patents lack either fixed or variable fees. This result is in line with the hypothesis of Dechenaux *et al.* (2007).

CONCLUDING REMARKS

In this chapter, I have described and analyzed *how* patents are commercialized and what implications this choice has for the performance of commercialization and renewal of patents. Specific emphasis has been on new start-up firms, which have been compared with other modes, i.e. patents which are sold, licensed and commercialized in existing firms. The empirical analysis uses a detailed dataset on Swedish patents owned by small and medium-sized firms and individual inventors. The dataset is based on a survey, where the response rate is 80%. In this database it is possible to follow the commercialization process of patents, for example, if, when and how the patent was commercialized, the performance in profit terms of the commercialization and the renewal schemes.

Descriptive statistics show that around 60% of the patents are commercialized. The rate is higher for firms (70%) than for individuals (50%). Most of the commercialized patents are commercialized in the same firm where the invention was created, whereas 14% are commercialized in new start-up firms. The new firms are almost exclusively started up by individual inventors, who neither had firms nor employees earlier. Also women and inventors who have more similar patents are more likely to commercialize their patents in new firms. To sell or license patents is disfavored by the high transaction and search costs in the market for arm's length contracts, which depends on asymmetrical information problems. The inventors know much more about the patent than external manufacturing firms. Theory argues that when business angels or private venture capital firms are involved already from the beginning, there should be a higher probability that patents are sold or licensed, since these intermediates have networks with external manufacturing firms. This view is supported by descriptive statistics but not by econometrical estimations.

The mode of commercialization is statistically related to the performance of the commercialization in profit-terms. The results from estimations show that the performance is significantly higher if somebody else than the inventor is responsible for the commercialization. This is not surprising as the invention and innovation stages require quite different skills. However, the performance is improved if the inventors are engaged by the entrepreneur during the commercialization. Inventions need to be adapted to market conditions before commercialization and inventors often have tacit knowledge that is necessary. The main result is that inventors are important as knowledge transmitters, but are not successful as firm creators.

When analyzing renewal of patents, it turns out that patents commercialized in new and existing firms as well as acquired/licensed patents with both fixed and variable fees are renewed significantly longer than non-commercialized patents. Among these commercialization modes, there is no significant difference. However, acquired/licensed patents that lack either variable or fixed fees are not renewed longer than non-commercialized patents. This depends on moral hazard problems with respect to inventor and/or firm effort.

The good performance of patents in new firms in terms of renewal contrasts with the poor performance in terms of profitability. This might depend on the fact that many individual inventors are over-optimistic and renew their patents for longer periods than what is optimal. Previous research has given such indications that individuals who start new firms are over-optimistic (de Meza and Southey 1996; Fraser and Greene, 2006).

REFERENCES

Anton, J.J. and D.A. Yao, 1994, 'Expropriation and Inventions: Appropriable Rents and the Absence of Property Rights', *American Economic Review*, 84(1), 190-209.

Association of University Technology Managers, 1998, *AUTM Licensing Survey*, Association of Technology Managers, Norwalk, CT.

Bottazzi, L., M. DaRin and T. Hellmann, 2004, 'The Changing Face of the European Venture Capital Industry: Facts and Analysis', *Journal of Private Equity*, 8, n.1.

Braunerhjelm, P., 1999, 'Venture capital, mångfald och tillväxt', (Venture Capital, Variety and Growth), *Ekonomisk Debatt*, 27(4), 213-22.

Braunerhjelm, P. and R. Svensson, 2007, 'The Inventors Role: Was Schumpeter Right?', *Journal of Evolutionary Economics*, Forthcoming.

Dechenaux, E., M. Thursby and J, Thursby, 2007, 'Shirking, Sharing Risk and Shelving: The Role öf University License Contracts', Discussion paper, Ken State University.

De Meza, D. and Southey, C., 1996, 'The Borrower's Curse: Optimism, Finance and Entrepreneurship', *Economic Journal*, 106, 375-86.

EU, 2001, *Towards a European Research Area. Key Figures 2001*, Office for Official Publications of the European Communities, Luxemburg.

Fraser, S. and Greene, F.J., 2006, 'The Effects of Experience on Entrepreneurial Optimism and Uncertainty', *Economica*, 73, 169-92.

Gans, J.S., D.H. Hsu and S. Stern, 2002, 'When Does Start-Up Innovation Spur the Gale of Creative Destruction?', *RAND Journal of Economics*, 33, 571-86.

Gans, J.S. and S. Stern, 2003, 'The Product Market and the Market for Ideas: Commercialization Strategies for Technology Entrepreneurs', *Research Policy*, 32(2), 333-50.

Gompers, P., and Lerner, J., 2001, 'The Venture Capital Revolution', *Journal of Economic Perspective*, No. 2, pp. 145-168.

Griliches, Z., 1990, 'Patent Statistics as Economic Indicators: A Survey', *Journal of Economic Literature*, 28, 1661-1707.

Kaplan S. N. and P. Strömberg, 2001, 'Venture Capitals As Principals: Contracting, Screening, and Monitoring', *American Economic Review*, 91, 426-30.

Norbäck, P.J., and L. Persson, 2008, 'The Organization of the Innovation Industry: Entrepreneurs, Venture Capitalists and Oligopolists, IFN Discussion paper.

Pakes, A., 1986, 'Patents as Options: Some Estimates of the Value of Holding European Patent Stocks', *Econometrica*, 54, 755-84.

Pavitt, K., 1991, 'What Makes Basic Research Economically Useful?', *Research Policy*, 20, 109-19.

Rosenberg, N., 1990, 'Why Do Firms Do Basic Research (with their own money)?', *Research Policy*, 19, 165-74.

Schankerman, M. and A. Pakes, 1986, 'Estimates of the Value of Patent Rights in European Countries during the Post-1950 Period', *Economic Journal*, 96, 1052-76.

Schumpeter, J.A., 1911 [1934], *The Theory of Economic Development*, Harvard University Press, Cambridge, Mass.

Svensson, R., 2002, 'Commercialization of Swedish Patents: A Pilot Study in the Medical and Hygiene Sectors', IUI Working paper No. 583, IUI, Stockholm.

Svensson, R., 2007a, 'Commercialization of Patents and External Financing during the R&D-Phase', *Research Policy*, 36(7), 1052-69.

Svensson, R., 2007b, 'The Performance of Licensed and Acquired Patents with Different Payment Terms: Evidence from Patent Renewal Data', IFN Working paper, Research Institute of Industrial Economics, Stockholm.

Svensson, R., 2008, 'Does External Financing Influence How Patents are Commercialized?', Discussion paper, Research Institute of Industrial Economics, Stockholm.

Venkataraman, S. & Sarasvathy, S.D. (2001). Strategy and Entrepreneurship: Outlines of an untold story. In M. A. Hitt, J. Freeman and J. S. Harrison (Eds.) *Handbook of Strategic Management*. Oxford, UK, Blackwell.

3. Entrepreneurial Human Capital: a Real Options Perspective

Karl Wennberg

In 2003, Torsten Jansson won the Swedish 'Entrepreneur of the Year' award. His firm, New Wave Group, is a true success story starting with a young Swede who, after finishing 2-year high school in the mid-80's, started a rural clothing company focusing on leisure and company clothing. Today, New Wave Group is listed on the Swedish Stock Exchange and has grown by an annual average of 38 percent, with a return on equity between 20 and 25 percent. Torsten is still the majority owner. When we interviewed Torsten, he mentions what he conceived as the key points of his strategy to success:

'It is often necessary to kill your darlings. This is something we have learned the hard way. My strategy has been to establish us on several markets and thus spread the risks of being negatively affected by economic downturns. I believe one should not be afraid to venture into new markets, but at the same time it's necessary to be able to cut losses and quickly exit a market or a project that fails to generate value. ... At the same time, Swedish culture is often not forgiving someone who fails. Sometimes it is best to face the truth and close down earlier rather than throwing good money after bad; after all there are plenty of good business ideas out there. But if you get a whole load of debts and then [go bankrupt], many people will suffer, not only the banks but also your customers, suppliers and employees. It is more difficult doing a comeback like we were able to. A key reason [for our turnaround] was the loyalty of employees and customers that we never bailed on.'

This story indicates that entrepreneurs, such as Torsten Jansson, who manage to establish a new venture and grow it into a successful firm, often, have experience from prior start-up attempts. Numerous empirical studies of entrepreneurship in various countries also indicate that prior experience with entrepreneurship is a strong recurrent pattern that seems to positively impact the success of subsequent venturing activities. Because entrepreneurship in the form of establishing and growing a new independent firm can be seen as a fundamental career choice, entrepreneurship researchers have frequently drawn upon the economic theory of human capital, a common framework for studying how education and various labor market experiences affect an individual's productivity and career choices. Based on findings that prior entrepreneurial experience is a strong predictor of both subsequent venturing attempts and the performance of these ventures, the emerging entrepreneurship literature has argued that prior experience in entrepreneurships constitutes a specific type of 'entrepreneurial human capital'.

Yet, several questions remain for entrepreneurship research to ponder: What *is* entrepreneurial human capital? How, specifically, does it affect individuals who initiate new ventures and how does it affect the long-term development of these ventures? And since entrepreneurship is inherently a very uncertain endeavor, how can we conceptualize entrepreneurs' decisions if they cannot make decisions based on rational financial calculations of known alternatives with a specific net present value, which are assumed in most of the economic literature on human capital?

This chapter tries to advance entrepreneurial human capital as a theoretical construct, and provides new empirical evidence to support the ideas that are proposed. It therefore provides two distinct contributions to the growing literature on entrepreneurial human capital. Empirically, this study highlights the distinction between how entrepreneurial human capital affects entrepreneurial *entry*, *performance* and *continuation* (i.e. non-exit).

This is of high importance since most research on entrepreneurial human capital is limited to measuring the effects of prior entrepreneurship on subsequent re-entry or 'progress in the nascent venturing process' (Davidsson and Honig, 2003). Theoretically, it shows how an 'investment under uncertainty' perspective can be used to integrate the theory of entrepreneurship (as the discovery and exploitation of market opportunities) and the economic theories of human capital (as a determinant of individuals' productivity).

The chapter is outlined as follows: first it follows a theoretical outline of the process by which individuals enter into and exit from entrepreneurship. The core of this process is the discovery and the exploitation of entrepreneurial opportunities with an unknown value. I call this process the entrepreneurial process. The first theory section describes how this process can be conceptualized from an 'investment under uncertainty' perspective. The second theory section discusses earlier studies of human capital and entrepreneurship, from which I derive hypotheses of how general human capital shape the entrepreneurial process. The third theory section focuses specifically on entrepreneurial human capital and how this can be hypothesized to shape the entrepreneurial process. The fourth theory section introduces the theory of real options and proposes several novel hypotheses of how real options heuristics shape the entrepreneurial process. After this follows a method section where I outline the data and methods used to test the hypotheses. The results are then presented, and the final section discusses the findings with their strengths and limitations, and proposes some avenues for further research.

THE ENTREPRENEURIAL PROCESS AND INVESTMENTS UNDER UNCERTAINTY

Recent conceptual developments in the field of entrepreneurship highlight the intersection of opportunities and enterprising individuals as critical for entrepreneurship (Shane & Venkataraman, 2000). The exploitation of such opportunity is defined by three characteristics: (i) the ability to discover versus the ability to exploit (ii), the entrepreneur's opportunity cost, and (iii) the uncertainty of the outcome from engaging in entrepreneurship (Shane, 2003). In this chapter, I focus primarily on the last two characteristics of the entrepreneurial process: opportunity costs and uncertainty associated with entrepreneurship. For a given opportunity and equally capable individuals, those individuals with low opportunity costs should be more likely to engage in entrepreneurship (Amit, Muller, & Cockburn, 1995). However, there is an important difference between having an insight about what may constitute a valuable opportunity, and having the knowledge about how to exploit this opportunity. For example, some individuals will be apt to discover opportunities and might engage in entrepreneurship to exploit these, but are less capable of building these ideas into profitable firms. Other individuals are less 'alert' to entrepreneurial opportunities (Kirzner, 1973) and will be more hesitant before engaging in entrepreneurship, but might be skilled in managing the uncertainty of exploiting the opportunity by building a new firm and establishing the firm on a competitive market. These differences are relevant for explaining differences between how entrepreneurial human capital affects the individuals' propensity to enter, to exit, and their performance as entrepreneurs. While most existing research assume that higher entrepreneurial human capital will affect all parts of the entrepreneurial process (i.e. the entry, exit, and performance of entrepreneurs) in the same positive direction, this chapter suggests that entrepreneurial human capital is intimately associated to the relative level of uncertainty that exists in different market spaces. It is proposed and empirically demonstrated that individuals with high entrepreneurial human capital operate under a real options heuristics that allows them to rapidly engage in entrepreneurship to test and verify the value of the opportunities that they discover, meaning that they are both more likely to engage in entrepreneurship and more likely to abandon their ventures.

From a rational decision-making perspective, people will exploit an opportunity if they believe that the expected monetary and psychological value, plus their required premium for uncertainty, exceeds the value of the alternatives. However, they do not know in advance whether exploiting this opportunity is going to be profitable. The accuracy of an entrepreneur's confidence in the value of an opportunity can only be tested on the market. The exploitation of an opportunity is characterized by the uncertainty associated with attracting resources, organizing the venture, and designing a functioning business model that attracts customers. Entrepreneurs therefore, have to develop strategies to handle the uncertainty related to the exploitation of an opportunity. Their choice of strategy will have an impact on the decision of whether to exploit, as well as how the opportunity is exploited. Uncertainty-*sharing* strategies suggest that entrepreneurs should work in close liaison with customers and suppliers in order to develop products and jointly share the financial risk (Sarasvathy, 2001). Uncertainty-*reducing* strategies suggest that entrepreneurs should decide only to make small initial commitments when unsure of their chances of success, providing the entrepreneur with a real option to invest more if early feedback about the value of the opportunity is promising (Venkataraman & Sarasvathy, 2001). The benefit of an uncertainty-sharing strategy stems from the resources that entrepreneurs might get from cooperation and networking with potential partners (Wennberg & Berglund, 2006). However, entrepreneurs with close professional and personal ties to other stakeholder are at increased risk of escalating their commitment beyond what is financially warranted (Hayward, Shepherd & Griffin, 2006). The benefit of an uncertainty-sharing strategy must therefore be weighed against the potential danger of pursuing an unprofitable opportunity too long. Conversely, uncertainty-reducing strategies prescribe that entrepreneurs should try to exploit a potential upside but 'cut their losses' (McGrath, 1999). Such strategies prescribe that entrepreneurs should strive to develop the opportunity into a business proposition while at the same time gather feedback from the market on the viability of this business proposition (Lévesque, Choi, & Shepherd, 2004). If this feedback is negative, the entrepreneur should close down in order to avoid further losses. The relative superiority of uncertainty-sharing versus uncertainty-reducing strategies most likely depends on context and it is difficult to make genera-lizeable statement about either one. Nevertheless, an interesting consequence of the different logics of uncertainty-sharing versus uncertainty-reducing strategies is that entrepreneurs with an uncertainty-sharing strategy are more likely to pursue unprofitable opportunities for too long (i.e. type-1 errors) whereas entrepreneurs with an uncertainty-reducing strategy are more likely to abandon potentially profitable opportunities too early (i.e. type-2 errors). This would suggest that if the uncertainty-reducing strategy is more viable in the long-term, entrepreneurs will have more prior start-up attempts if they are using real options strategies. Although this possibility has not yet been proposed in the literature, it is not an improbable one since people with a history of starting a venture are likely to continue to identify and exploit entrepreneurial opportunities (Shane, 2003; Shepherd, Douglas, & Shanley, 2000). In this chapter, I therefore propose a theoretical framework where individuals' human capital in liaison with their ability to manage the uncertainty of the entrepreneurial process where an 'investment under uncertainty' logic – a real options heuristics – shapes the process, by which people enter into and exit from entrepreneurship.

How does general human capital shape the entrepreneurial process?

The theory of human capital (Becker, 1964) uses economic logic to study, among other things, individual career choices such as choosing between employment and self-employment. Human capital theory follows mainstream economic logic by viewing individuals' choice of occupation or employment as a choice that maximizes their long-term economic and psychic utility. Human capital theory also distinguishes between general and specific human capital. General human capital is made up of skills that are useful in a variety of work settings. Specific human capital is made up of skills that are more specialized and valuable in a particular context, but less valuable in the general labor market. We can think of four types of human capital that are relevant for entrepreneurship: *general human capital* – for example primary education, *industry-specific human capital* – for example knowledge on how business is conducted and how products can be sold within that specific industry (Neal, 1995), *firm specific human capital* – for example knowledge of how a specific organization functions, and *entrepreneurial human capital* – skills relevant for establishing and running a new firm (Iyigun & Owen, 1998). According to Mincer (1958) the two major human capital concepts are education and accumulated labor market experience.

Much of the research on human capital in entrepreneurship highlights the distinction between general human capital and entrepreneurial human capital. While general human capital is composed of several factors such as education and work experience, entrepreneurial human capital is mostly only measured by an indicator variable of whether an individual has past experience in entrepreneurship. However, such an indicator does not tell us what type of prior experience in entrepreneurship is important, nor why this is so. Also, many low performing entrepreneurs continue indefinitely in their ventures (Wiklund, Delmar, & Sjöberg, 2004). It seems counterintuitive that an individual with prolonged low-performance venturing should have 'higher' entrepreneurial human capital than someone who rapidly, after engaging in entrepreneurship, achieves high financial performance and then divests of his/her firm. In this chapter, I therefore measure entrepreneurial human capital by counting the number of prior venturing experiences in entrepreneurship. Also,

I look at both entry into and persistence in entrepreneurship while at the same time controlling for financial performance.

Recent years have seen a spur of studies on the role of human capital in entrepreneurship. Researchers have, among other things, investigated how human capital affect people's inclination to engage in entrepreneurship (Bates, 1995; Davidsson & Honig, 2003; Evans & Leighton, 1989), exit or persist as entrepreneurs (Bates, 1990; Gimeno, Folta, Cooper, & Woo, 1997; Preisendörfer & Voss, 1990), as well as their financial performance (Gimeno et al., 1997; Honig, 2001). The findings of these and other studies are sometimes in conflict with each other and there is a vivid debate in the literature on how human capital affects entrepreneurial entry, exit, and performance (Van Praag, 2005). A meta-analysis by Van Der Sluis, Van Praag, and Vijverberg (2004) on 94 available studies of entrepreneurs reveals that in two thirds of all the studies, educational extent has an unambiguous and significantly positive effect on entrepreneurial performance. This effect was somewhat larger in the U.S. than in Europe or in the other countries studied.

People with more specific human capital such as extensive education and work experience are generally considered more likely to perform better in entrepreneurship (Bates, 1990; Brüderl, Preisendörfer, & Ziegler, 1992). With higher education, people have better access to information that allows them to identify valuable opportunities. The social processes and societal positions attained due to higher education, increases the likelihood that advantageously placed individuals will discover entrepreneurial opportunities, sometimes by active search and sometimes simply by being in the right place at the right time with the right knowledge (Baker, Miner, & Eesley, 2003). It is likely that an individual's general human capital will affect the likelihood that he or she discovers an opportunity since human capital provides individuals with more knowledge that can be beneficial in identifying new opportunities and ways of exploiting these opportunities (Wiklund et al., 2004). I therefore expect that general human capital in the form of a longer education will be positively associated with entrepreneurial entry:

Hypothesis 1: Higher general human capital will increase the likelihood of entry into entrepreneurship.

However, there exists some confusion in the literature as to how 'specific' types of human capital such as work experience from a particular industry, affect people's entry into, and persistence in, entrepreneurship. Davidsson and Honig (2003) suggest that the effect of general human capital on entrepreneurial processes such as entry, exit, and performance might be confounded by a number of complicating factors. For example, different types of human capital may be more important at different stages of the entrepreneurial process. This indicates a problem in the literature on entrepreneurial human capital since most of the available studies are limited to certain stages of the entrepreneurial process (Preisendörfer & Voss, 1990). Looking at several pieces of the puzzle at the same time complicates the picture further. For example, Gimeno, and colleagues (1997) demonstrated that the relationship between continuation and education is non-linear with high education increasing performance, but not continuation. A likely reason for this effect is that whereas individuals with higher human capital have better capabilities to successfully manage a firm, they also have higher opportunity costs (Gimeno et al., 1997; Wiklund et al., 2004). This chapter tries to overcome these problems by using a longitudinal design where I look simultaneously at how human capital influences both entrepreneurial continuation and performance.

How does entrepreneurial human capital shape the entrepreneurial process?

Coff (2005) defines entrepreneurial human capital as '*the set of knowledge and skills that individuals can bring to bear to create and exploit market opportunities*'. Since the central research question in human capital literature is return on investment, a similarly important question for entrepreneurial human capital should be: what is the return on investment in entrepreneurial human capital? In other words, how can increases in entrepreneurial human capital lead to successful new ventures (Coff, 2005)? According to Iyigin and Owen (1998) entrepreneurial human capital is the result of skills gained from experiences in entrepreneurship. Shane and Khurana suggested that prior entrepreneurial experience provides the entrepreneur with tacit skills and knowledge such as how to organize and finance a new firm, how to hire and lead people, but do not explicitly investigate what these skills are (Shane & Khurana, 2003). The theoretical work by Iyigin and Owen also suggests that industry-specific skills as well as more or less successful experience in entrepreneurship should be investigated. There seems to be a consistent finding in the literature that prior entrepreneurial experience is a strong predictor of subsequent entry (Bates, 1995; Carroll & Mosakowski, 1987; Evans & Leigton, 1989; Wiklund et al., 2004). I therefore believe that the accumulated length of prior experiences, i.e. whether an individual has experience from one, two or several earlier ventures should increase the likelihood of subsequent entry. This forms the logic behind a second hypothesis:

Hypothesis 2: Higher entrepreneurial human capital will increase the likelihood of entry into entrepreneurship.

In his article on entrepreneurial human capital, Coff (2005) cites the arguments made by labor economist Oi (1999) that entrepreneurship is too risky an endeavor to be considered a distinct human capital construct since individuals cannot make rational decisions on how much to invest. Coff therefore suggests that an 'investment under uncertainty' perspective, such as real options theory, might be a fruitful way to advance our thinking on entrepreneurial human capital. This study follows Coff's suggestion by applying real options as theoretical perspective where utility-maximizing individuals choose between paid employment or entrepreneurship in an uncertain market characterized by imperfect information.

How do real options shape the entrepreneurial process?

Real options theory argues that potentially profitable investments should be explored whenever possible, while at the same time limiting the commitment of resources that are tied to the specific investment. According to Kogut and Kulatikala (2001), a real option is defined as 'an investment decision that is characterized by uncertainty, the provision of future managerial discretion to exercise at the appropriate time, and irreversibility' (p.746). Real options analysis is a popular tool for determining the relative attractiveness of different investments under conditions of uncertainty. The focus on uncertainty, managerial discretion, and irreversibility share three fundamental connections to entrepreneurship theory. First, theories of entrepreneurship, such as Knight's (1921) framework, frequently centers around 'non-insurable risk' (i.e. uncertainty) as the key determinant of why certain market opportunities are left unexplored by existing firms, and why only some individuals are willing to bear the risk associated with exploring such opportunities. Second, entrepreneurship theory highlights the importance of individual agents that engage in new enterprising activities that established firms do not pursue. These individuals start new firms that to a large extent are formed by their personal goals, skills, and ambitions – in other words they as founders exert an exceptionally high level of discretion in how they choose to pursue their strategic goals. Third, entrepreneurial individuals place a high personal stake by leaving what they did before, and investing time and resources to establish a new firm – time and resources that most often are irreversible investments in that they cannot be re-used for other purposes. Applying real options logic to entrepreneurship indicates that the trade-off between the uncertainty and the irreversibly of an investment in a new venture should allow entrepreneurs to generate more information about the real value of an opportunity before making additional investments (Choi & Shepherd, 2004). This chapter therefore does not focus on the ability to recognize an opportunity but on the choice of how to exploit it in the presence of dueling options. Real options theory stems from Myers' observation that a company value results from both, (1) assets in place, and (2) opportunities to purchase real assets at potentially favorable prices in the future. Founded on the option valuation model of Blacks and Scholes, management research tends not to employ a formal valuation model of real options but rather uses real options analyses in analogous terms. Although the value of real options may be difficult to calculate precisely, there is ample evidence that the managers of public firms (Kogut & Kulatilaka, 2001) as well as entrepreneurs (Cave & Minty, 2004; O'Brien, Folta, & Johnson, 2003; Wennberg, Folta, & Delmar, 2006) often employ a 'real options heuristic'. That is, their strategic decisions might not constitute financial options in the sense of having a calculated value and duration attached to these; rather their decisions are formed by the uncertainty and irreversibility of the specific investment decision, implying real options logic. In empirical tests of such real options heuristics, previous literature has focused on two specific attributes of the Blacks and Scholes formula: uncertainty (volatility), and irreversibility (duration time). Existing real options models of the investment/entry decision have focused on the costs associated with the irreversibility of, or sunk, capital, indicating that these costs amount to a commitment value called an *option to defer* (O'Brien et al., 2003). The logic behind the option to defer is that if entry can be delayed, and it involves sunk costs that cannot be recovered in the event of subsequent exit, there might be gains in delaying the entry decision in face of uncertain outcomes. As irreversibility increases, the value of the option to defer increases, lowering the likelihood of entry. I use these predictions to formulate a test whether entrepreneurs make use of a real option heuristic:

Hypothesis 3: Irreversibility will exhibit a negative effect on entrepreneurial entry, decreasing the likelihood of entry as irreversibility increases.

Most initial investment, such as entry into entrepreneurship or an incumbent firm's entry into a new industry subfield, can be characterized by a dual option framework where the option to defer exists in combination with an option to grow (O'Brien et al., 2003). Where the value of defer options stems from the postponement of irreversible investments to gather more information (second-mover advantage), the value of growth options stem from the opportunity that an initial investment will provide valuable opportunities to expand further in the future (first-mover advantage). From this perspective, the growth options for entrepreneurs constitute the possibility to make small initial investments in product or service development, production capacity, and in the development of sales and distribution networks to assess the feasibility of the business opportunity. Kulatilaka and Perrotti (1998) suggest that these different options will dominate the entry decision at different levels of uncertainty. At intermediate levels of uncertainty, the option to defer will be the most valuable, inducing possible entrepreneurs to postpone their entry decision, and thus to lower the likelihood of entry. At high levels of uncertainty, the option of growth will be the most valuable, inducing possible entrepreneurs to enter immediately for the possibility of future growth. The trade-off between deferral and growth options indicates that likelihood of entry will be negatively influenced in equal measures by intermediate levels of uncertainty, but positively influenced by high levels of uncertainty, indicating a non-monotonic effect. I use these predictions as a second hypothesized test of a real option heuristic:

Hypothesis 4: Uncertainty will exhibit a non-monotonic and U-shaped effect on entrepreneurial entry, decreasing the likelihood of entry as uncertainty increases up to a point where very high levels of uncertainty will increase the likelihood of entry.

Up until this point, the suggested effects of human capital and real options heuristics have been hypothesized to affect entry into entrepreneurship. But as I have argued, different types of human capital may be important at different stages of the entrepreneurial process. From a real options perspective, entrepreneurs should be quick to invest in exploring attractive opportunities, however the real options heuristic suggests that entrepreneurs should stage investment into the new venture so as to be able to disband quickly if the opportunity proves not to be valuable or to be too difficult to exploit. In this sense, a real options heuristic provides a way for entrepreneurs to test the value of a plausible business opportunity (Delmar, Wennberg, & Hellerstedt, 2006). Then, the successful entrepreneur will have more prior start-up attempts if she or he is operating under a real options heuristic. Prior research suggests that people with a history of starting new ventures will continue to identify and exploit entrepreneurial opportunities (Shane, 2003; Shepherd, Douglas & Shanley, 2000), but to date there is very little research suggesting that entrepreneurial human capital has anything but a positive affect on all parts of the entrepreneurial process (the study by Gimeno et al., 1997 is a rare exception). If entrepreneurs really do make use of a real option heuristic, entrepreneurial human capital should not only be positively associated with entry, but should also be positively associated with exit. This forms the base for my fifth and final hypothesis:

Hypothesis 5: Higher entrepreneurial human capital will increase the probability of exit.

METHOD OF STUDY

Data

The primary source of data for this study is 'Longitudinell databas om utbildning, inkomster och sysselsättning' (LOUISE), an extensive longitudinal database maintained by Statistics Sweden. LOUISE includes detailed demographic information such as sex, age, extent and type of education, employment, and family situation of all inhabitants in Sweden. It also includes variables from the fiscal authorities such as earnings and wealth. This database was supplemented with publicly available information on characteristics of specific industries and regions, drawn from Statistics Sweden's publicly available databases at www.scb.se.

Dependent variables

Similarly to Holtz-Eakin, Joulfaian and Rosen (1994) I used tax sheets to identify self-employed entrepreneurs. The sample frame includes all Swedish individuals who during the period 1989-2002 were employed or self-employed in any of the 33 industries that are the focus of this study (see Appendix 3.1). Industries were delineated by the two digit SIC-equivalent industry codes. I excluded some industries with low or no entry barriers such as agriculture, fishing, retailing, transportation, and hotel and restaurant firms, which are dominated by small and/or part-time firms such as home-based catering firms and taxi services. I also had to exclude a small number of industries, such as finance and specialized education, which were of theoretical interest but where neither an uncertainty measure nor the financial control variables were available. The sample is therefore a population study including all individuals in the relevant industries (N=897,554). The proportion of self-employed entrepreneurs in the sample exceeded six percent; however the annual proportions of *entries* were only 1.62 percent. A methodological problem of investigating such 'rare events' is that discrete choice techniques such as logit or probit will underestimate the probability of rare outcomes (King & Zeng, 2001), in this case entry into entrepreneurship. To account for this problem and also to make data manipulation and analysis more efficient, I used state-based sampling (Manski & McFadden, 1981) by modeling the entry decision with a series of multivariate logistic regression models that compare instances of entry with a 10 percent random sample of all the non-entries. State-based sampling yields unbiased and consistent coefficients for all variables except the constant term which makes hypothesis testing unproblematic (Manski & McFadden, 1981). However, with a biased constant the model will have low predictive accuracy. A feasible way to correct the constant is by subtracting from it the log of the proportion of all entries in sample/proportion of all non-entries in the sample.[1] The final sample consisted of 14,515 instances of entry (14.12 percent) and 88,304 randomly sampled non-entries (85.88 percent).

The first dependent variable, *entry*, is a dichotomous indicator of whether an individual entered entrepreneurship at some time during 1997 and was not active as a self-employed entrepreneur during the preceding two years. As an entrepreneur, I define an individual who reports income from a company in which they work at least part-time and in which they have a significant ownership stake. The study includes self-employed entrepreneurs regardless of the legal form of their corporation, i.e. incorporations as well as partnerships and sole proprietorships are included. The second dependent variable, *exit*, is a time-varying indicator of whether an individual persists as self-employed during each of the following years 1998-2002.

Independent Variables

Education: Following human capital theory of labor market productivity, I expected education to have a positive effect on entrepreneurial entry. I measured years of education as the general length of an education (such as nine years of elementary school plus three years of high school) provided by educational codes in LOUISE.

Prior experience from entrepreneurship is considered a strong predictor of subsequent entry (Bates, 1995; Carroll & Mosakowski, 1987; Davidsson & Honig, 2003). I used the available data on individuals' labor market activities 1989-1996 to create a variable of prior entrepreneurial venturing counting the occasions of prior entries into self-employment. I first allowed all occasion where there was at least a one-year gap between the spells of self-employment to constitute a prior venturing activity. However, the data indicated that several individuals clearly entered and exited the same industry at the same location at close intervals; perhaps closing and starting the same proprietorship firm (see also Wiklund et al., 2004). I therefore added the requirement that there must be at least a two-year gap between spells of self-employment in *the same industry* and *at the same location* to constitute a single venturing activity.[2]

---

[1] In this case, ln(0.1/1.00) is added to the constant term, since we include one-tenth of all non-entries, together with all entries.

[2] Since this variable is measured from 1989 onwards, it is 'truncated'. This indicates a risk of underestimating the effect of the variance in the variable at the positive end of the distribution (i.e. we cannot distinguish between 4 prior spells and 2 prior spells of experience). Unless the variable has non-linear effects, any bias caused by the truncation of this variable is therefore likely to cause us to underestimate the effect of entrepreneurial experience, not overestimate it.

Uncertainty is a crucial characterization of the entrepreneurial process. Commonly, measures reflecting uncertainty are based on some variation in output such as stock price or GDP (O'Brien et al., 2003). However, this way of conceptualizing uncertainty as variation in an output suffers from two deficiencies: first, it does not capture trends in the data. Trends in the data will increase the variance, but it does constitute an element of uncertainty if they are predictable. It is therefore necessary to seek a measure of uncertainty that only considers variance about a predicted trend. Second, variation in an output does not account for the possibility that the variance is non-constant over time, i.e. heteroskedastic (Bollerslev, 1986). To deal with these two problems, uncertainty was measured as the conditional variance generated from a generalized autoregressive conditional heteroskedasticity (GARCH) model (Bollerslev, 1986). This model produced a time-varying estimate of uncertainty about the actual trend. I used publicly available data on industry-level investment levels, measured quarterly from 1990 to 1997. It should be pointed out that since managers are able to control variation in inputs, not all of this variance will reflect uncertainty (Foss & Laursen, 2005). Yet, to some extent this is also the case of output measures such as sales, stock returns or profitability. What I seek is an approximation for time-varying uncertainty related to entrepreneurial opportunities in different industry contexts. For this purpose, the GARCH model provided a unique estimate of uncertainty for each of the thirty-three industries in focus. I also include the squared term of uncertainty to investigate its potential non-linear effects. The squared uncertain term indicates the existence of growth options in an industry (O'Brien et al., 2003).

Irreversibility: A concern is that the effect of industry-specific uncertainty does not properly capture the theoretical arguments that the effects of uncertainty should be particularly high for entrepreneurs entering in industries that require significant capital outlay. Specifically, prior research indicated that the negative influence of uncertainty on investing in the venture might be greater for investment decisions that carries higher irrevocably capital outlays (O'Brien et al., 2003). I approximate for industry-level irreversibility by two variables: the *level of fixed assets* and the *level of leverage* within an industry. Entry decisions are generally considered more irreversible for industries that are characterized by extensive entry barriers. I used a measure of fixed relative to total asset in the industry to capture this effect, the theoretical rationale being that fixed assets such as buildings, machinery and equipment are less easily liquidated in face of adverse performance compared to other assets such as current inventories or accounts payable (Lambson & Jensen, 1998). Regardless of the type of assets that new firms invest in, industry leverage level may serve as another useful indication of the salvage value of assets. Assets with high salvage value can support a high debt ration, while

Variable	Mean	S.D.	Min	Max	1	2	3	4	5	6	7	8	9	10
1 Entry	0.141	0.348	0	1	1									
2 Entrepren. experience Years	0.096	0.352	0	3	0.077	1								
3 education	12.289	2.399	0	20	0.047	0.001	1							
4 Industry. experience	1.298	0.594	0	2.303	-0.176	0.005	0.013	1						
5 Uncertainty	68574	143638	25.475	1062854	-0.053	-0.045	0.001	0.066	1					
6 Uncertainty^2 inverse	2.53+10E	1.36+11E	648.985	1.13+13E	-0.036	-0.034	0.005	0.036	0.941	1				
7 leverage	0.790	0.059	0.611	1	-0.069	-0.076	0.061	0.059	-0.031	-0.088	1			
8 Fixed assets	0.407	0.123	0.190	2.472	-0.053	-0.039	-0.034	0.122	0.492	0.397	-0.390	1		
9 Age	38.386	12.503	0	71	0.079	0.161	-0.002	0.293	-0.009	-0.012	-0.037	0.041	1	
10 Net result (log)	343,520	423,210	8.23+9E	4.23-9E	n/a	0.121	0.031	0.108	0.023	0.010	-0.137	0.101	0.041	1

Note: All correlations exceeding ± 0.012 significant at the 5% level.

Table 3.1 Variables and correlation matrix

assets with low salvage value will have to rely on equity financing (Williamson, 1985). For example, the overwhelming majority of Swedish IT firms started during the dot-com bubble relied solely on equity financing since they rarely provide loan managers with asset security. Investments required to enter high leverage industries should therefore be more reversible than the investments required to enter low leverage industries. Consistent with investment research such as Gompers (1995), the inverse leverage variable was calculated as the inverse of the industry's long-term debt divided by total book assets. All independent variables together with their means and standard deviation are listed in Table 3.1.

Control variables

I include a set of individual-level, industry-level, and geographical-level variables known to affect people's probability to enter and continue in entrepreneurship. Measures of *family net wealth* was included to control 'tax sheltering' effects, i.e. the possibility that an affluent person will set up for income optimization purposes (Henreksson, 2005; Holtz-Eakin et al., 1994). *Gender* and *number of children* under 18 years living in the household, as well as dummy variables for ethnic background were included. Preliminary analyses indicated that certain ethnic backgrounds had a positive or negative effect on likelihood of entry and I therefore collapsed similar regions of birth into five dummy variables: *Swedish*, *Nordic* (Scandinavia), *Western* (Europe and North America) *Eastern* (Eastern Europe), and *Other* (Africa, Asia). I also include a control for the number of unemployment days in 1996 since the unemployed face widely different opportunity costs in terms of alternatives on the labor market. I account for industry-level factors that might be correlated with the present value of the entry opportunities. The general attractiveness of an industry was captured by the variable *industry profitability*, which measures the industry's average pre-tax result. *Industry size* and *R&D intensity* was captured by the logged total revenues and R&D investments per employee within the specific industry. Because start-ups are generally attracted to growing markets, I include the variable *population growth* that measures the local county's net growth in population. I also control for *population density* per region, and a measure of *county tenure* which functions as a coarse proxy for the social network that comes from living for many years in the same region. Finally, I controlled the local bankruptcy rate.

Statistical analyses

The hypotheses were tested in a two-step procedure. To investigate the first four hypotheses, which predict that the theoretically derived variables will affect individuals' probability to enter into entrepreneurship, I estimated a series of logistic regression models comparing all entries with the random sample of non-entries. To test the fifth hypothesis, I calculated survival tables for the 14,515 entrepreneurs that did enter in 1997 up until 2002. To compare the effects of entrepreneurial human capital on the entrepreneurs that exit or continue I used between-group significance tests of the survival functions. Specifically, I used Breslow's generalized wilcoxon test that is derived from the proportional hazard model which makes it possible to compare groups with unequal duration in a particular state, such as groups that exit versus groups that remain in entrepreneurship (Breslow, 1970). Since this is a simpler bivariate type of test, the results were verified by unreported multivariate hazard models using all of the independent and control variables in table 3.1 as control variables.

RESULTS

The results of the logistic regression model are shown below in table 3.2. The first model introduces the control variables, which with the exception of age are suppressed to save space. The second model introduces the human capital variables, the third model includes the real options variables, and the fourth and final model include all variables. The change in log-likelihood value for models 2, 3, and 4 are positive and significant, indicating that the theoretically derived variables add explanatory power to the model. The largest gain in log-likelihood, variance explained (Pseudo R2) and classification accuracy is model 2 which introduced the human capital variables.

I first investigated the effects of individual's general human capital on entrepreneurial entry. The human capital variables are introduced in the second model in table 3.2. Consistent with much prior research, higher education exhibits a strong and significantly positive effect on entry. I therefore find support for the first hypotheses; higher education raises the likelihood of entering into entrepreneurship. However, the effects are not very strong: Computing marginal odds ratios from the logistic regression estimates, I find that if all variables are held constant at their means, one additional year of schooling increases the likelihood of entry by 1 percent.

A key part of this study is to validate and extend prior studies of entrepreneurial human capital. Following the earlier literature, I measured entrepreneurial human capital as the prior experience in entrepreneurship together with relevant industry experience. However, instead of simply using an indicator variable of experience/no experience, I looked at prior occasions of starting and running a small firm. Looking again at the second model in Table 3.2, prior entrepreneurial experience appeared as the strongest positive predictors of entry. The marginal effects reveal that each spell of earlier experience from entrepreneurship increased the likelihood of entry by 3-5 percent. I also hypothesized that relevant industry experience would positively impact entry. Surprisingly, the effect of industry experience is very strong and significant – but in the opposite direction as hypothesized. This means that I cannot affirm hypothesis two – while prior entrepreneurial experience has a positive effect on the likelihood of entry, the negative effect of industry experience is much stronger: Holding all other variables constant at their means, each additional year of earlier industry experience decrease the likelihood of entry by 5-8 percent. This indicates that research should avoid lumping together, industry and entrepreneurial experience when conceptualizing entrepreneurial human capital, or, Swedish entrepreneurs are different than entrepreneurs studied earlier in other countries in that they for

	Base model	Human capital model	Real Options model	Full model
Constant	18,117***	21,854***	16,728***	19,351***
	(3,623)	(0,393)	(5,688)	(0,339)
Entrepren. experience		0.275***		0.259***
		(0.025)		(0.025)
Years education		0.083***		0.070***
		(0.005)		(0.005)
Industry, experience		-1.207***		-1.179***
		(0.024)		(0.024)
Uncertainty			-0.373***	-0.233***
(coeff.* 10^{-6})			(0.040)	(0.041)
Uncertainty ^{2}			0.005***	0.003***
(coeff.* 10^{-9})			(0.000)	(0.000)
Inverse leverage			-3.751***	-3.420***
			(0.266)	(0.272)
Fixed assets			-1.042***	-0.805***
			(0.158)	(0.159)
Age	0.026***	0.033***	0.025***	0.032***
	(0.001)	(0.001)	(0.001)	(0.001)
Observations	88304	88304	88304	88304
Log-likelihood:	-35594.5	-33601.7	-35205.9	-33350.23
Pseudo-R2:	0.036	0.090	0.056	0.106
Correctly classified cases:	80.90%	81.37%	80.96%	82.71%
Δ Log-likelihood:		3985.64***	777.32***	4468.57***

Note: Huber-White Standard errors in parentheses, control variables except age suppressed. ΔLR is for the improvement in model fit versus base model. *p>05; **p>0.01; ***p>.001 (two-tailed).

Table 3.2 Logit models on entry into entrepreneurship

some reason enter different industries than from which they have experience. I return to this issue in the discussion section.

Looking at the real option effects introduced in model 3, I first investigate the effect of industry-level irreversibility on the likelihood of entry. It is evident in model 3 that both the level of fixed assets and the level of inverse leverage have negative influence on entry. I therefore confirm Hypothesis 3: higher levels of irreversibility lowers the likelihood of entry, consistent with the theory behind the option to defer. Since the absolute levels of fixed assets and inverse leverage are based on proportions, their incremental marginal effects provide no interpretable value. In Table 3.3 below, I therefore demonstrate the marginal effect on entry by proportional changes in the irreversibility and uncertainty variables, ranging from one to two standard deviations of change in the independent variables. As can be seen in Table 3.3, holding all other variables constant, a one standard increase change in inverse leverage lowers the likelihood of entry by 3-7 percent. A one standard increase change in fixed assets similarly lowers the likelihood of entry by 2-3 percent.

Variable	1 St.Dev.	2 St.Dev.
Uncertainty	–4,4%.	–8,8%
Uncertainty ^{2}	+5,3%	+10,6%
Inverse leverage	–3,7%.	–7,4%.
Fixed assets	–2,3%.	–4,6%.

Table 3.3 Change in probability of entry after a relative change in independent variable

Turning finally to investigate how industry-specific uncertainty affects the likelihood of entry, I look at the linear and squared terms of uncertainty that are also introduced in model 3 of Table 3.2. Since the incremental values of uncertainty in the study does not constitute a meaningful value but only an estimate of volatility in each industry, uncertainty takes on values from 25-46 up until over one million. The coefficients for uncertainty and uncertainty-squared are therefore raised to the power of 10 several times for ease of interpretability. It is apparent from model 3 that industry-specific uncertainty, computed from the GARCH volatility model, had a significantly negative effect on the probability to enter. This provides additional support for the use of a real options heuristics in this study of Swedish entrepreneurs. Conversely, I find that the squared term of uncertainty, approximating for the presence of growth options in an industry, is negatively related to entry. This second finding is consistent with real options theory that the value of growth options should overtake the value of deferral options at high levels of uncertainty. I therefore find support for Hypothesis 4. As can be seen in Table

3.3, a, one standard change in uncertainty lowers the likelihood of entry by 4 percent whereas a one standard increase in uncertainty-squared increases the likelihood of entry by 5-3 percent. It should be remembered however that this second effect seems to be apparent only at very high levels of uncertainty.

Bivariate life table analysis

Figure 3.1 presents the exit patterns of the 14,515 entrepreneurs that in 1997 entered any of the 33 industries studied. Almost 50 percent exited within two years after entry, and after five years, more than two thirds of the sample exited from entrepreneurship. These figures are somewhat higher than the general pattern of self-employment duration found in Sweden (Delmar, Sjöberg, & Wiklund, 2003) as well as studies pertaining to Great Britain (Taylor, 1999) and the United States (Van Praag, 2005), but the differences are much smaller for the five-year exit rate compared to the two-year exit rate. For ease of interpretation, in this more simple bivariate analysis of the effect of entrepreneurial human capital on exit from entrepreneurship, I, similar to most prior studies, measure experience by giving all individuals with some prior experience in entrepreneurship an indicator variable, regardless of whether the individuals have had one, two or three spell of experience in entrepreneurship. I compare the exit rates of these 'experienced' entrepreneurs with the 'non-experienced' entrepreneurs by plotting two different Kaplan-Meier survival graphs in Figure 3.1.

From the two different Kaplan-Meier survival graphs in Figure 3.1, experienced entrepreneurs clearly seem to have higher exit rates. After little more than one year in entrepreneurship, 40.58 percent of the entrepreneurs with prior experience had exited, compared to 34.31 percent of non-experienced entrepreneurs. After one year, the difference in survival function is also significant in the expected direction (Chi-2 statistic: 43.23). However, the difference in survival function between entrepreneurs with and without prior experience diminished as they age. After five years in entrepreneurship, the remaining difference is very small with 32.25 percent of non-experienced entrepreneurs remaining compared to 30.16 of experienced entrepreneurs. This is an indication that after a few years, most entrepreneurs have been able to assess their business opportunity and whether they are able to establish a firm or not, and the real option heuristic effect has played out its role. Nevertheless, the difference between the survival functions of experienced and non-experienced entrepreneurs is still significant across all years of study (Chi-2 statistic: 18.73). A key finding of this study, which was not documented in the earlier research on entrepreneurial human capital is that prior entrepreneurial experience can be a strong predictor of *both* subsequent re-entry and exit from the new venture. This finding verifies the fifth and final hypothesis, adding to the accumulating evidence that entrepreneur use real options heuristic in their decision-making.

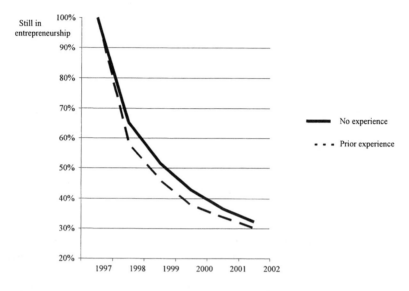

Note: Total number of entries: 14,515. 95 percent confidence interval is within the boundaries of the lines. Analysis time is year.

Figure 3.1 Kaplan-Meier graph on exit from entrepreneurship

DISCUSSION

This chapter started with the observation that an accumulating number of entrepreneurship studies have focused on the role of entrepreneurial human capital, often conceptualized as prior entrepreneurial experience, and investigated how this affect subsequent entrepreneurial processes that a person engages in. In this chapter I have argued that an 'investment under uncertainty' perspective offers a way to conceptualize how human capital affect the entrepreneurial process since individuals acting as entrepreneurs on an uncertain market cannot make predictable decisions on how much to invest. To verify these ideas, I studied processes of entrepreneurial entry and exit in a large sample of Swedish entrepreneurs, using theories of entrepreneurial human capital and real options to present testable hypotheses. I found that general human capital in the form of education and entrepreneurial human capital in the form of prior experiences in entrepreneurship were positively related to the likelihood that an individual would enter entrepreneurship. However, industry experience had a strong negative effect of entry. One possible conclusion is that industry-specific experiences are more valuable in subsequent employment rather than for entering self-employment as an entrepreneur. Another possible conclusion is that some specific institutional framework in Sweden, possibly its tenure-based system of job security, makes the opportunity cost of leaving employment too high for individuals with extensive experience at a single workplace (Henreksson, 2005). If these patterns are evident also in other countries, this would indicate that future research should avoid lumping together industry and entrepreneurial experience when conceptualizing entrepreneurial human capital. More cross-national research on this issue is therefore needed.

I found that the variables used to approximate for the presence of real options heuristics: uncertainty and irreversibility, had negative effects on the probability of entry, consistent with the existence of an option to defer. Also, the squared term of uncertainty was positively associated with the probability of entry, indicating that entrepreneurs are driven by growth options that at some level become more valuable than the option to defer investment. Much economic and management research has demonstrated the importance of entrepreneurial human capital in the form of prior entrepreneurial experience for individuals to engage yet again in entrepreneurship (Davidsson & Honig, 2003; Taylor, 1996). In this study I find the same patterns, however it was also apparent that individuals with prior experience are more likely to abandon their ventures at an early stage. I interpret this finding as consistent with the investment under uncertainty perspective: entrepreneurs with extensive prior experience have accumulated specific skills that allow them to excel in certain tasks, however they cannot forecast *ex ante* whether a particular opportunity will appear to be valuable or not. Individuals with high entrepreneurial human capital therefore seem to use real option strategies in that they more frequently identify and exploit new opportunities, and also they are more likely to abandon their ventures if the opportunity does not prove valuable enough. The benefit of these strategies to experienced entrepreneurs is the possibility of rapidly entering and exiting industries to test different business opportunities. Entrepreneurial human capital therefore seems to affect both the discovery and the exploitation side of business opportunities (Shane, 2003). These findings are associated with the emerging research streams on 'serial' or 'renascent' entrepreneurship. For example, Stam, Audretsch, and Meijaard (2006) similarly found that ex-entrepreneurs whose prior firms had survived more than three years, were not more likely to re-enter entrepreneurship than those who kept their firms only for a shorter period. More research assessing the roles of entrepreneurial human capital on serial/renascent entrepreneurship under a real options perspective is certainly warranted.

CONCLUSIONS AND LIMITATIONS

Using literature in economics and strategy, this chapter proposes that an 'investment under uncertainty' perspective offers a way to think about individuals' investment in human capital and how this should affect the entrepreneurial process. By showing that the entry and exit decisions is not only affected by entrepreneurs human capital but also by the industry-level uncertainty and irreversibility, the chapter offers some empirical evidence that real options logic affects entrepreneurs' entry and exit decisions. While some prior research has found similar patterns for entrepreneurial entry, this study is to the best of my knowledge the first to indicate that exit is positively associated with prior entrepreneurial experience. This is a counterintuitive result from a human capital perspective, but a result that is fully in the line with a real options perspective.

This study also comes with several limitations, all of which offers important pathways for future research attempts. A first limitation is that similar to most entrepreneurship research, I did not account for the fact that people with higher unobserved ability might be particularly prone to engage in entrepreneurship. An important path for economic oriented research in entrepreneurship would therefore be to collect data that could be used as an instrument to approximate for unobserved ability, for example score on intelligence or aptitude tests (Van Praag, 2005).

A second limitation of this study is that the variables used are not very detailed. Seeking an inclusive and unbiased sample with a large set of control variables to allow for comprehensive analyses, I used labor market databases that by definition are quite coarse. For example, the performance variable I controlled was limited to personal earnings of self-employed entrepreneurs. It is possible that outcomes other than earnings such as firm growth or successful development of new products are more important for entrepreneurs, at least in the short run. Future research should therefore be aimed at collecting more diverse types of outcome variables to empirically scrutinize the model of entrepreneurial human capital. Also, the predictor variables used to test the theoretical model of entrepreneurial human capital was limited to work position and length and type of industry experience. While it was found that prior experience from entrepreneurship and industry experience from several different sectors did have an effect on subsequent entrepreneurial entry and exit processes, this leaves an important question unanswered: what type of activities do people accumulate through entrepreneurial human capital in order to become successful entrepreneurs? Research on entrepreneurial career experience have suggested that owner-manager activities such as business planning, hand-to-hand marketing and negotiation skills may be such activities (Politis, 2005), but detailed empirical research on this topic is still lacking. Inductive research methods such as job content analysis or observational studies of practicing entrepreneurs (see e.g. Landberg, this volume) could provide some useful suggestions.

I am grateful to Russell Coff for intellectual input and to Tim Folta and Frédéric Delmar for help on a related project. Veronica Höök kindly checked the language. All errors remain my own.

Appendix: Industries in the sample

SIC-2	Industry	Number of entries
15	Manufacture of food products and beverages	155
16	Manufacture of tobacco products	2
17	Manufacture of textiles	51
18	Manufacture of wearing apparel; dressing and dyeing of fur	40
19	Tanning and dressing of leather; manufacture of luggage, handbags, saddlery, harness and footwear	15
20	Wood products	166
21	Pulp and paper	73
22	Publishing, printing and reproduction of recorded media	496
23	Manufacture of coke, refined petroleum products and nuclear fuel	4
24	Manufacture of chemicals products and pharmaceuticals	136
25	Manufacture of rubber and plastic products	82
26	Manufacture of other non-metallic mineral products	42
27	Manufacture and casting of metals	44
28	Manufacture of fabricated metal products, except machinery and equipment	280
29	Manufacture of machinery and equipment n.e.c.	370
30	Manufacture of office machinery and computers	55
31	Manufacture of electrical machinery and apparatus n.e.c.	179
32	Manufacture of radio, television and communication equipment and apparatus	277
33	Manufacture of medical, precision and optical instruments, watches and clocks	194
34	Manufacture of motor vehicles, trailers and semi-trailers	298
35	Manufacture of other transport equipment	118
36	Manufacture of furniture; manufacturing n.e.c.	139
37	Recycling	4
40	Gas, water and electricity	58
45	Construction and other engineering activities; technical testing and analysis	1130
50	Sale, maintenance and repair of motor vehicles and motorcycles; retail sale of automotive fuel	277
51	Wholesale trade and commission trade, except of motor vehicles and motorcycles	1143
52	Retail trade, except of motor vehicles and motorcycles; repair of personal and household goods	1348
71	Renting of machinery and equipment without operator and of personal and household goods	84

72	Computers and related activities	1272
73	Research and development	448
74	Business services	5510
90	Sanitation services	25

REFERENCES

Amit, R., Muller, E., & Cockburn, I. (1995). Opportunity costs and entrepreneurial activity. *Journal of Business Venturing, 10*(2), 95-106.

Baker, T., Miner, A. S., & Eesley, D. T. (2003). Improvising firms, Bricolage, account giving and improvisational competencies in the founding process. *Research Policy, 32*(2), 255.

Bates, T. (1990). Entrepreneur human capital and small business longevity. *The Review of Economics and Statistics, 72*(4), 551-559.

Bates, T. (1995). Entrepreneurship entry across industry groups. *Journal of Business Venturing, 10*(2), 143-156.

Becker, G. S. (1964). *Human capital, a theoretical and empirical analysis, with special reference to education* (2. ed.). New York. National Bureau of Economic Research.

Bollerslev, T. (1986). Generalized autoregressive conditional heteroskedasticity. *Journal of Econometrics, 31*, 307-327.

Breslow, N. (1970). A generalized Kruskal-Wallis test for comparing K samples subject to unequal patterns of censorship. *Biometrika, 57*(3), 579-594.

Brüderl, J., Preisendörfer, P., & Ziegler, R. (1992). Survival Chances of newly founded business organizations. *American Sociological Review, 57*(April), 227-242.

Carroll, G. & Mosakowski, E. (1987). The career dynamics of Self-Employment. *Administrative Science Quarterly, 32* (4): 570-589.

Cave, F. & Minty, A. (2004). How Do Entrepreneurs View Opportunities, Rose Tinted Spectacles or the Real Options Lens?, *Journal of Private Equity, 7*, 60-67.

Choi, Y. R. & Shepherd, D. A. (2004). Entrepreneurs' Decisions to Exploit Opportunities. *Journal of Management, 30*(3), 377-395.

Coff, R. (2005). Entrepreneurial human capital. In M. A. Hitt & R. D. Ireland (Eds.), *Blackwell Encyclopedia of Management*, Volume III, Entrepreneurship. Malden, MA, Blackwell.

Davidsson, P. & Honig, B. (2003). The role of social and human capital among nascent entrepreneurs. *Journal of Business Venturing, 18*(3), 301-331.

Delmar, F., Hellerstedt, K., & Wennberg, K. (2006). The evolution of firms created by the science and technology labor force in Sweden 1990-2000. In J. Ulhöi. & P.R. Christensen (Eds.). *Managing Complexity and Change in SMEs* (pp 69-102). Cheltenham, UK and Northampton, MA, USA: Edward Elgar.

Delmar, F., Sjöberg, K. & Wiklund J. (2003). *The involvement in self-employment among the Swedish science and technology labor force between 1990 and 2000*. Stockholm: ITPS.

Evans, D. S. & Leighton, L. S. (1989). Some Empirical Aspects of Entrepreneurship. *The American Economic Review*, *79*(3), 519-535.

Foss, N. & Laursen, K. (2005). Performance Pay, Delegation, and Multitasking Under Uncertainty and Innovativeness, an Empirical Investigation. *Journal of Economic Behavior and Organization*, *58*, 246–276.

Gimeno, J., Folta, T. B., Cooper, A. C., & Woo, C. Y. (1997). Survival of the fittest? Entrepreneurial human capital and the persistence of underperforming firms. *Administrative Science Quarterly*, *42*(4), 750-783.

Gompers, P. A. (1995). Optimal investment, monitoring and the staging of venture capital. *Journal of Finance*, *50*(5), 1461-1489.

Hayward, M., Shepherd, D.A., & Griffin, D. (2006). A hubris theory of entrepreneurship. *Management Science,* *52*(2): 160-172.

Henreksson, M. (2005). Entrepreneurship, a weak link in the welfare state? *Industrial and Corporate Change, 14*(3), 437-467.

Holtz-Eakin, D., Joulfaian, D., & Rosen, H. S. (1994). Sticking it out, Entrepreneurial survival and liquidity constraints. *Journal of Political Economy*, *102*(1), 53.

Honig, B. (2001). Human capital and structural upheaval, A study of manufacturing firms in the west bank. *Journal of Business Venturing*, *16*(6), 575-594.

Iyigun, M. & Owen, A. (1998). Risk, entrepreneurship and human capital accumulation. *American Economic Review*, *88*, 454-457.

King, G. & Zeng, L. (2001). Logistic Regression in Rare Events Data, *Political Analysis*, *9*(2), 137-163.

Kirzner, I. M. (1973). *Competition and Entrepreneurship*. Chicago: University of Chicago Press.

Knight, F. (1921) *Risk, Uncertainty, and Profit*. Boston: Houghton-Mifflin.

Kogut, B. & Kulatilaka, N. (2001). Capabilities as real options. *Organization Science*, *12*(6), 744-758.

Kulatilaka, N. & Perrotti, E. C. (1998). Strategic growth options. *Management Science*, *44*(8), 1021-1031.

Lambson, V. E. & Jensen F. E. (1998). Sunk costs and firm value variability, theory and evidence. *American Economic Review*, *88*, 307–313.

Landberg, A. (2009). Refueling or Running Dry: Entrepreneurs' Energetic Resources and the Start-up Process. In C. Holmquist & J.Wiklund (Eds.) Entrepreneurship and the Creation of Small Firms (pp. 149-179). Cheltenham, UK and Northampton, MA, USA: Edward Elgar.

Lévesque, M., Choi, Y. R., & Shepherd, D. (2004). *Exploration or Exploitation? Decision Rules for Entrepreneurs of New Ventures.* Cleveland: Case Western Reserve University.

Manski C. & McFadden, D. (1981). Alternative Estimators and Sample Designs for Discrete Choice Analysis. In C. Manski and D. McFadden (Eds.) *Structural Analysis and Discrete Data with Econometric Applications.* Boston: MIT Press.

Mincer, J. (1958). Investment in Human Capital and Personal Income Distribution. *Journal of Political Economy, 66*(4), 281-302.

McGrath, R.G. (1999). Falling forward: Real options reasoning and entrepreneurial failure. *Academy of Management Review, 24*(1): 13-30.

Neal, D. (1995). Industry-Specific Human Capital, Evidence from Displaced Workers. *Journal of Labor Economics, 13*(4), 653-677.

O'Brien, J. P., Folta, T. B., & Johnson, D. R. (2003). A real options perspective on entrepreneurial entry in the face of uncertainty. *Managerial and Decision Economics, 24,* 515-533.

Oi, W. (1999). The Hearty and Cheery State. *Contemporary Economic Policy, 17,* 138-146.

Politis, D. (2005). The Process of Entrepreneurial Learning, A Conceptual Framework. *Entrepreneurship Theory & Practice, 29*(4), 399-424.

Preisendörfer, P. & Voss, T. (1990). Organizational Mortality of Small Firms, The Effects of Entrepreneurial Age and Human Capital. *Organization Studies, 11*(1), 107-129.

Sarasvathy, S.D. (2001). Causation and effecuation: Toward a theoretical shift from economic inevitability to entrepreneurial contingency. *Academy of Management Review, 26*(2): 243-263.

Shane, S. (2003). *A General Theory of Entrepreneurship: The Individual-Opportunity Nexus.* Cheltenham, UK and Northampton, MA, USA: Edward Elgar.

Shane, S. & Venkataraman, S. (2000). The promise of entrepreneurship as a field of research. *Academy of Management Review, 25*(1), 217-266.

Shane S. & Khurana, R. (2003). Bringing individuals back in: the effects of career experience on new firm founding. *Industrial and Corporate Change,* 12:519–543

Shepherd, D. A., Douglas, E. J., & Shanley, M. (2000). New venture survival: Ignorance, external shocks, and risk reduction strategies. *Journal of Business Venturing, 15*(5-6), 393-410.

Stam, E., Audretsch, D. & Meijaard, J. (2006). Renascent Entrepreneurship. In E. Zacharacis et al. (Eds). *Frontiers of Entrepreneurship Research 2006* (pp. 174-187). Babson Park, MA: Babson College.

Taylor, M. P. (1999). Survival of the fittest, An analysis of entrepreneurship duration in Britain. *The Economic Journal, 109*(March), 140-155.

van der Sluis, J., Van Praag, C. M., & Vijverberg, W. (2004). Education and Entrepreneurship in Industrialized Countries, A Meta-analysis. Tinbergen Institute Discussion Paper.

Van Praag, C. M. 2005. *Successful Entrepreneurship, Confronting Economic Theory with Empirical Evidence.* Cheltenham, UK and Northampton, MA, USA: Edward Elgar.

Wennberg, K. & Berglund, H. (2006). Social Networking and the Development of New Ventures. In Beyerlein, M. (Eds). *Innovation through Collaboration. Advances in Interdisciplinary Studies of Work, Vol.12* (pp. 203–225). JAI Press.

Wennberg, K. Folta, T. & Delmar, F. (2006). A real options model of step-wise entry into self-employment. In E. Zacharacis et al. (Eds). *Frontiers of Entrepreneurship Research 2006* (pp. 119-132). Babson Park, MA: Babson College.

Venkataraman, S. & Sarasvathy, S.D. (2001). Strategy and Entrepreneurship: Outlines of an untold story. In M. A. Hitt, J. Freeman and J. S. Harrison (Eds.) *Handbook of Strategic Management.* Oxford, UK: Blackwell.

Westhead, P. & Wright, M. (1998). Novice, Portfolio and Serial Founders Located in Rural and Urban Areas. *Entrepreneurship Theory and Practice, 22*(4), 63-100.

Wiklund, J., Delmar, F., & Sjöberg, K. (2004). *Selection of the Fittest? How Human Capital Affects High-Potential Entrepreneurship.* Paper presented at the Academy of Management Meeting, New Orleans.

Williamson, O. E. (1985). *The Economic Institutions of Capitalism.* New York: Free Press.

4. New Ventures' Entry Strategies: a Comparison of Academic and Non-Academic Business Startups

Sari Roininen and Håkan Ylinenpää

INTRODUCTION

Although previously studied, one of the least understood features of modern societies is the process of creating a new venture (Reynolds & White, 1997). Even less studied is the phenomenon that this chapter highlights: 'differences between different categories of start-ups'. As Deakins (1999) notes, every new venture is unique and the facilitating factors that might lead to a successful business start-up vary. Basic factors that might imply different start-up processes emanate from the nature or specific characteristics of the product/ service that the firm seeks to commercialize, the markets that new ventures target, and the resources and market entry strategies that are required for commercialization.

In focus here is the difference between knowledge-intensive academic spin-offs and non-academic new business start-ups. A main concern in this chapter is how different product and market characteristics may be related to different market entry strategies and different modes of acquiring and organizing the firm's resources during the start-up process as well as to different consequences in terms of firm growth and revenues. We address this theme by comparing two types of entrepreneurial endeavours: the start-up process of academic spin-offs (requiring specific and high-level knowledge) versus the start-up process of a non-academic company (requiring a lower level of specialized expertise).

Following Shane, Locke and Collin's (2003; 259) definition, we define entrepreneurial endeavours as 'the processes by which opportunities to create future goods and services are discovered, evaluated, and exploited'. In other words, we focus on the development of a new venture where one or more founders formulate, commercialize, and further develop their business idea. The following text starts by developing a theoretical framework of reference for the chapter, basically building on previous research by Deakins (1999) and Lindholm Dahlstrand (2004). In the succeeding section we describe the methodology utilized for collecting the case-study based evidence by the case study results. We then conclude by discussing the results and research implications of the study.

A THEORETICAL FRAMEWORK

Start-up process

As Bygrave (1989) states: 'every firm's start-up process is a disjointed, discontinuous and unique event'. Lindholm Dahlstrand (2004) has shown that the start-up process involves different intangible success factors. Therefore, there is no ready-made solution to the issue of 'how to successfully start a new company'. However, some stages or phases in a start-up process are common for all new ventures. This has induced several researchers to try to 'map' the start-up process. A typical and well-spread model depicting differrent phases in the start-up process was developed in 1999 by Deakins (and later utilized and further developed by Lindholm Dahlstrand, 2004). This model, which has been adopted as a theoretical framework for this chapter, includes five different phases of the new venture creation process: the idea formulation, opportunity recognition, pre-start planning and preparation for the venture start-up, the venture establishment and launch, and, finally, post-entry development.

Audretsch, Houweling and Thurik (2004), Deakins (1999), Lindholm Dahlstrand (2004), Shane (2000) and Venkataraman (1997), all point out that the idea formulation in a venture's start-up process, to a high degree, is dependent on the entrepreneur's prior knowledge and experience. Lindholm Dahlstrand (2004) concludes that many Swedish technology-based ventures are created based on knowledge from the entrepreneur's earlier company experience or from employment or studies at a university. In addition, entrepreneurs can make use of their established networks (both social and work-related) and their knowledge about markets in order to acquire competitive advantages and financial support (ibid). The track record of a venture or an entrepreneur is crucial for establishing credibility among established actors like investors, customers and suppliers (Cooper, 2002; Hitt, Ireland, Camp & Sexton, 2002). From this perspective, ventures started by younger entrepreneurs may, regardless of whether they are high-tech or low-tech, find it harder to create a new venture because of their lack of developed networks and track records.

A key factor in the start-up process is to transform the developed idea into a business opportunity (Deakins 1999; Lindholm Dahlstrand, 2004). An important factor for transforming an idea into a vital venture is the individual's inner drive. Adizes (1987), Crant (1996), Klofsten (1998) and Shane et al. (2003) state that individual motivation, inner drive, and personal engagement in the new venture needs to be above the level of a hobby activity in order to succeed. The individual motivation is far more important for a new venture than is a flawless business idea.

In a pre-start phase the entrepreneur needs to investigate the opportunities for business financing. This is especially important for a technology-based venture (Deakins, 1999; Lindholm Dahlstrand, 2004). In addition, in order to succeed it is equally important to do market research that indicates to the entrepreneur and his/her stakeholders that there is a profitable market for the new venture (Deakins, 1999). Specifically, the selection of a market segment is important in order to maintain the core focus of the product/service (Klofsten, 1998), something that is particularly important for high technology ventures. In this stage the entrepreneur also has to prepare for the venture's organization, which, according to Sexton and Kasarda (1992) and Storey (1994), can benefit from a team of founders instead of a single founder. This is due to the fact that several founders also may facilitate access to a broader range of networks and expertise. In team-based new ventures it is however important that the knowledge and experience of the team are complementary, and that their personal characteristics match one another (Lindholm Dahlstrand, 2004). As an alternative to recruiting staff on their own payroll, new ventures should consider building alliances and coalitions with external actors (Klofsten, 1998).

When a venture is about to enter a market, timing is essential to the venture's success (Deakins, 1999; Lindholm Dahlstrand, 2004). This is particularly significant for a new venture that launches new products to be able to make use of the first mover advantages, i.e. it is easier for an innovator to achieve larger market shares than it is for its followers (Grimm & Smith, 1997; Lee, Lee & Pennings, 2001). A presumption is of course that the market is mature enough and ready, or that the venture with limited efforts can influence it to accept and demand the new product. To launch a new product may also necessitate new ventures to educate customers about how to make full use of their products, which is associated with higher expenses (Lindholm Dahlstrand, 2004). Further, if the new product is introduced to an immature market, the pioneer customers' demand needs to be strong enough for them to be willing to pay for the product (Lazonick, 2005), and there are always risks for followers as soon as the market matures (Porter, 1985). During this phase, resources such as patent holdings, brand equity, and other potentially valuable resources (Mosakowski, 2002) as well as knowledge based on elaborate market research can be essential and protective for the idea (Lindholm Dahlstrand, 2004).

As soon as a new venture has been established, the venture will develop its relations with its stakeholders and other actors. The venture's most important task is to build up its track record and liability in order to attract customers, obtain required financing, and to be able to get credit from suppliers (Deakins, 1999; Lindholm Dahlstrand, 2004). To facilitate the start-up processes and the ventures' credibility, the firms can also build alliances (Lee et al., 2001) with customers in an early phase, where customers may take part in product development and act as investors. These allied customers should in particular be those who need the product/service the most (Klofsten, 1998). To build awareness among customers, the venture has to distribute information about the product on a long-term basis, especially if the product is innovative (Klofsten, 1998; Kotler, Armstrong, Wong & Saunders, 1996). Generally speaking, building different kinds of networks is important during this phase, because ventures that manage to build reliable networks with people holding important positions often have a higher likelihood of succeeding (Politis, 2005).

Antecedents for entrepreneurial endeavours

Entrepreneurial events and processes may also be studied with a point of departure in the product/service that is offered to a market (supply side) or in the 'the market-opportunity seeking behaviour' (Hendry, Arthur & Jones, 1995) that opportunity recognition and exploitation involve (demand side). This classic 'divide' has paved the way for two research streams in entrepreneurship research: (1) Research that, following Schumpeter (1934), has been interested in how new market offerings (new products, new production methods, new ways of organizing business activities) cause 'creative destruction' by facilitating for innovators to gain competitive advantage on the market; (2) Research that, building on Kirzner (1973) and others, has been more interested in how entrepreneurs seize imbalances and opportunities on the market and exploit them for their own benefit. Even if most modern research in the field understands these two streams as 'two sides of the same coin', they involve fundamental differences. 'Schumpeterian' entrepreneurship research may hence be understood to more highlight the role of 'technology push' (e.g. new innovative products based on new knowledge or new combinations of knowledge) and the entrepreneurial role of destroying existing market structures by introducing more favourable solutions to customers' problems (thereby creating 'imbalances' in a previously stable but less dynamic economy). 'Kirznerian' entrepreneurship research, on the other hand, underlines the function of the entrepreneur as someone who exploits an unfilled market need (market pull) and thereby creates a 'balance' between demand and supply on the market. Although not transparent, the distinction between innovation and opportunity recognition relates to another dichotomized concept: the difference between proactive and reactive entrepreneurs. Crant (1996) suggests that individuals and firms with proactive motives have better qualifications to create new prosperous ventures since they create their own competitive environment, identify new opportunities and act upon them with persistence. With innovative advantages the venture can achieve high returns if they are fast and first on the market (Lee et al., 2001). Such first movers are those who first introduce new products or services, which brings 'monopoly profits' until imitators or substitutes come out on the market (Grimm & Smith, 1997). On the other hand, several studies on e.g. product development have identified the risk associated with a 'pioneering strategy', implying that a more reactive 'follower strategy' is beneficial for long-term firm growth and revenues (Bain 1956; Bodin, 2000; Cooper & Kleinschmidt, 1993). Recognizing that in practice, innovation and opportunity recognition are often interwoven concepts, we still find the distinction between these two basic types of entrepreneurial endeavours (as well as the degree of maturity of the targeted market) as an initially interesting theoretical building block for this chapter.

Previous research hence states that entrepreneurs discover opportunities related to their prior information and knowledge, such as education, work experience or other means (cf. also Audretsch et al., 2004; Klofsten, 1998; Politis, 2005; Roberts, 1991; Venkataraman, 1997). Information and prior experience influence the entrepreneur's ability to comprehend, interpret and apply new information in ways that those lacking that prior information cannot replicate (Roberts, 1991). Entrepreneurs will therefore normally start new firms in an attempt to exploit different ideas based on their previous knowledge and experience. Shane (2000) and Shane and Venkataraman (2000) state that the source of entrepreneurship lies in the difference in information about opportunities, and that individual differences influence how these individuals discover opportunities. This is in line with the Austrian framework argument that discoveries of entrepreneurial opportunities depend, to a certain extent, on the distribution of information in society, where the possession of the distinctive information allows people to see different opportunities (Kirzner, 1973). Moreover, the discovery of entrepreneurial opportunities is an ability to identify commercial opportunities rather than an optimizing process; therefore the entrepreneur needs to see new means-ends relationships in order to combine existing concepts and information into new ideas (Shane & Venkataraman, 2000).

Opportunities are however not always (or even primarily) discovered and exploited by a stand-alone-company. With the intention of competing effectively on markets, small firms are increasingly using alliances and networks both to get access to information (e.g. market or technology information; cf. Ylinenpää, 1999), and to acquire and build necessary resources and capabilities (Hitt et al., 2002; Johansson, 2006; Westerberg & Ylinenpää, 2006; Wincent & Westerberg, 2006). This allows firms to compete in markets without first possessing all the resources needed (Cooper, 2002), and enhances new ventures' chance of survival and eventual success (Baum, Calabrese & Silverman, 2000). Moreover, networks can create legitimacy for new firms, especially if they are focused on creating a new market or a niche within an established market, since alliances can lead to exchange relationships with entrepreneurial firms' customers (Cooper, 2002). In addition, Cooper states that ideas for new ventures often lead to the formation of social networks, and that the creation of new ventures is based on network ties of either an individual or of entrepreneurial teams. Thus, networks are sources of as well as means for exploiting entrepreneurial opportunities.

Strategic alliances as well as strategic networks have, according to Hitt et al. (2002), become highly popular means for entering international markets, and according to Deakins (1999), new ventures need to establish network relations with, e.g. partners and/or key customers that help them break into new markets. This is specifically important for new ventures aiming for an international market (McDougall & Oviatt, 2000). New information technology facilitating international transactions and the opening of new global markets have led to an increasing number of small ventures entering international markets (Ireland & Hitt, 1999). In this international entry, Lu and Beamish (2001) found that small firms experience greater profits when they engage in alliances with local partners on the new markets. To summarize, previous research in the field suggest that engaging in strategic partnerships seem to be crucial, especially for exploiting new entrepreneurial opportunities.

An emerging theoretical framework

From the literature review, a theoretical framework serving as a guide for empirical analysis may be generated. The context of this framework is a time-based sequential model for 'normal' or 'ideal' new venture creation processes, developed on the basis of Deakins (1999) and Lindholm Dahlstrand (2004). The focus of the framework consists of key concepts that we have identified as important for developing a better understanding of our research purpose: to identify how different product and market characteristics may be understood to relate to different market entry strategies and different modes of acquiring and organizing the firm's resources (resource configuration)

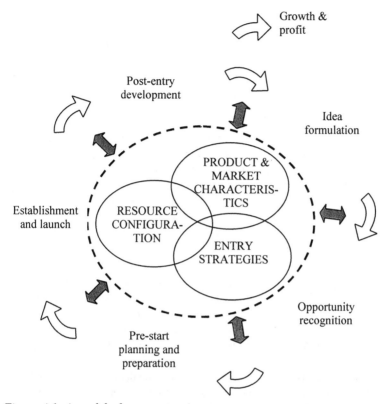

Figure 4.1 A model of new venture's start-up process

during the start-up process as well as to different outcomes in terms of firm growth and profit. The basic idea of the framework is that the mode of resource configuration, the entry strategy and the product/market characteristics affect the new venture's start-up process. At the same time the start-up process per se can affect the entry strategy, the resource configuration, and product and market characteristics. This is illustrated in Figure 4.1 by two-way arrows.

In other words, the nature of a firm's resources (i.e. its tangible as well as its intangible resources) can affect the idea formulation, the way the firm recognizes opportunities, the planning and the factual start-up of a new venture, the market approach and how the venture is developed during and after its launch on the market. Likewise, the chosen entry strategy and the characteristics of both the venture's products/services and markets affect decisions referring to the planning and implementation of the new business concept. At the same time, the start-up process with its activities and events (and not least, the learning that such experiences often involve) affect the

emergent entry strategy, required resources and the final product development, since market research and different preparations may call for modifi-
cations and strategic shifts along the way.

METHOD

In order to arrive at a proper understanding of the new venture creation process, we need a more holistic understanding of the phenomenon, an understanding that takes an interest in both the process itself and in important
factors related to the phenomenon under study (cf. Bouchikhi, 1993). A new
venture's start-up process consists of several integrated phases with various
factors affecting these phases. To be able to get a holistic understanding of
the phenomenon, we need to study all phases and factors affecting the process
(cf. Miles & Huberman 1994). For this purpose, case studies, is an
appropriate research strategy since such an approach facilitates a holistic
understanding of the phenomenon in itself and of how different factors relate
to each other (Guba & Lincoln, 1989; Patton, 1990). First of all, case studies
are essential when an investigator wants to *describe* a course of events in a
real-life context. Second, case studies are relevant when the investigator tries
to *explain* the presumed casual links in complex, real-life settings (cf. Miles
& Huberman, 1994; Yin, 2003). Since the intention of this study is to analyze
and compare two types of start-up processes (academic spin-offs and non-
academic venture creation) and to explain why these start-up processes may
evolve following different logics and trajectories, a case-study approach was
chosen.

   The criteria used for selecting case-study firms and categories were that
they should have operated for at least three years from the start; that the firms
were either manufacturing or service companies; that the firms were
developed in different environments (different situational and contextual
conditions) and finally, that the growth rate varied. These criteria were
chosen in order to get more thorough and varying information about different
ventures'/categories' start-up processes as well as about different influencing
factors with the intention of being able to identify patterns (Miles &
Huberman, 1994). In addition, a three year frame of firm survival is regarded
essential in this study due to the fact that the start-ups would, by then, have
gained knowledge and experience, increasing their likelihood of survival and
further growth (c.f. Jovanovic, 1982; Pakes & Ericson, 1998), and have had
time to build its own history and experiences resulting in the firms being
capable of answering the research questions in this study. Case studies were
conducted in three academic spin-offs:

- *X-Tech,* with a business concept to offer people (basically engineers in different companies) the opportunity to interact and cooperate through their computers where people are able to talk to and see each other, chat, share documents, use a whiteboard and surf the web together, regardless of their geographical location (15 employees and a turnover of 1.060.000 €).
- *Y-Tech,* with a business concept to offer research-project and EU-project participants, the opportunity to cooperate using distance-spanning information technology, enabling them to work with and share documents, manage, control and plan the project through a custom-made project tool on the Internet (4 employees and a turnover of 420.000 €).
- *Z-Tech,* with a business concept to offer companies a 3-D motor, which they can integrate into their products (games), and to offer people opportunities to play virtually advanced games on the Internet (no employees and a turnover of 213.000 €).

And in three non-academic ventures:

- *A-Trade,* with a business concept to offer software that increases computer performance, and complete computer sets and appurtenant services, foremost to computer enthusiasts but also to other interested customers, primarily on a national market (3 employees and a turnover of 1440.000 €).
- *B-Trade,* with a business concept to offer kiosk products of good quality and with a high degree of service to a local market (2 employees and a turnover of 530.000 €).
- *C-Trade,* with a business concept to offer designed products with optimal design and function to private persons, organizations, wholesalers, etc (no employees and a turnover of 10.600 €).

The empirical data was collected through personal and open-ended interviews with founders of the ventures where they described their start-up process and different factors and events that influenced this process.

The personal interviews were semi-structured and the respondents were told to recall and describe how they had progressed through their professional lives from completion of their education until the time of the study, and to explain decisions taken during their careers and how these decisions affected their future career prospects. A major reason for using a semi-structured approach was to get more detailed information and to ensure that the discussion was driven by what the respondents felt was important in order to stay as close as possible to their lived experience. However, to avoid that due to forgetfulness, post-rationalization or other circumstances, the respondents left out important information referring to e.g., different phases of their development processes, and more specific questions were asked. In order to validate the information, every interview was concluded by constructing a 'rich picture' (Miles & Huberman, 1994) where a time line was drawn on a paper and different events and experiences that influenced the respondents' decisions were noted. Each interview lasted about two to three hours. In addition, information was also obtained from the ventures' websites, from a business database and by studying printed materials about the ventures.

FINDINGS

As could be expected, the start-up processes in the two categories of new ventures reveal both similarities and differences. In this chapter, we will focus on differences between academic spin-offs and non-academic ventures related to the theoretical characteristics in a start-up process depicted in Figure 4.1 (product characteristics, market characteristics and entry strategies, and resource configuration respectively), and also how to address the out-put of this process in terms of growth and profit level of the studied companies.

Product Characteristics

The original business concept in all *academic spin-off* companies originated directly or indirectly from academic research. This means that the products and services offered were knowledge-intensive and preferably high-tech. The founders of the academic spin-offs recognized an opportunity to create a product-based business based on their previous experiences and knowledge, and they developed a product for some years in parallel with their previous positions as researchers or students. Due to the significant time required for developing market-ready products, all three academic spin-offs started their businesses by offering services such as consulting services as a complement to their product offers in order to generate a required cash flow. These knowledge-based services connected to the product have been essential for the product users and enabled the companies to develop additional services generating important revenues. The products/services were moreover developed in cooperation with the parent university, where the university served both as a pioneer user and a demanding customer.

The *non-academic* new ventures' business concept originated from the founders' recognition of a market opportunity signalling an unfilled market need. This need was exploited by offering to the market, already known products and by using the founders' previous knowledge, experience or interest. Two of the ventures, A-Trade and B-Trade, sold products manufactured by suppliers. The third venture, C-Trade, designed its own products in order to improve or modify already known products, which were then in turn manufactured and sold by other companies that the founder got into contact with through her personal network that she built up over time and through her relations with a community support program for new ventures.

Market Characteristics and Entry Strategies

The aim of all *academic spin-off* ventures was to achieve world leadership in their specific niche – and to earn money. Recognizing the limited size of the regional and national market, these new ventures chose to market their products on an international market from the very beginning. One of the ventures, Z-Tech, had to restructure their business idea and modify their product twice, since they learnt that they did not have the competitive advantage required to successfully compete with the existing large international companies. The firms' innovative products were offered to an often immature market and, as a consequence, these ventures normally had to educate their costumers on how (and why) to use the product. In order to reach their customers and to offer them the product and service, X-Tech, five years after their start-up hired two retailers in the US who knew the market, and then one in Europe a year later. Z-Tech had difficulties in addressing their target customers but they got into contact with Sun Microsystems early in their start-up process and received assistance from them for marketing, since Z-Tech had based their product on Sun Microsystems's technology and refined the use of it (which Sun Microsystems had not been able to do themselves). Y-Tech, finally, had recently started to look for a partner to cooperate with in sales in order to increase their market shares.

The *non-academic* new ventures' products were, on the other hand, offered to a general and often local or national market providing sufficient revenues in line with the ambitions of the founders to make a living. In one of the firms (A-Trade), however, the initial business concept was developed and the ambitions expanded when they, through their customers and via different computer forums on the Internet, learned that there was a need for a specific new software product enabling the firm also to sell outside the national market through a web-based shop. Also C-Trade with the purpose of reaching a broader market started to cooperate with a retailer in the national capital a couple of years after their start-up.

Resource configuration

The *academic spin-offs'* specialized and high-tech business concepts required significant investments in product development and refinement, normally spanning over several years. This entailed a considerable need for (external) funding to finance staff/man-hours, product material and production equipment (e.g. computers, servers, software). Due to their limited creditability and track record, all spin-off firms have had to put a lot of effort into identifying and acquiring external funding. This was especially evident in Z-Tech, whose founders were young students, whereas the founders of X-Tech and Y-Tech with their longer experience had a higher credibility in attracting external venture capital. In order to acquire external funding, all academic spin-off companies early on founded a limited company. Moreover, all spin-off ventures were started by several (two to four) founders where different competences could be seen as complementary assets in the new ventures. Functions such as marketing, accounting, administration and responsibility for the firm's retailers were hence shared among the founders. After the venture start-up, both X-Tech and Y-Tech have hired four to six new staff members for product development work. When these new ventures after some time also appointed a professional board of directors, they got access to a valuable function for management support – a mentoring support they would actually have needed already from the beginning but could not afford to pay for. Through their professional board of directors, the founders now got access to strategic guidance and business advice from experienced persons who knew the business and could broaden their networks and personal relations. Z-Tech has not yet been able to appoint a professional board of directors, but has meanwhile got in touch with people who are willing to give at least some advice.

Contrary to the academic spin-off companies, the requirements for investments were limited among *non-academic* new ventures. This enabled the firms to start their companies on the basis of their own personal savings and with the general support given by government subsidies to the people starting a new company of their own. Moreover, all non-academic companies were started by single founders. The limited need for external funding and the fact that all companies started up as solo-entrepreneurs (Hult & Ramström, 2000) , involved a simple structure wherein all companies started as (and still are) private firms and not limited companies. This also meant that the firms have no management support in terms of a professional board of directors. All founders perceived themselves to be the most important resource for their new ventures, but had, to various degrees, also acquired or accessed external resources and expertise to the firm. Only the founder of B-Trade had a high creditability and track record due to his prior occupation and enterprising within the line of business and therefore had no difficulties in getting external funding and trust from suppliers and banks. In addition, B-Trade's founder had an established network that helped him with problem-solving, which was something that C-Trade's founder established during the start-up process. A-

Trade and B-Trade hired external members of staff after their start-up to work with sales and other tasks, whereas C-Trade still operates alone.

Growth and profit

Due to the *academic spin-off* ventures' significant product development and personnel costs, it took several years before X-Tech and Y-Tech could report any net profits, while Z-Tech still after three years has not achieved the funding or reached the market shares and sales needed. During the post-entry development (here three to five years from start-up), X-Tech grew significantly from employing its four founders to 23 employees; a number that due to outsourcing of accounting, invoicing and marketing functions has today been reduced to just 15. During this period of time the venture's annual turnover increased from 530 to 640 thousand euro, and increased further to nearly 1.1 million euro in 2005. Y-Tech also increased their turnover to nearly half a million euro in 2004 and employed four persons, whereas Z-Tech has no employees and has increased its turnover from 159 to 213 thousand euro. It should be noted, however, that Z-Tech has not been in operation for more than three years, while the other firms in this group have run their businesses for seven and six years respectively.

Based on the fact that all *non-academic* firms offered products well known to the market and that only limited initial investments were required, these ventures could attain a net profit already from their first year of operation. While B-Trade and C-Trade have consolidated their companies on a level that provides revenues enough for a decent living, A-Trade stands out as an expansive exception: during the post-entry development (the three to five years from start-up), the annual turnover of A-Trade has increased from 270 thousand euro to 1.4 million euro and employment of three persons as a consequence of their changed and developed business concept. Due to the increased sales, and because of the benefits a limited company may offer, the founder now considers reorganising the venture into a joint-stock company. Although both B-Trade and C-Trade have increased their turnover (B-Trade has increased its turnover by 20% to 530 thousand euro with two employees and C-Trade has doubled its turnover to 10.6 thousand euro but still has no employees), they are in this specific respect not close to the level of A-Trade's development.

ANALYSIS

Table 4.1 summarizes the study's findings, indicating that academic spin-offs and non-academic ventures have different start-up processes, characteristics and outcomes. As already stated, the academic spin-offs' innovative products originated from university research, whereas the non-academic ventures' products were known to the market. This difference may be related to Schumpeter's (1934) and Kirzner's (1973) views on how entrepreneurs discover and exploit business opportunities, where the academic spin-offs enter a market through innovations that require change in customer behaviour (Walsh, Kirchhoff & Newbert, 2002), while the non-academic firms enter by discovering and satisfying existing market demands. While the academic spin-off may be understood to follow a market entry strategy characterized as 'technology push' (implying e.g. higher investments, international markets already from the start, a need for education of customers and longer pay-off

Academic Spin-Offs	*Characteristics*	*Non-Academic Ventures*
High-tech/knowledge-based New to the market	Product	Low-tech-based Known to the market
Specific market niche requiring a broad market International/global market	Market	General market, often addressed with geographic specialization Local/regional market
Technology push Collaboration as a means of international market entry Proactive including education of new customers	Entry strategy	Market pull Normally relying on their own resources Reactive; "filling a hole on the market"
Substantial need for external funding More advanced structure: - several founders - a specialized management team and hired experts - professional board of directors, - limited company organization	Resource configuration	No or limited need for external funding Simple structure: - one owner-manager - no professional board of directors - private firm organization
Planned growth and long pay-off period involving an increasing demand for financial and other resources No profit during the first years	Growth & profit	Early growth stabilizing the firm as a "bread-and-butter company" or emergent growth as a result of oppor- tunity recognition Net profit from year one

Table 4.1 Contrasting the start-up process of non-academic ventures and academic spin-offs

periods), the strategy of the non-academic firms in this study relies on 'market pull' satisfying an existing market need with more or less well-known products and services. From this perspective, the entrepreneurs with their roots in academic research manifest more of a proactive 'Schumpeterian entrepreneurship' aiming for 'exploration' (March 1991) of new business concepts, while the entrepreneurs starting what we in this chapter have labelled 'non-academic firms', reflect more of a reactive and 'Kirznerian mode of entrepreneurship' seeking to 'exploit' existing market opportunities (ibid.).

As the case of A-Trade demonstrates, however, the start-up process itself involves learning and opens new windows of opportunities, enabling firms to redefine their business concepts along the way, where mere opportunity exploitation based on offering customers already existing solutions to their needs is combined with at least some degree of innovative product development. However, when after the start-up A-Trade changed its business idea and offered 'a product new to the market' to a specific market niche, this innovative product was initiated by the founding entrepreneur not based on 'technology push' but on 'market pull' by recognizing an opportunity on the market that current products did not satisfy.

Whether the new venture has its origin in 'technology push' or 'market pull' also has implications for how the new venture configures its resources in order to enter its target markets. Knowledge-intensive and often high-tech companies generally require more resources for product development and (international) marketing, implying a need for external funding, long-term investments and a more advanced structure of the firm itself. Non-academic firms, normally targeting a regional or local 'market hole' with products and services already known to the customer, may rely on their own resources, a shorter time to market and pay-off, and a more simple structure of the firm. This was manifested in this study by all academic spin-offs choosing to start a limited company with a management team (many founders) and at least an ambition to appoint a professional board of directors, in order to achieve the funding required and to access important knowledge resources, while the non-academic firms relied on the owner-manager him/herself and a more simple firm structure. As pointed out by e.g. Sexton and Kasarda (1992) and Storey (1994), access to different types of knowledge and expertise is important during the start-up process. If the new venture develops and exploits new and knowledge-based products/services, the importance of building a management/expert team with complementary knowledge in different functions and roles is even more highlighted (cf. Klofsten 1998; Lindholm Dahlstrand 2004), since one person alone seldom possesses all the competences required. Organizing a professional board of directors is from this perspective a gateway to a broader range of expertise that a new venture may access. In the present study, this strategy was employed only by the more knowledge-based firms represented by academic spin-offs.

To build networks and alliances may hence be regarded as a means of extending the boundaries of the firm itself, thereby making external resources accessible to the firm. In this study, the academic spin-offs, being more innovative than the more traditional non-academic firms, target an international market in order to attain higher profit. These 'born global firms', due to their more sophisticated and advanced products and services, can hence not rely on a local, regional or even national market (cf. Boter and Holmquist, 1996). As a result, alliance building for entering international target markets was an essential ingredient in these firms' market strategies (cf. Hitt et al., 2002). X-Tech thus engaged two retailers in the US that knew the specific demands of their target market, while Y-Tech was looking for collaboration with a sales company to help them reach a larger market. Z-Tech early on initiated cooperation with a large corporation (Sun Microsystems) in order to attract attention from their desired customer segment and to be able to demonstrate the benefits of their products. Such activities were considerably lower among the non-academic firms since they targeted a local or regional market and relied more on their own in-house resources.

The growth of a firm may be regarded as both an input and an output of a start-up process: *input* in terms of what motives and ambitions the founding entrepreneurs have for starting the new company and *output* in terms of the factual growth of the new venture. From the literature in the field (e.g. Davidsson 1989; Westerberg 1998), we know that the entrepreneurs' own motives and ambitions are crucial as input-factors for whether the new venture will grow or not. In this study, all academic spin-offs aimed already from start at world leadership in their specific niche – and at earning money. The non-academic firms, on the other hand, were started as means of generating an income for the founder him/herself. When studying the firms' growth processes, it was also obvious that the academic spin-offs followed a more growth-oriented and planned trajectory, whereas the non-academic ventures seemed to be satisfied with stabilizing as a so called 'bread-and-butter-company'. One exception among the non-academic ventures already noted is A-Trade, which has experienced a high growth rate since after the start-up the venture developed its business idea into a more growth-oriented trajectory. According to Mintzberg and Waters (1985), this growth-oriented trajectory may be understood as 'an emergent strategy' based on the learning the entrepreneur experienced during her/his start-up, where the process (depicted in Figure 4.1) per se, fertilized a reorientation of the firm's business concept.

Despite the fact that the academic spin-offs in this study all clearly expressed their ambitions towards world leadership and earning (a lot of) money, it is only the non-academic firms that so far can report net profits. The academic spin-offs' innovative products, which they offer to an international niche and often immature market, require significantly higher investments than market offers from non-academic firms (cf. Lindholm Dahlstrand, 2004). As a consequence, academic spin-offs' normally invite external funding into a joint-stock company (which non-academic firms often avoid), and often reach profitability later than non-academic firms (which often require net revenues already from the first year). In the search for 'first mover advantage' (Grimm & Smith, 1997; Lee et al., 2001), timing is however essential. For new innovative products to succeed on the market, the market should 'be ready' or at least be possible to influence with limited efforts (e.g. through education), in order to build a market demand. According to Shane (2001), innovations and a first-mover-strategy can be an advantage for a venture, while others (e.g. Cooper & Kleinschmidt, 1993) have pointed out that inappropriate timing may act as a barrier to the market as well. Whether the investments made in the academic spin-off companies in this study will pay off and be more profitable on a long-term basis than in the non-academic firms, is however an issue for further study.

CONCLUSIONS

The main aim of this chapter has been to analyze and compare the start-up processes of two different categories of firms: academic spin-offs requiring specific and high-level knowledge and partnership with other companies and/or organizations adhering to high professional demands, versus the process of starting a 'traditional', non-academic new company (requiring a lower level of specialized expertise and cooperation with partners). A main question we have tried to answer is how different product and market characteristics may be understood to relate to different market entry strategies and different modes of acquiring and organizing the firm's resources during the start-up process, as well as to different consequences in terms of firm growth and revenues. The concluded findings depicting entry strategies and their observed relations to the level of knowledge intensity and technology are presented in Figure 4.2.

Following a 'technology-push' entry strategy in the commercialization of high technology product/service on a normally international and immature market, calls for customer education and specific marketing approaches; a strategy which is expensive and time-consuming. Moreover, a 'technology-push' entry strategy also requires a combination of different kinds of expertise during the start-up process for business and product development, and strategic planning. This is an 'explorative challenge' far more complicated and demanding than for new ventures exploiting a product known to the market using a market-pull strategy. New ventures derived from university research and/or educations have a more significant need for resources than non-academic new ventures. To enable the commercialization of the academic spin-offs' more high-technology or knowledge-intensive products, these ventures were to a higher degree dependent on external competencies for their competitiveness and on long-term investments from venture capitalists for financing the resource-demanding product development and refinement. While non-academic new ventures addressing the market with a market-pull strategy face a less complicated and more 'exploitative' challenge, we have in this study also shown that the start-up process, per se, may involve a learning process, as when A-Trade during the start-up process recognizes new windows of opportunities and therefore changes its business concept towards more innovative products/services (a shift depicted by a broken arrow in Figure 4.2).

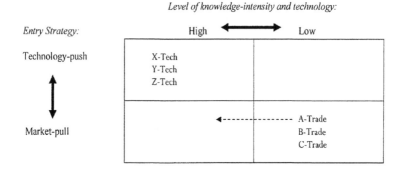

Figure 4.2 Studied new ventures by employed entry strategy, level of knowledge intensity and technology

Adopting a resource-based view of new venture creation and development, a new venture's performance to a great extent may be attributed to the resources they hold (Penrose, 1959) where valuable, rare and inimitable resources could yield competitive advantage (c.f. Barney, 1991; Ylinenpää, 1999; Yli-Renko, Autio & Sapienza 2001). A strategy for managing situations where in-house resources are insufficient is, of course, to obtain the necessary knowledge, information and resources through networks and alliances (cf. Cooper, 2002; Hitt et al., 2002; Wincent & Westerberg, 2006). For the academic spin-offs in this study, cooperation with the university was important for their product development as well as a place where they could start to build up their networks and get access to customers. Alliance building was also an essential ingredient in the spin-off firms' strategy for entering their international target markets (cf. Hitt et al., 2002) by cooperating with existing companies in promoting and selling their products. Moreover, by organizing a professional board of directors early on, the academic spin-off companies got access to important expertise and their personal networks. Thus, by using alliances and networks, the academic spin-offs got access to the necessary resources and capabilities required for competing effectively on their markets without first owning all the resources needed (cf. Cooper, 2002; Wincent & Westerberg, 2006), and hence they were able to survive and grow despite their own lack of significant firm-specific resources. To build networks and alliances may accordingly be regarded as a means of extending the boundaries of the ventures themselves, where such activities were considerably lower among the non-academic firms targeting a local or regional market and relying more on their own in-house resources.

To conclude, the start-up process and further development of academic spin-offs may be understood as a process that to a significant degree is different from the start of more 'traditional' business ventures. In fact, the results from this study yield an understanding of the start-up process as being centred around the entrepreneur and his/her organization in non-academic firms, while the start-up process for academic spin-offs to a significantly higher degree involves manoeuvring and acting in a wider context together with (or in opposition to) other significant factors. Thus the start-up process must be understood in its specific context. While starting a traditional small firm highlights the key word 'organization' for serving a local or regional market with already known products and services, start-up of academic new ventures is best understood by the verbs 'organizing' and 'networking' in their endeavour to reach an international and often immature market with new products and services. In other words, when serving local markets a traditional firm can coordinate and systemise its activities in doors to achieve its objects due to its simplicity, following classic and straight-forward concepts on how to build a suitable organization. Academic spin-offs, on the other hand, often have to interact with other players in order to attain vital resources building a competitive advantage and when they target customers not aware of needing the specific, and often complicated, products that are being offered. This inter-organizational process of academic spin-offs involves the challenge of mobilizing both traded and untraded resources, 'beyond the limits set by the resources they currently control' (Jarillo, 1989: 135), resulting in situation-specific solutions based on organizing, networking and negotiating relations with their partners. In this respect, new business venturing with its roots in academia may be better understood as collective entrepreneurship (Johannisson 2000), where the new firm serves as 'a nexus for traded and untraded interdependences' (Storper, 1995: 125), than a mere intra-organizational endeavour involving primarily the entrepreneur and his/her organization.

IMPLICATIONS

The findings presented in Table 4.1 depict two very different start-up processes, and may serve as a basis for drawing interesting implications for practice, policy-makers and academic research. For entrepreneurs interested in starting a new venture, this chapter highlights challenges to be overcome during the start-up process and how these relate to the nature of the business concept (especially the degree of knowledge invested in the venture's products and services). In comparison to non-academic start-up ventures, knowledge-based ventures face a more complex start-up process, which requires specific, complementary and extended resources in the form of funding, skills and knowledge to manage. These resources can be obtained through networks and alliances with other companies, and through key individuals such as members of the firm's board of directors. To conclude, starting a knowledge-based academic spin-off company requires a different set of management strategies and practices compared to starting a more traditional small business.

For policy-makers and organizations active in supporting new venture creation, this chapter has hopefully manifested the dangers of generalizing business start-up as a uniform process. In fact, entrepreneurs and business concepts are different (Bygrave 1989) and benefit from different kinds and degrees of assistance during their start-up processes. For academic spin-offs, access to long-term external venture capital is critical, while non-academic start-ups may to a higher degree rely on internal funding. Academic spin-offs, also to a greater extent, are dependent on firm-specific resources (e.g. specialized mentoring support) in contrast to non-academic ventures, which may manage their start-up processes themselves or in combination with general new venture creation support. For policy-makers and support organisations this implies different support functions and activities, when e.g. designing incubators for new venture creation.

For the academic community, this chapter may have contributed more in-depth knowledge of factors and processes involved when comparing knowledge-intensive new ventures with more 'traditional' business start-ups. The empirical results from this study highlight that different factors affect different type of new ventures' start-up processes. One interesting result emerging from this study is the contrast between non-academic solo entrepreneurs, to a very high degree relying on the resources and skills of one single person (The Entrepreneur), versus the more or less 'collective mode of entrepreneurship', involving both internal and external partners, that characterizes academic spin-off start-up processes. The new ventures' different business concept is another appealing result where academic spin-offs are shown to be more focused on innovative products or services than non-academic new ventures. This could be related to the entrepreneurs' decisions to explore or exploit a business idea, where exploration might be more focused on technology and exploitation on markets (Holmquist, 2006) – a difference in turn having effect on the start-up processes itself.

Future research should benefit from elaborating on this theme, investigating what factors and conditions that affect different ventures' start-up process by utilizing qualitative, in-depth approaches as well as quantitative approaches and a more robust database. Adopting a learning perspective, it would also be interesting to study more thoroughly the 'experiential learning' taking place during the process of discovering, planning and exploiting a business opportunity – in this study, most significantly demonstrated by the case of A-Trade. Related to this is the function of previous learning and experiences: Do 'habitual entrepreneurs' behave differently than 'first time entrepreneurs'? Following the approach taken in this chapter, it should also be important to develop a more holistic understanding of the new venture creation process, involving e.g. entrepreneurial motivation and individual capabilities as factors taken more into consideration. Having in mind that this study relies on analytical generalization building on localized empirical data, theoretical concepts deducted from international research and comparisons with previous research findings, the results should have a bearing also outside the studied context. It would however be interesting to further study if (and in that case how) institutional factors such as national laws and regulations or factors related to different local or regional cultures may impact on the start-up processes we have addressed in this study.

REFERENCES

Adizes, I. (1987). *Corporate life cycles: how and why corporations grow and die and what to do about it.* Englewood Cliffs: Prentice Hall.

Audretsch, D.B., Houweling, P. & Thurik, A.R. (2004). Industry evolution: diversity, selection and the role of learning. *International Small Business Journal*, 22 (4): 331-348.

Bain, J. (1956). *Barriers to new competition.* Cambridge: Harvard University Press.

Barney, J.B. (1991). Firm resources and sustained competitive advantage. *Journal of Management*, 17(1): 99-120.

Baum, J.A.C., Calabrese, T., & Silverman, B.S. (2000). Don't go it alone: alliance network composition and startups' performance in Canadian biotechnology. *Strategic Management Journal*, 21(3): 267-294.

Bouchikhi, H. (1993). A constructivists framework for understanding entrepreneurship performance. *Organization Studies*, 14 (4): 549-570.

Bodin, J. (2000). *Perpetual product development. A study of small technology-driven firms.* Doctoral dissertation, Umeå University.

Boter, H. & Homquist,C. (1996). Industry characteristics and internationalization processes in small firms. *Journal of Business Venturing,* 11(6): 471-487.

Bygrave, W.D. (1989). The entrepreneurship paradigm (1): a philosophical look at its research methodologies. *Entrepreneurship Theory and Practice,* 14 (1): 7-26.

Cooper, R.G. & Kleinschmidt, E.J. (1993). Major new products: What distinguishes the winners in the chemical industry? *Journal of Product Innovation Management,* 10(2): 90-111.

Cooper, A.C. (2002). 'Networks, alliances, and entrepreneurship'. In Hitt M.A., Ireland, R.D., Camp, S.M., Sexton, D.L (Ed.) *Strategic entrepreneurship: Creating a new mindset:* 203-222. Oxford, Blackwell Publisher.

Crant, M.J. (1996). The proactive personality as a predictor of entrepreneurial intentions. *Journal of Small Business Management*, 34(3): 42-49.

Davidsson, P. (1989). *Continued entrepreneurship and small firm growth.* Doctoral dissertation, Stockholm School of Economics.

Deakins, D. (1999). *Entrepreneurship and Small Firms.* Berkshire: McGraw-Hill Publishing Company.

Grimm, C.M. & Smith, K.G. (1997). *Strategy as action: Industry rivalry and coordination.* Cincinatti: SouthWestern.

Guba, E.G., & Lincoln, Y.S. (1989). *Fourth generation evaluation.* Newbury Park: SAGE.

Hendry, C., Arthur, M.B. and Jones, A.M. (1995). *Strategy through people – Adaption and learning in the small-medium enterprise.* London: Routledge.

Hitt, M.A., Ireland, R.D., Camp, S.M. & Sexton, D.L. (2002). *Strategic entrepreneurship: Creating a new mindset.* Oxford: Blackwell Publisher.

Hult, E-B, & Ramström, D. (2000). *The Swedish solo-entrepreneur, extension and characteristics.* Paper presented at the 11th Nordic conference on small business research, Aarhus.

Holmquist, C. (2006). Entreprenörskap och ledning. In H. Ylinenpää, B. Johansson & J.Johansson (Eds.) *Ledning i småföretag,* Lund: Studentlitteratur.

Ireland, R.D. & Hitt, M.A. (1999). Achieving and maintaining strategic competitiveness in the 21st century: the role of strategic leadership. *Academy of Management Executive,* 13(1): 43-57.

Jarillo, J.C. (1989). Entrepreneurship and growth: The strategic use of external resources. *Journal of Business Venturing,* 4(2):133-147.

Johannisson B. (2000). Modernising the Industrial District: Rejuvenation or Managerial Colonisation? In Vatne, E. & Taylor, M. (eds.), *The Networked Firm in a Global World.* Ashgate: Aldershot, 283-308.

Johansson, J. (2006). *Mindre verkstadsföretags jakt på konkurrensfördelar genom strategiska allianser – om överföring av kunskapsrelaterade resurser och dess strategiska betydelse.* Licentiate thesis, Luleå University of Technology.

Jovanovic, B. (1982). Selection and the evolution of industry. *Econometrica,* 50(3): 649-670.

Kirzner, I.M. (1973). *Competition and entrepreneurship.* Chicago: The University of Chicago Press.

Klofsten, M. (1998). *Affärsplattformen: entreprenören och företagets första år.* Stockholm: SNS Förlag.

Kotler, P., Armstrong, G., Wong, W. & Saunders, J. (1996). *Principles of marketing.* London: Prentice Hall.

Lazonick, W. (2005). The innovative firm. In J. Fagerberg, D. Mowery & Nelson, R., (Eds.), *The oxford handbook of innovation.* Oxford: Oxford University Press.

Lee, C., Lee, K., & Pennings, J.M. (2001). Internal capabilities, external networks, and performance: a study on technology-based ventures. *Strategic Management Journal,* 22(6-7): 615-640.

Lindholm Dahlstrand, Å. (2004). *Teknikbaserat nyföretagande: tillväxt och affärsutveckling.* Lund: Studentlitteratur.

Lu, J.W. & Beamish, P.W. (2001). The internationalization and performance of SMEs. *Strategic Management Journal,* 22(6-7): 565-586.

March, J.M. (1991). Exploration and Exploitation in Organizational Learning. *Organization Science,* 2: 71-87.

McDougall, P.O & Oviatt, B.M. (2000). International entrepreneurship: The intersection two research paths. *Academy of Management Journal*, 43(5): 902-908.

Miles, M.B. & Huberman, A.M. (1994), *Qualitative Data Analysis: An Expanded Sourcebook*, 2 ed. SAGE, Thousand Oaks.

Mintzberg, H. & Waters, J.A. (1985). On strategies, deliberate and emergent. *Strategic Management Journal*, 6: 257-272.

Mosakowski, E. (2002). Overcoming resource disadvantages in entrepreneurial firms: When less is more. In Hitt, M.A., Ireland, R.D., Camp, S.M. & Sexton, D.L. (Eds.), *Strategic Entrepreneurship: Creating a New Mindset:* 106-126. Oxford: Blackwell Publisher.

Pakes, A. & Ericson, R. (1998). Empirical implications of alternative models of firm dynamics. *Journal of Economic Theory*, 79(1): 1-45.

Patton, M.Q. (1990). *Qualitative evaluation and research methods.* 2 ed., Thousand Oaks: SAGE.

Penrose, E.T. (1959). *The theory of the growth of the firm.* New York: Wiley.

Politis, D. (2005). *Entrepreneurship, career experience and learning.* Doctoral dissertation, SIRE: Halmstad University.

Porter, M. (1985). *Competitive advantage.* New York: Free Press.

Reynolds, P.D. & White, S.B. (1997). *The entrepreneurial process.* Westport: Quorum Books.

Roberts, E. (1991). *Entrepreneurs in high technology: Lessons from MIT and beyond.* New York: Oxford University Press.

Schumpeter, J. (1934). *The Theory of Economic Development.* London: Oxford University Press.

Sexton, D.L. & Kasarda, J.D. (1992). *The state of the art of entrepreneurship.* Boston: PWS-Kent Publishing.

Shane, S, & Venkataraman, S. (2000). The promise of entrepreneurship as a field of research. *Academy of Management Review*, 25(1): 217-226.

Shane, S. (2000). Prior knowledge and the discovery of entrepreneurial opportunities. *Organization Science*, 11(4): 448-469.

Shane, S. (2001). Technology regimes and new firm formation. *Management Science*, 47(9): 1173-1190.

Shane, S., Locke, E.A. & Collins, C.J. (2003). Entrepreneurial motivation. *Human Resource Management Review*, 13(2): 257-279.

Storey, D.J. (1994). *Understanding the small business sector.* New York: Routledge.

Storper, M. (1995). The resurgence of regional economies, ten years later. In Edquist, C. & McKelvey, M., 2000, *Systems of innovation: growth, competitiveness and employment,* Vol. 1: 125-155. Cheltenham, UK and Northampton, MA, USA: Edward Elgar.

Venkataraman, S. (1997). The distinctive domain of entrepreneurship research: an editor's perspective. In Katz, J., Brockhaus, R. (Eds.) *Advances in Entrepreneurship, Firm Emergence, and Growth.* Greenwich: JAI Press.

Walsh, S.T., Kirchhoff, B.A., & Newbert, S. (2002). Differentiating market strategies for disruptive technologies, *IEEE Transactions on Engineering Management,* 49 (4): 341-351.

Westerberg, M. (1998). *Managing in turbulence – An empirical study of small firms operating in a turbulent environment.* Doctoral dissertation, Luleå University of Technology.

Westerberg, M. & Ylinenpää, H. (2006). Samverkan i mindre företag i Sverige. In Ylinenpää, H., Johansson, B. & Johansson, J. (Eds.), *Ledning i småföretag,* vol. 1: 273-297. Lund: Studentlitteratur.

Wincent, J. & Westerberg, M. (2006). Resource Contribution from Entrepreneurial Firms in Strategic SME networks. *Journal of Entrepreneurship and Innovation,* 7(1): 23-31.

Yin, R.K. (2003). *Case study research: design and methods.* 3 ed., Thousand Oaks: SAGE.

Ylinenpää, H. (1999). Competence Management and Small Firm Performance. In B. Johannisson, & H. Landström (Eds.), *Images of Entrepreneurship and Small Business – Emergent Swedish Contributions to Academic Research,* vol. 1: 217-240. Lund: Studentlitteratur.

Yli-Renko, H., Autio, E., & Sapienza, H.J. (2001). Social capital, knowledge acquisition, and knowledge exploitation in young technology-based firms. *Strategic Management Journal,* 22(6-7): 587-613.

5. How Human Capital Affects Self-Employment among the Science and Technology Labor Force

Johan Wiklund, Frédéric Delmar and Karin Hellerstedt

INTRODUCTION

It is frequently argued that a key to the economic vitality of a nation is related to the commercialization of opportunities based on new knowledge. Indeed, the commercial exploitation of science and technology based opportunities has been argued to be increasingly important to the economic development of nations and regions (Acs, 2002). More specifically, Baumol (1993) and followers (e.g., Murphy, Shleifer, & Vishny, 1991) argue that at the core of economic development lies the engagement in entrepreneurship by the science and technology labor force. This group of individuals is expected to have a higher probability to pursue entrepreneurial opportunities based on new technology (Baumol, 1993; Henrekson and Rosenberg, 2001). This is because people have access to different information and process it differently depending on idiosyncratic knowledge (Shane, 2000). Therefore, the ability to discover and exploit opportunities depends largely on previous education and work experience. Thanks to long education and advanced work experience, the science and technology labor force possesses substantial human capital, which could provide unique qualities for starting and operating new ventures with the potential of creating substantial growth and economic value. Further, among this labor force, the incentive structure for becoming self-employed is likely to depend less on necessity and un-employment and more on the potential of large gains, because income opportunities are likely to be substantial in wage work. However, studies that directly address the engagement in entrepreneurship of the science and technology labor force are limited. Instead, indirect proxies, such as the college enrollment in engineering, have been used (see e.g., Murphy et al., 1991 for a discussion).

Taking a first step in addressing the engagement in entrepreneurship of the science and technology labor force, we use the framework of occupational choice. Entrepreneurship is typically not considered as a work alternative in the occupational choice literature (see e.g., Carroll & Mosakowski, 1987), although claims are made that occupational choices included are exhaustive (Keane & Wolpin, 1997). Therefore, by considering entrepreneurship of the science and technology labor force as an occupational choice, we add both to the occupational choice literature and to entrepreneurship research.

Human capital theory has frequently been utilized to understand the occupational choices that people make. Central to human capital theory is the fact that the returns on different investments in human capital will vary depending on occupational choices. For example, it has been suggested that the returns on wage experience is higher in continued wage work than in self-employment (Evans & Leighton, 1989). The basic premise of this chapter is that there are differences in what generates utility for entrepreneurship compared to other occupations, and that this affects if people choose entrepreneurship or other occupations. Investments in human capital provide greater utility for entrepreneurship and other investments provide greater utility for other occupations. Human capital theory has also been used to understand individuals' transitions into self-employment (Davidsson & Honig, 2003). The argument being that individuals with more and higher quality human capital are more likely to enter self-employment.

In this chapter, our aim is to analyze self-employment among the science and technology labor force in Sweden and what factors are correlated to self-employment. We examine the first time entry into self-employment among the Swedish science and technology labor force, i.e., people who have a three-year or longer university education in engineering, science, or medicine. We utilize a unique dataset, where we follow three cohorts of graduates (1991, 1993, and 1995) and their subsequent entry into self-employment. This population is highly interesting since their human capital, based on their educational background, is likely to relate to the type of opportunities they exploit. In that sense one could expect this labor force to be critical for the transfer of scientific knowledge into commercial activity through the start-up of new independent companies. In other words, it is a population that could be expected to engage in entrepreneurship with a higher potential for economic growth.

By conducting this study, we make several contributions to the literature. First, viewing entrepreneurship as a career choice and utilizing human capital theory, we provide a solid theoretical embedment for empirical findings, such as the effect of experience or education on the probability of becoming self-employed. Second, we consider that starting and operating a business is associated with an opportunity cost in terms of foregone income from alternative occupations. Third, we believe that it is important to investigate the involvement in self-employment among the science and technology labor force since it is a group believed to be important for economic development (Baumol, 1993).

The chapter proceeds as follows: in the next section we present theory on human capital and relevant previous research. This discussion leads to a formulation of hypotheses that will be tested. Following that, we present our data, measures and variables, as well as analysis techniques. Thereafter, the results of our analyses are presented, followed by a discussion section. The chapter ends with our conclusions.

THEORY AND HYPOTHESES

Human Capital and Self-Employment

Human capital theory posits that individuals with more or higher quality human capital achieve higher performance in executing relevant tasks (Becker, 1975). Applying human capital theory to entrepreneurship, we should expect a positive association between an individual's human capital and the likelihood that he or she discovers an opportunity because greater human capital provides individuals with more knowledge that can assist them in identifying opportunities and knowledge of ways to best exploit opportunities once they have been discovered. However, the decision whether or not to exploit an opportunity involves weighing the value of the opportunity against the costs of exploiting it, and comparing this to the outcomes of other possible courses of action (Shane & Venkataraman, 2000). That is, because people have other work alternatives, there is an opportunity cost associated with the exploitation of an opportunity. Highly educated individuals with relevant experience likely have many career options other than going into self-employment. Therefore, such individuals are likely to discover more opportunities and are better suited for exploiting them once discovered. But the incentives for taking action and starting a new firm may be small unless the potential value of the business opportunity is substantial (Honig, 1998), because they have several other career options. This suggests that while the ability of discovering and exploiting business opportunities in independent businesses may be generally high among the science and technology labor force, the incentives for doing so may be low unless the potential value of the business opportunity is substantial.

Scholars have started to examine the importance of human capital for entering self-employment as well as how it affects the subsequent performance of the new venture (Bates, 1995; Bowen & Hisrich, 1986; Davidsson & Honig, 2003; Evans & Jovanovic, 1989; Evans & Leighton, 1989; Gimeno,

Folta, Cooper, & Woo, 1997; Honig, 1998; Rauch & Frese, 2000; Snell & Dean, 1992). However, while this literature has made substantial contributions to our understanding of the relationship between human capital and self-employment, it has not sufficiently considered the fact that human capital does not only provide the individual with skills and knowledge that can be used for running an independent business, but it may also be applied in other employment options. Therefore, in order to understand who does and does not become self-employed, it is important to study the opportunity cost of doing so.

From a human capital theory perspective, then, one would expect the science and technology labor force to primarily start businesses that have a high potential for providing substantial value for the individual. In essence, this is the theoretical argument for the interest in their entrepreneurship. Building on this general framework of the relationship between human capital and self-employment, in the following we develop hypotheses for how various aspects of human capital affect the likelihood that individuals in the science and technology labor force enter into self-employment.

Entrepreneurial Experience

To a large extent, entrepreneurs learn by doing, i.e. entrepreneurial skills are honed by investing time in working as self-employed (Iyigun et al., 1998). In the entrepreneurship literature, the most frequently investigated aspect of human capital is previous start-up experience. This experience may provide entrepreneurs with expertise in running an independent business and provide benchmarks for judging the relevance of information (Cooper, Folta, & Woo, 1995). It can lead to an understanding of the 'real' value of potential opportunities; speed up the business creation process; and enhance performance (Davidsson & Honig, 2003). Individuals with entrepreneurial experience are likely to accumulate human capital particularly valuable to self-employment while this experience probably is less useful in the context of wage work and therefore less valued by an employer. Stated differently, the payoff of entrepreneurial experience is likely to be larger in self-employment than in wage work. This is supported by previous empirical research, which has found previous entrepreneurial experience to be a predictor of future engagement in entrepreneurship (Bates, 1995; Davidsson & Honig, 2003). We believe that this expectation will hold also for the science and technology labor force. Thus we hypothesize the following:

Hypothesis 1: The probability of becoming self-employed is higher among individuals with previous self-employment experience.

Switching Jobs

An important distinction can be made between general and specific human capital. Specific human capital is developed through training and experience with particular work tasks in a specific job. Therefore, specific human capital is valuable in that particular context but has few applications outside of it. The investments individuals and firms make in specific human capital explains why workers with specific skills are less likely to switch jobs, and typically are the last ones to be laid off during a downturn in the economy (Becker, 1975). Therefore, as an individual remains with a job for a long time, the opportunity cost associated with switching jobs increases. On the other hand, someone who frequently changes jobs develops less specific human capital, and has a lower opportunity cost associated with future job changes. Frequent job changes may also be associated with developing more general skills and knowledge because the skills developed at different jobs are not identical. General human capital facilitates the integration and accumulation of new knowledge, which provides individuals with a larger opportunity set (cf. Gimeno et al., 1997), which increases chances of discovering new business opportunities. Several studies support the notion that job switching increases the likelihood of becoming self-employed (Evans & Leighton, 1989; Taniguchi, 2002). Taken together, this suggests that people who switch jobs frequently have a lower opportunity cost associated with becoming self-employed and are more likely to discover entrepreneurial opportunities. Furthermore, this diversity in experiences can provide individuals with both important experiences that are valuable for self-employment and more likely to pay off in self-employment. This leads to the following hypothesis:

Hypothesis 2: The probability of becoming self-employed increases with the number of job changes.

Labor-Market Experience

Previous research suggests that wage experience carries a higher return in wage work than in self-employment (Evans & Leighton, 1989) and that the returns are diminishing with increased experience (Mincer, 1974). Consistent with this argument, individuals should become less likely to turn to self-employment, the more work experience they accumulate, because the opportunity cost of entrepreneurship increases and the returns diminish. On the other hand, people who become self-employed need to acquire information about profitable business opportunities in order to start their own business. Individuals typically discover and exploit opportunities that are related to the knowledge they already possess (Shane, 2000; Venkataraman, 1997), and work experience is an important source of gaining relevant knowledge. However, while work-experience is likely to be of value to entrepreneurship, this does not overthrow the general argument that the opportunity cost of entering self-employment increases with longer work experience. Thus:

Hypothesis 3: The probability of becoming self-employed decreases with longer labor-market experience.

Length of Education

It has often been pointed out that entrepreneurs are either highly educated or they are not. Since the population in which we are interested has higher levels of education, we believe it is important to distinguish between those with post-graduate education to those without it. Post-graduate studies equip the individuals with substantial human capital over and above under-graduate levels of education, which can be exploited through self-employment. For example, university research can lead to the acquisition of knowledge than can be protected via patenting. One important way to exploit such knowledge is through the start-up of a new firm (cf. Shane, 2000). Further, the value of research training is likely to pay off at a relatively low number of very qualified research intensive firms. Therefore, the number of employment alternatives for research trained individuals where this training pays off is likely to be small, which reduces the opportunity cost of self-employment. This is confirmed by empirical data on employment in Scandinavia, where less than ten percent of individuals with post-graduate education work in the private sector (Autio & Ahola, 1996). Also, many individuals with post-graduate education work at universities (over 50 percent in Scandinavia, see Autio & Ahola 1996), and universities allow – and to an increasing extent even encourage – their employees to start businesses while remaining employed at the university. This is reflected by the rapid increase in self-employment among individuals with post-graduate education (Tether & Storey, 1998). From a human capital perspective, a high level of education also means higher levels of human capital. The theory assumes that more human capital is better (Davidsson & Honig, 2003). However, Davidsson and Honig (2003) discuss that prior research has produced mixed results concerning education. Often there has been a non-linear relationship between length of education and probability of becoming self-employed (cf. Davidsson & Honig, 2003). This could prove to be important for the specific population we are interested in. However, the vast majority of studies still predict that longer education results in higher human capital, which in turn increases the likelihood of entering self-employment. Even if prior research offers mixed results, we would expect those with post-graduate education to be more prone to become self-employed than those without. Thus:

Hypothesis 4: The probability of becoming self-employed is higher among individuals with post-graduate education than among individuals without such education.

Income

The current income of an individual is an indicator of how well his or her human capital pays off in financial terms (Becker, 1975). Because of market imperfection such as sluggish labor markets, discrimination and perceptual biases among those determining salaries, income differences are not likely to exactly reflect differences in human capital (Becker, 1993). Individuals may therefore have occupations where they earn less than they would in other occupations. In other words, if remaining in low paid occupations, these individuals have a cost in terms of the forgone value of the time spent on investments in human capital. This creates incentives for switching jobs, such as moving into self-employment. The decision of whether to exploit a business opportunity through self-employment involves weighing the value of the opportunity against the costs of exploiting it, and comparing this to the outcomes of other possible courses of action (Shane & Venkataraman, 2000). A lower salary in present occupation means giving up less money and thus a lower opportunity cost, suggesting that the relative attractiveness of becoming self-employed is larger. Thus:

Hypothesis 5: The probability of becoming self-employed decreases with increases in annual income from current job.

Age

In accordance with previous research (Gimeno et al., 1997), age can serve as a proxy for human capital in terms of experience and on-the-job training (cf. Becker, 1993). Generally, we would expect older individuals to possess more human capital, which would make them better equipped to run their own business. On the other hand, there is a cost associated with the switching between two alternative occupations, because over time individuals acquire specific human capital that can not be transferred from one occupation to another (Becker, 1975; 1993). The switching cost includes the efforts and expenses that the individual would need to undertake in job searches and re-training. Older individuals have a shorter time period to recover the costs associated with switching jobs because of their shorter time left in the labor market. This should make older individuals less prone to switch occupations. Because human capital increases with age, individuals can reap greater benefits from being self-employed as they grow older. But the cost of switching to self-employment will also increase with age. Bates (1995) found that across industries there was an inverse U-shape between age and self-employment entry. The effect of increased age seemed to level off at around 40 years (Bates, 1995). In a similar vein, Bates (1990) found an inversed U-shape between age and firm survival. Davidsson & Honig (2003) account for age effects and the potential negative effects of increased age. They do not however, consider a possible inverse U-shaped relationship. In sum, research suggests that age is a proxy for human capital, but a large share of conducted studies do not account for a non-linear impact. Furthermore, several studies that include age squared do not provide a theoretical argument for doing so. An argument supporting such empirical findings is that the opportunity cost of switching between employment and self-employment increases with age. We see no reason for why the science and technology labor force should be different from the general population in this respect. Therefore, we expect the relationship between age and self-employment to have an inverse U-shape. Thus:

Hypothesis 6: The relationship between age and self-employment has an inverse U-shape. The probability of becoming self-employed first increases with increases in age but then decreases as the individual grows older.

METHOD

Research Design and Sample

Inclusion in the sample is determined by the year for finishing a university education in science, medicine (excluding nurses) or engineering that is at least three years long. All individuals finishing their studies in 1991, 1993, or 1995 are included. By having these three cohorts we can control for age, period and cohort effects (Aldrich, 1999; Yamaguchi, 1991). For example, those included in our sample finish their studies before, during, and after the recession in 1992 to 1993, which could affect their probability of becoming self-employed. Moreover, we have no left censored cases and follow everyone from finishing their studies and onwards. Hence, we have full information and do not have problems with sample bias (Blossfeld & Rohwer, 1995). A total of 15,507 individuals met our inclusion criteria. For these individuals we have one observation each year for every variable included in the study.

Statistics Sweden has developed a number of longitudinal data registers following individuals on the basis of their personal number (the Swedish equivalent to the social security number), which remains unchanged during the life of a person. Working closely with register experts at Statistics Sweden, we cross referenced and combined several data registers in order to develop the dataset and the variables. All data come from official data registers such as tax registers, and are reported by individuals, employers, public agencies and so forth.

In order to follow how individuals transit into self-employment, the unit of analysis of this study is the individual and not the new firm. As many new firms are started by teams and many individuals buy or inherit existing firms, the number of individuals entering self-employment does not equal the number of new firms created during the period of observation.

Measures

Dependent variable

The dependent variable is entry into self-employment. Two criteria had to be fulfilled in order to consider an individual as self-employed. Any individual who operates a sole proprietorship or a partnership, or owns (part of) a close held limited liability company, reporting it as the major workplace fulfills the first criterion. The second criterion concerns not receiving a larger income from wage work than from self-employment. Many individuals operate a firm as a sideline to regular employment, partly because there are no costs associated with starting a sole proprietorship. Starting a firm as a sideline to regular employment does not represent a career change. It is only when an individual starts operating a firm as a main activity that we consider that person to be self-employed. This definition has advantages compared to previous studies of self-employment. First, we consider individuals who are self-employed irrespective of the organizational form they choose for their company. Second, we recognize that people can be simultaneously employed and operate a firm, and we provide a strict criterion for when they should be considered self-employed. We code the variable '0' when an individual is not self-employed and '1' the year the person becomes self-employed. We observe 717 entries into self-employment during the period of observation which correspond to 4.6% of the population.

Independent variables

We investigate the impact of four specific aspects of human capital; prior experience, length of education, personal income and age. Prior experience relates to past entrepreneurial experience, number of job changes and total labor market experience. Past entrepreneurial experience is measured as the number of years that individuals report being self-employed *but* receive a smaller income from self-employment than from wage work. During these years, self-employment is not the primary work activity (cf. the definition of self-employed above). Job change is measured as the total number of job changes a person makes. A maximum of one change per year is recorded. A change in the work place number indicates a job change and thus includes both changes within and between organizations. Finally, experience from the labor market was measured as the total number of years worked prior to becoming self-employed.

Length of education measures if the individual has a post-graduate education as opposed to an under-graduate or graduate education. Those with a post-graduate education were coded 1 and those without were coded 0. There are different approaches as to whether this variable should be measure as a continuous or a dichotomous variable (Davidsson & Honig, 2003; Carrol & Mosakowski, 1987). Due to the fact that all individuals in our population have at least three years of university education, we do not have a lot of variation on this variable. Therefore, the distribution forces us to use a dichotomous variable for length of education.

Income is based on the gross earned income that has been reported to the tax authorities on a yearly base. The independent variable age was calculated on the basis of birth date. As we expect the effect of age to have an inverse U-shape, we also include age squared.

Control variables
There are other aspects often highlighted to be important for predicting self-employment entries. Therefore, we include nine control variables. First, we account for the sex of the individual (Brush, 1992; Duchénaut, 1997; Holmquist & Sundin, 2002) measured as 0 for men and 1 for women. Second, we account for whether the individual is an immigrant (Davidsson & Honig, 2003; Storey, 1994). This variable was constructed based on country of birth, coded '1' for people born outside of Sweden and '0' for people born in Sweden. Third, access to financial capital (e.g., Taylor, 2001) was included. It is measured as a dummy variable with an individual in a household with a total wealth of more than one million Swedish crowns[1] coded as 1 and those with less wealth as 0. Fourth and fifth, two labor market status variables were constructed. The first signals if the individual is not working but receives taxable income (e.g., parental leave benefits or unemployment benefits). The second shows if the individual is not working and does not receive an income

---

[1] 1 Million Swedish Crowns corresponds to 125,000 USD and is the floor for capital taxation. Wealth is collectively declared and taxed by a household. This measure is therefore preferred over individual wealth.

(e.g., a housewife). Sixth, the type of education refers to the three sub-categories of the studied population, i.e. engineering, medicine and natural sciences. Two dummies have been created for natural sciences and medicine and in the model engineering is the reference group. Seventh, in order to account for family status, five family types were identified and dummies were created for the first four categories. These are cohabitation with children under 18 years; married with children under 18 years; single mother with children under 18 years; single father with children under 18 years; and other family status (e.g., single). Eight, working in different industries equips individuals with different experiences, which can affect the likelihood of entering entrepreneurship. Following Swedish practice (cf. Davidsson, Lindmark, & Olofsson, 1998), we created eight industry types based on ISIC codes and created dummy variables for the first seven categories. The industries were: High-technology manufacturing, Technology consultants, Other knowledge intensive services, Finance, Trade, Research and Development, Healthcare, and Other. Finally we control for when the individuals entered the population (i.e., finished their university studies). Two dummy variables were constructed, one for each year of entry (1993 and 1995). Individuals entering the population in 1991 represent the reference group.

RESULTS AND DISCUSSION

Analyses

There is always some probability that those who are not self-employed in a given year will enter self-employment the following year. Thus, it is impossible to establish a time-frame sufficiently long to ensure that the probability of every individual entering self-employment is zero. To deal with such situations, specific statistical techniques have been developed. We use event history analysis, which treats individuals not transiting into self-employment as censored in the year of their last observation. Unlike methods such as logistic regression, event history analysis generates unbiased estimates of the probability of entering self-employment for this type of data. Statistical tests of different distributional assumptions showed that our data best fit the standard Weibull distribution. Therefore, a Weibull hazard rate model with robust clustering on each individual is applied.

Table 5.1 below provides the descriptive statistics for all variables and Table A1 (Appendix A) shows the correlation matrix. The results of estimating the probability of entering self-employment at any time during the period of observation are found in Table 5.2 below. Hazard rates are displayed and show the probability change of entering self-employment caused by one unit change in the independent variables (estimated at the sample means). The probability decreases if the value is below 1 and increases if it is above 1.

As can be seen in the tables below, five of our six hypotheses are supported. We will briefly go through them one by one. According to Hypothesis 1 we expect that the probability of becoming self-employed is higher among individuals with previous self-employment experience. The hazard rate of

		Mean	Std.Dev.	Min	Max
1.	Self-employment	0.02	0.12	0.00	1.00
2.	SE experience	0.18	0.77	0.00	10.00
3.	Job changes	1.87	1.07	1.00	9.00
4.	Year worked	4.00	2.57	0.00	10.00
5.	Doct. Engineering	0.04	0.18	0.00	1.00
6.	Doct. nat.science	0.02	0.15	0.00	1.00
7.	Doct. Medicinec	0.02	0.14	0.00	1.00
8.	Salary	236549.50	160325.90	0.00	10900000.00
	Education				
9.	Nat. science	0.11	0.31	0.00	1.00
10.	Medicine	0.19	0.39	0.00	1.00
11.	Age	32.55	6.70	18.00	83.00
12.	Age square	1104.35	542.56	324.00	6889.00
13.	Sex	1.31	0.46	1.00	2.00
14.	Immigrant	0.18	0.38	0.00	1.00
	Social status				
15.	Not working but tax	0.05	0.22	0.00	1.00
16.	Not working no tax	0.06	0.23	0.00	1.00
17.	Net worth	0.04	0.19	0.00	1.00
18.	Married with young child	0.26	0.44	0.00	1.00
19.	Cohabit with young child	0.07	0.26	0.00	1.00
20.	Single father with young child	0.00	0.06	0.00	1.00
21.	Single mother with young child	0.01	0.11	0.00	1.00
	Industry				
22.	High-tech manufacturing	0.13	0.34	0.00	1.00
23.	Technology consultant	0.13	0.34	0.00	1.00
24.	Other knowledge-intensive industries	0.02	0.12	0.00	1.00
25.	Finance	0.02	0.13	0.00	1.00
26.	Trade	0.04	0.19	0.00	1.00
27.	R&D	0.07	0.26	0.00	1.00
28.	Healthcare	0.16	0.37	0.00	1.00
	Cohort				
29.	grad1993	0.31	0.46	0.00	1.00
30.	grad1995	0.31	0.46	0.00	1.00

Table 5.1 Descriptive statistics

PREDICTOR VARIABLES	
Entrepreneurial experience	1.47***
Job changes	1.21***
Labor market experience	0.85***
Length of education	1.08
Income	1.00***
Age	1.16***
Age square	0.99***
CONTROL VARIABLES	
Education	
Natural science	0.78
Medicine	1.90***
Labor Market Status	
Not working but tax	0.03***
Not working no tax	0.09***
Family Status	
Cohabit with young child	0.99
Married with young child	1.12
Single mother with young child	0.89
Single father with young child	0.50
Industry	
High-tech manufacturing	0.25***
Technology consultant	2.37***
Other knowledge-intensive industries	4.66***
Finance	0.49
Trade	1.19
R&D	0.14***
Healthcare	0.56***
Cohort	
grad1993	1.32**
grad1995	1.69***
Other	
Net worth	1.63**
Sex	0.52***
Immigrant	1.05
MODEL STATISTICS	
-Log Likelihood	2175.58
Chi- square	1904.42

Note: Values are hazard rates, *** = p< 0.001; ** = p< 0.01; * = p< 0.05 in two-tailed tests. The analysis file contains 111,826 individual-year observations, 15,507 cases and 717 entries into self-employment.

Table 5.2 Results of event history analyses predicting entry into full-time self-employment

1.47 (p < 0.001) means that there is a statistically significant effect of previous self-employment and entry into self-employment. The value of 1.47 implies that this effect is positive since it is above 1. Consequently, the results supports hypothesis 1. Hypothesis 2 predicts that the probability of becoming self-employed increases with the number of job changes. Also this hypothesis is supported since the effect is statistically significant and the hazard rate is above 1 (hazard rate 1.21; $p < 0.001$). Our results show that the probability of becoming self-employed diminishes with the number of years worked, which lends support to hypothesis 3. Here the hazard rate is below 1 indicating that the more years an individual has worked the less likely he or she is to enter self-employment (hazard rate 0.85; $p < 0.001$). Hypothesis 4, which states that the probability of becoming self-employed is higher among individuals with post-graduate education than among individuals without such education, is not supported by our findings (hazard rate 1.08; $p > 0.1$). Hypothesis 5 on the other hand is supported. According to this hypothesis the probability of becoming self-employed increases with decreased annual income from the individual's current job. As the hazard rate is above one and the p-value below 0.05 (hazard rate 1.01; $p < 0.001$) we can note that the higher income individuals receive from their employment, the less likely they are to actually become self-employed. Finally, the effects of age (hazard rate 1.16; $p < 0.001$) and age square (hazard rate 0.99; $p < 0.001$) support the inverse U-shaped relationship of Hypothesis 6. This suggests that up to a certain age the increase in age is positively associated with entry, but after leveling off, this effect instead becomes negative. Six of the control variables were also found to have an impact on the entry rates. Namely, education, labor market status, industry, cohort, sex, and net worth effects were all found to predict entry.

Entry into Self-Employment

In this chapter we set out to study the relationship between human capital and entry into self-employment among the science and technology labor force. We used unique longitudinal data and event history analysis to examine the work careers of 15,507 individuals with university education of three years or longer in medicine, natural sciences, or engineering. We predicted their first time entry into self-employment by observing their first six to ten years of labor market activity after finishing their studies. The data allowed us to take several aspects of human capital into account. In line with human capital theory, we argue that human capital equips individuals with more and better options for choosing an occupation, self-employment being one of the options. Previous entrepreneurship research has not sufficiently considered the fact that while individuals with more or better quality human capital may be better suited for self-employment, given that they desire self-employment, they also have many other employment alternatives, which may reduce their incentives for going into self-employment. We call these other alternatives the opportunity cost associated with self-employment. Based on this logic, no less than five out of our six hypotheses regarding entry into self-employment received support.

Our first hypothesis concerning the importance of entrepreneurial experience was supported. The longer a person is self-employed as a sideline to a regular job, thus accumulating experience, the higher the probability that the person will enter full-time self-employment. Previous research has found that self-employment of any length increases chances of subsequent self-employment (e.g., Bates, 1995; Davidsson & Honig, 2003). We complement and refine these findings by showing that part-time self-employment is sufficient for serving the purpose of gaining experience and that the longevity of this experience is important.

The relevance of job changes to entrepreneurship has not been considered enough in previous research. Interestingly, and in line with theory, our findings show that the more jobs an individual tries, the more likely he or she is to subsequently enter self-employment. We suggest that this is because job changes expose individuals to more diverse experiences, which increases their chances of discovering entrepreneurial opportunities, while the opportunity cost for becoming an entrepreneur decreases. This finding suggests that job mobility is positively associated with entrepreneurship within this population. Both job switching and entrepreneurship have been used as indicators of labor market dynamism and both are more common among highly educated individuals in the US than in Europe. It is possible that job mobility can, in part, explain the differences in entrepreneurship between the two continents.

We hypothesized and found a negative effect of labor-market experience on self-employment because the payoff to wage experience is higher in continued wage work than in self-employment. Increased labor market experience means that large investments have been made in the current career and these investments may be difficult to recover in self-employment. This finding shows the advantages of our research design. Previous research utilizing broad samples and techniques other than panel data analysis tend to find the opposite. Future research will have to resolve this seeming conflict of results. In light of our careful research design and the theoretical rationale for the relationship in terms of the opportunity cost of entering entrepreneurship, we believe our finding to be correct concerning the negative effect of labor-market experience on self-employment.

We hypothesized and found that lower income would be associated with higher probability of entering self-employment because individuals earning less would have stronger incentives for searching for other occupations where their human capital investments would pay off better (Amit, Muller, & Cockburn, 1995). This finding supports the idea that people who face work discrimination or for other reasons are restricted in their professional careers may find self-employment as a viable option (cf. Storey, 1994).

The effect of age square (over and above the effect of age) supports the relatively complex inverse U-shaped relationship between age and self-employment that we hypothesized. While older people have accumulated more human capital, the cost associated with switching to another career also increases with age. Previous uni-variate analyses of self-employment tend to find that entry into self-employment is most common somewhere around the age of 30 to 40 years in the population at large. In our research, we have provided a human capital theoretical rationale for this empirical observation and also modeled it in a multi-variate context, which is a contribution to the literature.

Implications for Research

Taken together, our findings complement entrepreneurship research that has emphasized the discovery of entrepreneurial opportunities (e.g., Kirzner, 1973; Shane, 2000). Human capital theory can help us understand why some people choose to exploit entrepreneurial opportunities while others do not. The population we study is likely to discover interesting high-potential opportunities (Baumol, 1993). However, based on human capital theory, we have shown that there may be incentives not to exploit opportunities that have been discovered, or not to even be alert to entrepreneurial opportunities because there is an opportunity cost associated with becoming an entrepreneur.

Viewing entrepreneurship as a career option, we find that highly educated individuals earning high salaries through long careers likely view entrepreneurship as an unattractive alternative. Entrepreneurship is different from other occupations because of the uncertainty it entails (Iyigun & Owen, 1999). The size of the entrepreneur's income is uncertain and largely depends on the success of the new venture, which is difficult to project with any accuracy, and the longevity of the job is uncertain because the failure rate among new ventures is very high. For many, entering entrepreneurship means giving up a certain income for uncertain entrepreneurial returns. As a result, the evaluation of entrepreneurial opportunities involves considerable uncertainty and it is difficult to estimate the utility of entrepreneurship as an occupational choice.

This chapter contributes to both entrepreneurship research and the human capital literature. Our research provides interesting implication for the strand of entrepreneurship interested in the relationship between sources of opportunities; their discovery, and exploitation. Entrepreneurship theory should take into consideration that opportunity discovery does not automatically lead to exploitation. The decision of whether or not to exploit an opportunity involves weighing the value of the opportunity against the costs of exploiting it, and comparing this to the outcomes of other possible courses of action (Shane & Venkataraman, 2000).

Those individuals with the highest probability of discovering valuable opportunities may also have the highest opportunity cost for entering self-employment and are less likely to engage in entrepreneurship unless they perceive the value of the opportunity to be substantial. As entrepreneurship is a highly uncertain business, it is possible that many of these individuals demand too large a risk premium in order to engage in entrepreneurship. Based on this study's findings, we suggest that further research must take the opportunity cost of exploiting opportunities into consideration. Further, as argued above, evaluating an entrepreneurial opportunity involves substantial uncertainty. Consequently, people likely evaluate the same opportunities differently based on idiosyncratic incentives and intentions. Therefore, the psychological approach is likely to be valuable in understanding why some people choose to exploit opportunities while others do not.

We also inform the strand in entrepreneurship that is interested in the effects of human capital. Previous research has not sufficiently taken into account that human capital is heterogeneous and that different strands of human capital affect occupational choices differently. That is, some aspects of human capital increase the probability of entering entrepreneurship while other aspects decrease the probability. We have made considerable efforts to eliminate methodological problems that have disturbed previous research. Hence, our results should be quite robust and provide important grounds for further research and theorizing.

Practical Implications

The level of entrepreneurship in a society can be affected by making decisions that change the supply of enterprising individuals, the demand for such individuals in terms of the prevalence of business opportunities (Correll, 2001; Thornton, 1999), or both. In this study, by controlling for education and the year of entering the labor force, we carefully control for the demand side while studying the supply of entrepreneurship. Several of our findings have important implications.

The return to entrepreneurship relative to other career options, as well as the chance of success, affects the opportunity cost of entering entrepreneurship and, thus, the likelihood that people become entrepreneurs. The individuals we study could probably start high-potential new ventures, but relatively few choose to become self-employed (4.6%). In order to reduce the opportunity cost and make self-employment more attractive, policy makers could increase the financial returns to self-employment and decrease the financial punishment for failure, if the aim is to increase the supply of entrepreneurship.

It appears that longer work experience decreases chances of becoming self-employed because the returns to wage experience are higher in wage work than in self-employment. This suggests that it is important to present entrepreneurship as a viable career option to young people leaving the university. Taken together with the finding that the experience of part-time self-employment has a positive effect on full-time self-employment, this suggests that one way to increase the supply of entrepreneurs among the science and technology labor force could be for universities to stimulate students to take entrepreneurship classes and start companies in parallel with their studies. It could provide them with the possibility of gaining entrepreneurial experience (i.e., knowledge that is needed to organize, manage, and market science-based entrepreneurial opportunities) and understanding the value of the opportunity being exploited, without taking the risk associated with leaving a job.

The result that frequent job changes positively affect the probability of entering self-employment suggests that a more dynamic labor market could positively influence entrepreneurship. At present, there are several labor market rigidities in Sweden. Someone who decides to leave a job becomes 'last in line' at other employers because Swedish labor market laws promote constantly remaining with the same employer. Further, leaving a job to become self-employed is associated with giving up social benefits. Even if in theory, there are social benefits for self-employed within Sweden, in practice they often do not materialize. If such rigidities could be removed, labor market dynamics and the relative attractiveness of self-employment would likely increase for this population.

Limitations

This chapter focuses solely on the science and technology labor force in Sweden. Thus, it is premature to infer our results to other parts of the Swedish labor market, or to other countries. While this design has considerable advantages because it allows better controlling for unobserved heterogeneity coming from different educational background, it also limits generalizability. We developed our hypotheses on the basis of general theory and findings. Given that we, to a large extent, received support for them indicates that we can generalize to other populations. However, in terms of education we would be hesitant to do so. In our study, education length did not appear to have an impact on self-employment entries. Since we study a group of individuals that all possess rather long educational degrees, this effect might not be observed.

It is likely that having more fine-grained measures of length of education and a population with more diversity on this variable, would produce other results concerning length of education, e.g. Davidsson and Honig (2003), on a sample of Swedish nascent entrepreneurs, found that length of education was positively related to the start-up process.

We carefully developed an indicator of self-employment. While we believe that this is a vast improvement over previous research, to some extent it may be a mixed blessing. Detailed analyses not presented in this chapter show that there is an enormous richness in the variety of opportunities exploited by the self-employed. In our analyses, we lumped all these opportunities together under the label 'self-employed'. Future research would benefit from more fine-grained analyses, controlling for the type of business started, the amount of time spent, income generated and so forth.

The reliance on secondary data has several advantages: it avoids response biases, which often leads to inflated results due to common method and common source variance; the measurement error of most variables is likely to be small; it is possible to include information that people are reluctant to divulge, such as income; non-response is virtually zero; and it is possible to conduct census studies. At the same time, there are also drawbacks with secondary data. The most important is that we were unable to tap several interesting variables. For example, we know nothing about the performance of the businesses that people operate. However, it is our intention to gather additional data on the businesses, including performance measures.

Finally, in our analyses we have fully utilized the fact that we have a panel study covering ten years. We have no left censored cases, and do not suffer from survival bias and problem with incomplete information. We study all relevant individuals from leaving university and onwards. Hence, we believe that our study provides useful methodological contributions to research on entry into self-employment, but, as touched upon above, the fact that many different types of self-employment are jointly analyzed probably attenuates results.

CONCLUSIONS

The science and technology labor force is important to the economic wellbeing of many nations. One important way these individuals contribute to economic development is through self-employment. In this chapter we examine how their human capital affects the likelihood of entering into and exiting from self-employment. Our findings suggest that human capital and occupational choice provide a valuable theoretical lens for understanding self-employment decisions. Human capital affects both the attractiveness of self-employment and of other job alternatives. Our findings have important implications for those interested in understanding the involvement in entrepreneurship by the science and technology labor force.

Acknowledgements: Handelsbanken Research Foundations, the Swedish Agency for Innovation Systems (Vinnova), the Swedish Foundation for Small Business Research, and the Swedish National Board for Industrial and Technological Development have financed this study. Their support is gratefully acknowledged.

Appendix A Table A1. Correlation matrix

	1	2	3	4	5	6	7	8	9	10	11	12	13	14	15	16	17	18	19	20	21	22	23	24	25	26	27	28	29	30
1	1.00																													
2	.10	1.00																												
3	.06	.12	1.00																											
4	.03	.17	.49	1.00																										
5	-.01	.04	.03	.12	1.00																									
6	-.01	.00	-.01	.05	-.03	1.00																								
7	.01	.04	.01	.02	-.03	-.02	1.00																							
8	-.11	.08	.22	.52	.04	-.01	.00	1.00																						
9	.00	-.03	-.03	-.10	-.07	-.01	-.05	-.17	1.00																					
10	.03	.05	-.02	.05	-.10	-.06	-.08	-.03	-.18	1.00																				
11	.10	.16	.15	.29	.04	-.08	.11	.17	-.03	.17	1.00																			
12	.10	.15	.11	.22	.03	.11	.22	.12	-.01	.15	.99	1.00																		
13	.01	.00	.00	.07	-.05	.09	.07	-.20	.10	.23	.00	.01	1.00																	
14	.04	.02	-.04	-.01	-.02	.08	.08	-.02	.66	.08	.28	.27	-.02	1.00																
15	-.02	-.03	-.04	-.06	-.05	.02	.01	-.29	-.02	-.01	-.04	-.03	.03	.04	1.00															
16	.03	-.05	-.10	-.24	-.02	.03	.05	-.33	-.05	-.01	.16	.18	.01	.19	-.01	1.00														
17	.04	.09	.05	-.24	.00	.01	.07	.09	.00	.00	.20	.20	.03	.04	-.01	.03	1.00													
18	.03	.08	.11	.10	.01	.04	.04	.09	-.05	.11	.18	.14	.02	.09	-.05	-.03	.06	1.00												
19	.01	.01	.01	.25	.04	.00	.05	.01	.01	.03	.03	.02	-.01	-.03	.00	-.03	-.01	-.17	1.00											
20	.00	.01	.00	.02	.00	.00	.00	.01	.01	.01	.05	.05	-.04	.01	.00	.01	.00	-.05	-.02	1.00										
21	.01	.02	.08	.08	-.01	-.01	.02	-.04	.01	.08	.08	.07	.15	.03	.01	.05	.00	-.06	-.03	-.01	1.00									
22	-.05	-.04	-.01	.05	.00	-.02	-.04	.11	-.04	-.04	-.16	-.07	-.07	-.02	-.06	-.09	.00	-.06	-.02	-.01	-.03	1.00								
23	.04	.02	.12	.08	-.02	-.03	-.06	.13	-.04	-.20	-.06	-.07	.10	-.06	-.05	-.09	.02	-.01	.01	.00	-.03	-.16	1.00							
24	.07	.02	.08	.03	-.01	-.01	.08	.08	.00	-.05	.00	.01	-.02	.01	.02	-.03	.01	.00	-.01	.00	.00	-.05	-.05	1.00						
25	.00	.00	-.01	.02	-.01	-.01	.07	.07	.00	-.06	-.06	-.04	.01	.00	.00	-.05	.02	-.01	-.01	.00	.00	-.05	-.08	-.02	1.00					
26	-.03	-.01	-.03	.01	-.03	.03	.05	.05	.10	-.01	-.01	-.04	-.03	.00	.00	-.06	.01	-.01	-.01	.00	.00	-.08	-.12	-.03	-.03	1.00				
27	-.03	.00	.02	-.02	.11	.15	.01	-.06	.19	-.09	-.09	-.04	.01	.06	.01	-.10	-.01	-.02	.04	-.01	-.01	-.12	-.18	-.04	-.04	-.10	1.00			
28	.01	.05	-.05	.04	-.09	.07	.05	.01	-.13	.79	.16	.14	.19	.00	.02	.00	.00	.11	.00	.01	.07	-.19	-.18	-.06	-.06	-.01	-.13	1.00		
29	.00	.02	-.02	.01	.01	-.01	.01	-.01	-.03	-.03	.03	.03	-.01	.06	.00	.01	.01	.01	.04	.01	.01	.00	-.01	.00	-.61	.01	.00	.02	1.00	
30	-.02	-.06	-.18	-.22	-.04	-.02	-.01	.03	.06	.08	-.12	-.11	.00	-.03	-.03	-.03	-.03	-.10	-.02	-.02	-.02	.01	.06	.01	.08	.01	.00	-.08	-.43	1.00

Note. Variable numbers correspond to Table 1. All correlations above or equal to .01 are significant at p< .05.

REFERENCES

Acs, Z. J. 2002. *Innovations and the growth of cities*. Cheltenham, UK and Northampton, MA, USA: Edward Elgar.

Aldrich, H. 1999. *Organizations evolving*. London: Sage Publications.

Amit, R., Muller, E., & Cockburn, I. 1995. Opportunity costs and entrepreneurial activity. *Journal of Business Venturing*, 10: 95-106.

Bates, T. 1990. Entrepreneur human capital inputs and small business longevity. *Review of Economics & Statistics*, 72(4): 551-559.

Bates, T. 1995. Self-employment entry across industry groups. *Journal of Business Venturing*, 10: 143-156.

Baumol, W. J. 1993. *Entrepreneurship, management and the structure of payoffs*. Cambridge, MA: MIT Press.

Becker, G. S. 1975. *Human capital*. Chicago, IL: Chicago University Press.

Becker, G.S. 1993. Nobel lecture: The economic way of looking at behavior. *The Journal of Political Economy*, 101(3): 385-409.

Blossfeld, H.-P., & Rohwer, G. 1995. *Techniques of event history analysis: New approaches to causal analysis*. Mahwah, New Jersey: Lawrence Erlbaum Associates.

Bowen, D. D., & Hisrich, R. D. 1986. The female entrepreneur: A career development perspective. *Academy of Management Review*, 11: 393-407.

Brush, C. G. 1992. Research on women business owners: Past trends, a new perspective and future directions. *Entrepreneurship Theory & Practice*, 16(4): 5-30.

Carroll, G. R., & Hannan, M. T. 2000. *The demography of corporations and industries*. Princeton, New Jersey: Princeton University Press.

Carroll, G. R., & Mosakowski, E. 1987. The career dynamics of self-employment. *Administrative Science Quarterly*, 32: 570-589.

Cooper, A. C., Folta, T. B., & Woo, C. 1995. Entrepreneurial information search. *Journal of Business Venturing*, 10: 107-120.

Correll, S. J. 2001. Gender and the career choice process: The role of biased self-assessments. *American Journal of Sociology*, 106(6): 1691-1730.

Davidsson, P., & Honig, B. 2003. The role of social and human capital among nascent entrepreneurs. *Journal of Business Venturing*, 18: 301-331.

Davidsson, P., & Lindmark, L., & Olofsson, C., 1998. The Extent of Overestimation of Small Firm Job Creation – An Empirical Examination of the Regression Bias, 1998, *Small Business Economics*, Volume 11, Number 1: 87-100, Springer Netherlands

Duchénaut, B. 1997. *Women entrepreneurs in SMEs*. Rennes, France: Euro PME.

Evans, D. S., & Jovanovic, B. 1989. An enstimation model of entrepreneurial choice under liquidity constraints. *Journal of Political Economy*, 97(4): 808-826.

Evans, D. S., & Leighton, L. S. 1989. Some empirical aspects of entrepreneurship. *The American Economic Review*, 79: 519-535.

Gimeno, J., Folta, T. B., Cooper, A. C., & Woo, C. Y. 1997. Survival of the fittest? Entrepreneurial human capital and the persistence of underperforming firms. *Administrative Science Quarterly*, 42: 750-783.

Henrekson, M., & Rosenberg, N. 2001, Designing Efficient Institutions for Scinece-Based Entreprenurship: Lesson from the US and Sweden, *The Journal of Technology Transfer*, Volume 26, Number 3: 207-231, Springer Netherlands

Holmquist, C., & Sundin, E. (Eds.). 2002. *Företagerskan: Om kvinnor och entreprenörskap*. Stockholm: SNS Förlag.

Honig, B. 1998. What determines success? Examining the human, financial, and social capital of Jamaican microentrepreneurs. *Journal of Business Venturing*, 13: 371-394.

Iyigun, M. F., & Owen, A. L. 1998. Risk, entrepreneurship, and human capital accumulation. *American Economic Review*, 88: 454-457.

Iyigun, M. F., & Owen, A. L. 1999. Entrepreneurs, professionals, and growth. *Journal of Economic Growth*, 4: 213-232.

Keane, M. P., & Wolpin, K. I. 1997. The career decisions of young men. *Journal of Political Economy*, 105: 473-522.

Kirzner, I. 1973. *Competition and entrepreneurship*. Chicago, IL: University of Chicago Press.

Mincer, J. 1974. *Schooling, experience and earnings*. New York: Columbia University Press.

Murphy, K. M., Shleifer, A., & Vishny, R. W. 1991. The allocation of talent: Implications for growth. *The Quarterly Journal of Economics*, 106: 503-530.

Rauch, A., & Frese, M. 2000. *Human capital of small scale business owners and business success: A longitudinal study of moderators and mediators*. Paper presented at the ICSB World Conference 2000, Brisbane, Australia.

Shane, S. & Venkataraman, S. 2000. The promise of entrepreneurship as a field of research. *Academy of Management Review*, 25(1): 217-226.

Shane, S. 2000. Prior knowledge and the discovery of entrepreneurial opportunities. *Organization Science*, 11(4): 448-469.

Snell, S.A., & Dean, J.W. 1992. Integrated manufacturing and human resource management: A human capital perspective. *Academy of Management Journal*, 35(3): 467-504.

Storey, D. J. 1994. *Understanding the small business sector*. London: Routledge.

Hiromi Taniguchi, "Determinants of Women's Entry into Self-Employment, "*Social Science Quarterly*, vol. 83, no. 3, 2002, pp.875–93.

Taylor, M. P. 2001. Self-employment and windfall gains in Britain: Evidence from panel data. *Economica,* 68: 539-565.

Tether, B.S. & Storey, D.J. 1998. Smaller firms and Europe's high technology sectors: A framework for analysis and some statistical evidence, *Research Policy*, 26(9): 947-971.

Thornton, P. H. 1999. The sociology of entrepreneurship. *Annual Review of Sociology*, 25: 19-46.

Venkataraman, S. (1997). The distinctive domain of entrepreneurship research. In J.A. Katz & R.H. Brockhaus Sr. (Eds.), *Advances in entrepreneurship, firm emergence and growth* (Vol. 3, pp. 119-138). Greenwich, CT:JAI Press.

Yamaguchi, K. (1991). *Event history analysis*. Newbury Park: Sage Publications.

6. The Framing of New Business Concepts in Established Corporations: an Explanatory Investigation

Christian Czernich and Ivo Zander

INTRODUCTION

Corporate entrepreneurship, or the process by which new business concepts are introduced and ultimately commercialized by established corporations, is at the heart of corporate renewal and a necessary requirement for the firm's long-term survival (Dougherty & Hardy, 1996; Hamel & Prahalad, 1994; Zahra & Covin, 1995). In most established companies, individual initiatives at lower organizational levels generate a stream of new business concepts that are potentially recognized and retained by the established organization. These new business concepts are typically promoted by an intrapreneur, whose task it is to develop a new concept into a commercially viable product or service, in the process 'selling' it and creating awareness its commercial potential to other organizational members.

Despite the fact that new business concepts are critical for the long-term survival of the corporation, their status is often precarious and only a small proportion of all new concepts can hope to survive and have a significant impact on organizational operations and strategy (Biggadike, 1979; Block, 1982). Intrapreneurs and their new business concepts must compete for the limited resources in the organization, transform inert organizational structures, and overcome the often incredulous attitudes among other organizationnal members (Burgelman, 1991; Kazanjian & Drazin, 1987; Lovas & Ghoshal, 2000; Sykes & Block, 1989). The success and survival of new business concepts in the established corporation requires the intrapreneur's persistent effort to attract and maintain the attention of others (Dutton et al., 2001; Pinchot, 1985), and to present or sell the new concept in a way that generates the support needed for its ultimate acceptance.

To attract attention and generate support for the new business concept, the intrapreneur can make use of framing when presenting and promoting the concept to other organizational members (Fiol, 1994). Framing aims at influencing the mental models through which others make sense of and evaluate new information. When successful, it supports the formation of a positive attitude towards the new concept, and ultimately results in the decision to have it retained by the organization. The way in which the intrapreneur presents and promotes a new business concept thereby can be of significant importance for its survival in the host corporation.

Although it has been suggested that intrapreneurs can utilize the strategic use of 'framing' in their attempts to promote new business concepts (Dutton et al., 2001; Howell & Higgins, 1990), empirical studies on the subject are scarce and have mostly relied upon single observations and case studies (e.g. Fiol, 1994; Pinchot, 1985). Hence, there is limited systematic knowledge about how intrapreneurs make use of framing as part of their new business venture activities. The present chapter sets out to fill this empirical void, offering more broad-based empirical evidence on how intrapreneurs actually go about framing their new business concepts. Specifically, the chapter explores how intrapreneurs present and promote their new business concepts in terms of the key categories threat, opportunity, novelty, and commonality (Ahuja & Lampert, 2001; Dutton & Jackson, 1987; Jackson & Dutton, 1988), as well as the implications of different framing approaches for the survival of new business concepts in the host corporations.

The chapter uses survey data on 49 new business concepts introduced in 18 Swedish corporations, generating information about how the intrapreneurs have framed their respective concepts in the corporate context. These new business concepts were generally judged to represent something significantly new in terms of technology or functionality, thus highlighting the potential need for framing to get them accepted and retained by the respective corporations. Starting from baseline information about the intrapreneurs' framing of their new business concepts in terms of threat, opportunity, novelty, and commonality, cluster analysis identifies three more specific framing approaches. Event history techniques are finally applied to explore the implications for survival of the new business concepts within the host corporations.

The results suggest the existence of a baseline approach to framing in which intrapreneurs emphasize the opportunity and novelty associated with their new business concepts. The framing of new business concepts as a response to a threat or something that resembles prior successful projects within the corporation is used more sparingly. Within this baseline approach, three specific framing approaches are identified, labeled active-strategic, active-optimistic, and passive. Whereas each group represents a distinctive combination of emphasis on opportunity, threat, novelty, and commonality, the most common combination is that of a high degree of emphasis on both opportunity and novelty. Results concerning the implications for survival of the new concepts within the host corporations reveal no differences in the effectiveness of the three different framing approaches.

The chapter consists of five main sections. The first section presents existing theoretical perspectives on framing and identifies those framing approaches and literature identified as presumably most effective in securing the survival of new business concepts inside the established corporation. The second section presents the sample, methodology, measurement of key variables, and main statistical methods, and it is followed by two sections that contain the results and an extended discussion. The final section contains a summary of findings and conclusions, as well as some suggestions for future research.

THEORETICAL PERSPECTIVES ON FRAMING

At the fundamental level, framing is concerned with how individuals attempt to construe the meaning and convey a picture of 'reality' to other people (Benford & Snow, 2000; Fiol, 1994). The objective is to generate attention to certain issues, problems, or projects and to construct mental models that help others make sense of and evaluate new information (Dutton & Ashford, 1993; Huber, 1991). In the words of Benford and Snow (2000: 614), framing in a social context thereby denotes 'an active, processual phenomenon that implies agency and contention at the level of reality construction.'

In the organizational context, the way in which managers interpret new issues, events, or projects determines their potential range of behavior (Huber, 1991; Kiesler & Sproull, 1982) and ultimately influences organizational action (Chattopadhyay, Glick & Huber, 2001; Daft & Weick, 1984; Dutton & Duncan, 1987; Dutton & Jackson, 1987; Milliken, 1990). Framing is particularly important when individuals at lower or middle levels of the organization seek attention to and support for issues that fall outside established practices and cognitive frames of top management. Successful framing thereby contributes to the implementation of projects that may change corporate strategy (Burgelman, 1991; Lovas & Ghoshal, 2000), introducing new products and services which may ultimately become accepted parts of the corporation's core activities (Burgelman, 1983).

One way of generating attention and constructing meaning is to employ certain cognitive categories and linguistic labels that help people make sense of new information. These categories are comprised of objects sharing similar attributes, allowing the communicator to use shortcuts in conveying the meaning and implications of new issues, events, or projects. Three such categories identified in the organizational and framing literature are threat, opportunity and novelty. Threat has been associated with negative outcomes, uncontrollable situations, and potential loss, whereas opportunity is associated with positive outcomes, controllable situations, and potential gain (Dutton & Jackson, 1987; Jackson & Dutton, 1988). Although these attributes have been identified as distinctly related to either threats or opportunities, threat and opportunity do not represent opposite or mutually excluding categories in all respects. For example, pressure to act and the need for quick action have been associated with both threats and opportunities (Jackson & Dutton, 1988), and whereas managers may perceive a threat from a new competing technology they may at the same time recognize that it offers an opportunity to enter a new field of significant future potential.

Novelty and how it is perceived is widely discussed in the literature on organizational change (e.g. Ahuja & Lampert, 2001; Kazanjian & Drazin, 1987; Piderit, 2000; Tyre & Hauptman, 1992), and it has two different connotations. It may refer to novelty in a general sense, emphasizing the extent to which an issue, object or event is equally novel to all observers (for example, trading over the Internet may at some point have been perceived as a generally novel way of doing business), but it may also be seen in relation to the current operations and practices of the individual organization. From this perspective, a particular event or object may represent a novel experience to one firm, whereas it is more or less aligned with established practices in another. The opposite of novelty is commonality, or the extent to which new issues, objects or events are aligned with already established perceptions and practices in the general or firm-specific sense.

Some empirical evidence suggests that individuals use framing intentionally and strategically. Dutton et al. (2001) show that so-called issue-sellers in organizations are very conscious about how they frame the issue they want to sell to top management. They also show that the way 'issue entrepreneurs' package an issue, for instance by making it appear more incremental than it actually is, or how they connect to other salient issues or important organizational goals influence the likelihood that the issue will have an organizational impact. Howell and Higgins (1990) show that champions of new ideas make use of a number of framing tactics to capture the attention of resource allocators and to convince them about the future potential of innovations. Innovators do so not only by formulating a compelling vision for what the concept might become, but also by linking the concept to larger principles and values held by the organization. In the more general setting of entrepreneurship, Hargadon and Douglas (2002) illustrate how Thomas Edison actively tried to shape perceptions of the electric light by presenting it in a way that made it seem less novel and threatening to the established gas-lighting system than it actually was.

The Framing of New Business Concepts in Established Corporations

While a distinction can be made between different objects of framing, including issues, problems, and projects (Dutton & Ashford, 1993), the present chapter is concerned with the framing of new business concepts introduced in established corporations. These new business concepts are specifically defined as products or services that have introduced something significantly new in terms of technology or functionality.

In the corporate entrepreneurship literature, framing is typically associated with key individuals or intrapreneurs at lower organizational levels and outside the organizational core (Galbraith, 1982; Antoncic & Hisrich, 2003), attempting to promote new business concepts among other organizational members in general and top management in particular (Burgelman, 1983).[1] It is concerned with how a new business concept is connected to changes and developments in the external environment; for example, whether it is to be seen as a response to an external threat or opportunity (Zahra, 1991), and how it is to be perceived in the light of ongoing internal operations and practices. The ultimate objective is to generate attention to the new business concept and to develop a collective understanding of it among various decision makers. This attention and understanding is intended to lead to positive attitudes, support, and ultimately the organization's retention of the new business concept and strategic renewal (Guth & Ginsberg, 1990).

Apart from generating attention and support for new business concepts, framing in the corporate entrepreneurship context often (but not necessarily) has the connotation that individuals strategically try to communicate pictures of reality that do not necessarily correspond to all 'objective' or known facts. Intrapreneurs thereby attempt to convey an appealing picture of new business concepts without resorting to outright misrepresentations of the objective and true facts. As an illustration, Pinchot (1985) describes how in response to evolving top priorities at GM, the lead intrapreneur, at one point, presented and 'sold' the Fiero sports car as a fuel-efficient car for commuters.

Although the framing literature is fundamentally concerned with creating and conveying a picture of reality to other people, it does generate some *a priori* expectations about what framing approaches should be most effective

---

[1] A probably more limited number of new ventures are the result of top-down processes, and it has been suggested that these processes are most prevalent and effective in the case of products and services that already at the outset are found to involve far-reaching strategic change which involves the entire corporation (Day, 1994; Stopford and Baden-Fuller, 1994). Although variation introduced through top-down processes may have important consequences for firm growth and long-term survival, the resulting new products and services and their potential retention will not be the main focus of this chapter.

in generating attention and support for new business concepts. The first expectation concerns the extent to which new business concepts are presented as a way to avoid threats or to take advantage of potential opportunities for the organization. It has been found that managers are more likely to pay attention to and respond to threats than to opportunities (Dutton & Jackson, 1987; Jackson & Dutton, 1988). In the more general context of strategic decisions, it has also been found that while there is marginal difference between the ultimate impact of framing based on adaptation (threat) or innovation (opportunity), the former appears to invoke much shorter strategic decision processes (Nutt, 1998). In order to attract attention to new business concepts in the first place, the most effective approach would be to frame new concepts as a necessary response to a threat from the environment, rather than emphasize how the concepts represent a new opportunity for the organization.

The second expectation is that framing new business concepts in a way that emphasizes their similarity to already existing operations and practices is more effective than presenting them as something novel. New business concepts framed in a way that makes top managers feel a greater sense of control have a higher probability of success in the project-selling process (Dutton & Duncan, 1987). Also, top managers are more likely to commit to new business concepts for which they feel they can provide valuable personal skills and input (Dutton & Ashford, 1993). Proponents of new business concepts also need to align the presentation of their projects with existing internal and external norms and beliefs about what is appropriate and legitimate (Dutton et al., 2001; Howell & Higgins, 1990; Lounsbury & Glynn, 2001). From these perspectives, new business concepts where commonality is emphasized are more likely to generate understanding and positive support than those framed in novelty terms.

Yet, assuming there is an initial preference for emphasizing threat rather than opportunity in the framing of new business concepts, the available literature has produced two competing hypotheses regarding the emphasis on novelty or commonality (Chattopadhyay et al., 2001; George et al., 2006; Gilbert, 2005). Arguments based on prospect theory suggest that the threat of a potential loss shifts attention towards novel solutions that tend to be riskier than established solutions and routines of the corporation. The most effective way of framing a new business concept would therefore be to emphasize that it responds to an environmental threat but also proposes a novel solution to mitigate this threat. In contrast, the threat-rigidity hypothesis suggests that any threats to individuals and organizations tend to be met with rigidity and the cementing of already established cognitive structures and behaviors. From this perspective, the appropriate framing of new business concepts should rely on the emphasis on threats to the organization, combined with a presentation of the new concepts as something which resembles or corresponds to already established operations and practices.

Although the extant literature suggests that some framing approaches are more successful than others, the various combinations of the threat/opportunity and novelty/commonality categories appear to involve some inherent trade-offs, originating in the need to generate both attention and support for new business concepts. Specifically, consistently emphasizing threat (and thus evoking feelings of uncontrollability) to get attention for a new business concept may lead to a loss of support during the implementation stage (Jackson & Dutton, 1988). In view of this, the ultimate success of framing may depend on the individual's ability to shift the emphasis and content of communication over time, and strategic framing implies that the individual alternates the use of framing categories in communicating with others. The skilled intrapreneur thereby consciously or unconsciously adapts communication and framing according to the receiver (Huber, 1991), attempting to generate the most favorable response from the broad and varied set of individuals who may be involved in the selection of new business concepts. Hence, in the process of promoting a new business concept the intrapreneur may emphasize both threat and opportunity, as well as novelty and commonality, depending on the particular situation and organizational position of the receiver.

Implications for Survival in the Host Corporation

While the framing and corporate entrepreneurship literature has generated some relatively clear expectations about successful framing approaches, in the present chapter the assessment of survival implications must remain limited and exploratory. This is partly because the full set of internal and external variables that influence the success of new business concepts in established corporations is potentially very large (e.g. McGrath, Venkataraman & MacMillan, 1994; Thornhill & Amit, 2000; Tsai, MacMillan & Low, 1991), requiring theoretical treatment and data well beyond the capacity of the present chapter. Also, while it can be expected that intrapreneurs who focus on threat and either novelty or commonality in their framing approaches will be more successful than others (Dutton & Jackson, 1987; Jackson & Dutton, 1988; Nutt, 1998), the performance and survival implications of any alternative framing approaches are essentially unknown.

As the main function of framing is to attract the attention of other organizational members and to improve the chances of getting support for the new business concept, the basic assumption is that framing activities do have an influence on the success of new business concepts. This success may then be measured in terms of the survival of new business concepts in the host organization (Nutt, 1998). It could perhaps be argued that any form of active framing produces more success than passive approaches, but this expectation depends on the extent to which intrapreneurs make use of the 'correct' framing approaches. Taken together, the assessment of survival implications concerns a largely unexplored issue in the corporate entrepreneurship literature, and in the present chapter data limitations only allow for a preliminary and rudimentary search for conspicuous differences in the effectiveness of different framing approaches.

METHODOLOGY

Sample and Data Collection

Sample. To analyze the framing of new business concepts in established corporations, the chapter draws upon a survey of the nature and fate of 49 new business concepts introduced in 18 Swedish corporations (for a similar approach, see Thornhill & Amit, 2000).

To be included in the sample, the new business concepts had to: (1) Represent the autonomous initiatives of employees of established corporations (as it turned out, these employees were mostly engineers), (2) concern a product or service that introduced something significantly new in terms of technology or functionality, and (3) have passed what Burgelman (1983: 226) calls the 'conceptual' or 'pre-venture' stages. Because the collection of data combined the use of interviews and surveys, the costs of data collection limited the sample to new business concepts that had originated in Swedish companies. It is notable that the sampling targeted and included both retained, spun-off, as also terminated new business ventures.

Because there are no publicly available lists of significantly new business concepts in established corporations, the new business concepts were identified through snowball sampling (Hair et al., 2003; for detailed information about the sampling process, see Appendix A). In the current study, such snowball sampling was combined with a convenience-sampling approach, i.e. cases were included in the sample whenever a new business concept which met the sampling criteria was identified during the course of the study. Observations were thus gathered from two main sources: personal contacts with managers and engineers who were directly asked whether they could act as respondents and/or knew about other concepts that fit the sampling criteria, and secondary data sources such as newspapers and magazines.

The 49 new business concepts were introduced in 18 Swedish corporations, at the time of data collection ranging in sales from USD 9 million to

USD 37 billion (median USD 7 billion). The largest number of observations pertaining to one individual host corporation was 8, the smallest one. The companies operated in a relatively diverse set of industries, by and large representative of the structure of Swedish industry, including industries such as IT and telecommunications, automotive vehicles, pharmaceuticals, steel, pulp and paper, and electrotechnical equipment. There is a relative dominance of firms in the IT and telecommunications industries (just under 25 per cent of all observations), and a fairly even distribution of firms across the remaining industries.

Data were collected from key informants, who were typically the primary inventors and champions of the new products or services associated with the new business concepts.[2] In the very few cases where the inventor was not the main champion of the concept and/or was not involved in commercialization attempts, the project manager who took over management of the venture was used as the key informant. The identified individuals were involved with the venture on a daily basis and can be expected to have possessed accurate and detailed knowledge about the nature of the new business concept and how it developed within the existing corporation. The majority of survey responses were collected during face-to-face meetings, in which an initial interview was followed by the completion of a 128-item questionnaire. In a limited number of cases, telephone interviews were also conducted. The questionnaire was filled out in a controlled setting and in the majority of cases in direct connection to the initial interview (for additional details about the data collection, see Appendix B).

One drawback of using key informants is that it introduces potential informant biases (Bagozzi, Yi & Phillips, 1991). Specifically, the views and perceptions of informants may be biased by their specific organizational roles, and their interpretation of certain events and circumstances may differ significantly from that of other persons within the same organization. Furthermore, informant reports might be distorted by memory failure, inaccurate recall or hindsight bias (Golden, 1992), which is a common problem in

---

[2] A number of individuals may be involved in the process of promoting and implementing new business concepts, including the original inventors of new products and services, 'champions' who may buy into the project and promote the new concept throughout the organization, and middle managers who connect the ventures with top management (e.g. Burgelman, 1983; Day, 1994; Galbraith, 1982; Howell and Higgins, 1990). In the great majority of cases examined in this chapter, and as found in other studies as well (Burgelman, 1983), the original inventor also remained the key champion throughout the new business venturing process. The term 'intrapreneur' thus refers to the person who came up with the new product or service concept and was also the key individual promoting it within the established corporation. It cannot be precluded that potentially different forms of framing occurred among other individuals involved in the development and promotion of the new business concept, but it has not been possible to account for these framing activities in the present study.

survey-based research (Doz, Olk & Smith-Ring, 2000). The main reason for not using multiple informants, and as experienced in similar prior studies (MacMillan, Block & Narasimha, 1986), was restricted access to well-informed additional respondents (Kumar, Stern & Anderson, 1993). It was initially attempted to obtain complementary information from middle- and top managers, but this approach proved impractical. Because of the sensitive nature and still precarious status of many of the business ventures, key informants were very reluctant to identify one or several additional sources of information, presumably out of fear that contacting these individuals might have uncontrollable and negative effects on the success of their concepts in the corporation.

The problems of hindsight bias and selective recall were somewhat reduced by the procedure of conducting an interview prior to the completion of the survey. During the interviews, respondents were asked to review the history of their new business concepts in considerable detail, which is likely to have activated their memory and permitted more accurate answers to the various questions in the survey. Another factor favoring recall was that the respondents were asked about a major event in their professional career. Such major events are likely to be associated with emotions, excitement and pride of having been involved in the new business ventures, all factors which can be expected to enhance the accuracy of recall.

Common method bias is of potential concern in studies relying upon key informants (Podsakoff, MacKenzie & Lee, 2003; Podsakoff & Organ, 1986). While it is not a significant problem in identifying intrapreneurs' framing approaches, it has a potential influence in the analyses of survival implications. However, the survival times employed in the present chapter represent a relatively objective and unambiguous measure of success. For analyses using survival times, problems associated with consistency motives were further mitigated as information about survival times was collected during the interviews that preceded the completion of the questionnaire (Podsakoff et al., 2003). Social-desirability problems should represent a minor concern, as responses were confidential and individual questions did not concern issues where respondents may have felt compelled to produce socially legitimate or desirable answers. Overall, however, restricted access to multiple respondents and potential common method bias both suggest caution in interpreting select analyses and empirical results.

Variables

The variables used for identifying general framing patterns among the investigated intrapreneurs were derived from the extant literature on framing and identical to those used as criterion variables in the cluster analysis. The measurement of all framing variables was based on a 7-point scale, ranging from 1 (totally disagree) to 7 (totally agree).

Threat. Two of the survey questions were designed to capture the threat aspect of the respondents' framing approaches, specifying the type of environmental change the new business concepts responded to. The first question addressed threat as a cognitive category, whereas the second question represented one of the attributes that have been associated with this category (Dutton & Jackson, 1987): (1) 'In conversations with people inside the company (but outside the venture team) the concept was portrayed as a response to a threat against the company', and (2) 'In conversations with people inside the company (but outside the venture team) it was emphasized how the concept could counteract a decline in company profits'.

Opportunity. Two survey questions were designed to reflect the opportunity aspect of the respondents' framing approaches, again differentiating between opportunity as a cognitive category and one of its attributes: (1) 'In conversations with people inside the company (but outside the venture team) the concept was portrayed as a response to a new market opportunity for the company', and (2) 'In conversations with people inside the company (but outside the venture team) it was emphasized how the concept could contribute to increasing profits for the company'.

Novelty. The novelty dimension of the respondents' framing approaches was measured by a question that captured the extent to which the new business concept was presented as novel in a general sense: 'In conversations with people inside the company (but outside the venture team) it was attempted to emphasize the degree of novelty of the concept'.

Commonality. While a low score on the novelty measure suggests an emphasis on the commonality dimension, reluctance to emphasize novelty does not necessarily mean that commonality is emphasized instead. A separate question therefore addressed the extent to which the new venture was presented as similar to earlier and successful projects: 'In conversations with people inside the company (but outside the venture team) similarities to earlier successful projects were emphasized'. Earlier successful projects are likely to have become retained and institutionalized in the form of established operations and practices (Burgelman, 1983), and similarity to earlier successful projects captures both procedural aspects (how launching and implementing the new business concept resembled earlier projects) and structural aspects (the degree of alignment with established operations and practices).

Survival. It is inherently difficult to assess the performance of new business concepts, especially in the early stages of development. In many cases, the new concepts are yet to reveal their commercial potential, and profitability measures tend to be highly ambiguous because of varying levels of investments throughout the development process.

To explore the implications of different framing approaches, the survival measure captured the length of the new business concepts' survival in the corporate context. This was a relatively objective measure, measured from the year in which the intrapreneur started investing serious and regular effort in developing the new business concept, and captured by the question 'what year did active development of the new business concept start?'. At the time of data collection, the status of the individual new business concepts could then be that they were either retained by the corporation (yet, by definition still at potential risk of being terminated), or terminated (a category which included both formally discontinued concepts and those that had been spun off).[3]

Statistical Methods

The first part of the empirical investigation maps out the intrapreneurs' framing of their new business concepts and also identifies specific groups of intrapreneurs in terms of their framing approaches.

The identification of groups of intrapreneurs with similar framing approaches is based on cluster analysis, using threat, opportunity, novelty, and commonality as the main criterion variables. Following the suggestions by Ketchen and Shook (1996), the cluster analysis uses a combination of hierarchical agglomerative and iterative partitioning methods (for similar applications, see e.g. Hadaway, 1989; Parker, 1997). The hierarchical agglomerative method was Ward's method, which has been commonly used in the social sciences and the strategic management literature (Aldenderfer & Blashfield, 1984; Ketchen & Shook, 1996). The iterative partitioning method was the k-means method. All analyses were made with the SPSS 14.0 statistical package.

While there is no definitive way of deciding upon the optimal number of clusters or groups, the presence of two framing dimensions and expectations

---

[3] In many cases, the intrapreneurs had conceived of the fundamental idea underlying the new business concept several years before the one defined as the year of introduction. During this period the intrapreneur only occasionally tinkered with the technology, often at home or during his/her spare time, trying to determine whether there might be a business opportunity associated with the concept. This pre-conceptual stage, comparable to what Burgelman (1983) refers to as the opportunity-definition stage, is not included in the calculation of survival times. Notably, serious and regular effort in developing the new business concept did not require any official recognition or support from the host organization. Survival time calculations did not include the first year of the new concept's existence, but did include the last year of observation, thus averaging out any errors that may arise from concepts being introduced at the very beginning of a year and last recoded at the end of any particular year (either as a surviving new business concept or as a terminated concept).

about the most effective framing approaches suggested there, could result in three to four groups of intrapreneurs in terms of their framing approaches. It was therefore decided to provisionally end the clustering procedure when three to four clusters had been identified, and that the ultimate decision would take into account a heuristic examination of the dendogram and examination of fusion or agglomeration coefficients.

Analyses of survival implications involved life-table analyses, which provide information about survival probabilities across the identified clusters of framing approaches.

RESULTS

Framing Approaches

Table 6.1 provides baseline information about the framing of new business concepts among the surveyed intrapreneurs.

The results show that the intrapreneurs in the sample generally emphasize opportunity rather than threat when presenting and promoting their new business concepts among other organizational members. Differences between the means of questions 1 and 3 as well as 2 and 4 are all significant at the 1 per cent level. Also, the new business concepts tend to be presented as novel, whereas their similarity to earlier successful projects is generally de-emphasized ($p<.01$).

While the descriptive statistics reveal the baseline tendencies in the framing of new business concepts among the respondents, cluster analysis provides additional information about the grouping of intrapreneurs according to their use of combinations of the threat, opportunity, novelty, and commonality categories. The first stage of the cluster analysis used Ward's method with squared Euclidean distances to identify preliminary clusters and seed points for the iterative partitioning analysis that followed. Although scale values were identical across individual questions and variances did not differ significantly across the variables, all variables were standardized to Z scores (thereby preventing variables with larger variances from having an artificially high influence on the cluster solution).[4] The resulting dendogram suggested that three to five clusters provided useful separations of observations and cluster solutions. The analysis of the agglomeration coefficient

---

[4] Analyses based on the non-standardized variables had a moderate effect on the number of cases in each of the identified clusters, but no substantial effect on the relative values of the criterion variables or cluster characteristics.

suggested a particularly pronounced jump between the three and two cluster solutions, and hence the three cluster solution was employed as a starting point for the subsequent k-means analysis.

Question (from 1 'totally disagree' to 7 'totally agree')	n	Mean	Median	Std. Dev.
Threat In conversations with people inside the company (but outside the venture team):				
1. The concept was portrayed as a response to a threat against the company	48	2.27	1	1.87
2. It was emphasized that the concept could counteract a decline in company profits	48	3.27	3	1.92
Opportunity In conversations with people inside the company (but outside the venture team):				
3. The concept was portrayed as a response to a new market opportunity for the company	49	5.41	6	1.80
4. It was emphasized how the new concept could contribute to corporate profitability	48	5.29	6	1.74
Novelty In conversations with people inside the company (but outside the venture team):				
5. It was attempted to emphasize the degree of novelty of the concept	49	4.73	5	1.89
Commonality In conversations with people inside the Company (but outside the venture team):				
6. Similarities to earlier successful projects were emphasized	48	2.35	2	1.73

Table 6.1 Baseline statistics framing variables

The k-means procedure used the clusters and cluster centroids identified by Ward's method and made an additional number of passes through the data. By making multiple passes through the data, the final solution is less impacted by outliers (to which Ward's method is sensitive) and the final solution optimizes within-cluster homogeneity and between-cluster heterogeneity (Ketchen & Shook, 1992). Yet, it requires that the number of clusters be determined *a priori*. The k-means procedure produced three refined groups of intrapreneurs in terms of their overall framing approaches (a total of four cases changed clusters as a result of the k-means procedure), differentiated by some but not all of the selected criterion variables (Table 6.2).

Members of the first cluster, comprising 15 intrapreneurs, follow what can be labeled an *active-strategic* framing approach. The most notable characteristic of this approach is the comparatively high emphasis on both threat and opportunity when connecting new business concepts to developments in the external environment (yet, in absolute terms, the emphasis on threat is moderate). Theoretically, threat and opportunity should represent somewhat opposing categories, and the observed use of both suggests that the intrapreneurs in the active-strategic group adapt their messages according to the specific situation and organizational position of the receiver; sometimes, the threat aspect is emphasized whereas at other times new market opportunities are highlighted. At the same time, results concerning the novelty category suggest that members of the active-strategic group put moderate emphasis on the novelty aspect, and that they rarely present the new business concepts as similar to existing and successful operations and practices in the corporation.

The second group of intrapreneurs, comprising 25 and thus the majority of the sample respondents, follow a framing approach that may be labeled *active-optimistic*. The relatively single-minded focus on opportunity rather than threat among members of this group suggests they see positive aspects and possibilities for gains as the most important and indeed sufficient element for gaining attention and support for their new business concepts. At the same time, perhaps consistent with the focus on the positive and likely gains, intrapreneurs in the active-optimistic group prefer to present their new business concepts as something novel. Presumably, intrapreneurs in the active-optimistic group expect other organizational members and top management to embrace similar and essentially positive attitudes towards new business concepts.

The third group of intrapreneurs, comprising the relatively small number of 6 intrapreneurs, is characterized by the absence of framing activity. Because this group emphasizes neither threat nor opportunity in association with their new business concepts and also tends to take a moderate position with respect to the concepts' degree of novelty, the adopted framing approach can be labeled *passive*. While it may be concluded that this group of intrapreneurs makes little use of framing in attempts to present and promote new business concepts, presumably with negative effects on their success rate, there is an alternative interpretation of the results. Specifically, it could be hypothesized that the passive group acts strategically in the sense that its members hide

Question (from 1 'totally disagree' to 7 'totally agree')	Cluster		
	1	**2**	**3**
	(n=15)	**(n=25)**	**(n=6)**
Threat In conversations with people inside the company (but outside the venture team):			
1. The concept was portrayed as a response to a threat against the company	4.40 (1.92)	1.40 (0.71)	1.00 (0.00)
2. It was emphasized that the concept could counteract a decline in company profits	4.07 (1.58)	3.32 (1.98)	1.17 (0.41)
Opportunity In conversations with people inside the Company (but outside the venture team):			
3. The concept was portrayed as a response to a new market opportunity for the company	5.73 (1.03)	6.20 (0.76)	1.83 (1.60)
4. It was emphasized how the new concept could contribute to corporate profitability	5.47 (1.25)	5.88 (1.13)	2.00 (1.55)
Novelty In conversations with people inside the company (but outside the venture team):			
5. It was attempted to emphasize the degree of novelty of the concept	3.53 (1.73)	5.92 (1.00)	3.17 (1.94)
Commonality In conversations with people inside the company (but outside the venture team):			
6. Similarities to earlier successful projects were emphasized	2.00 (1.36)	2.52 (1.69)	2.17 (2.40)

[a] Cluster solution includes only cases for which information across all criterion variables was available; n = 46.

Table 6.2 Identified clusters by criterion variables[a], raw score means (standard deviations within parentheses)

their efforts and operate 'under the radar screen' (Burgelman, 1983), attracting as little attention as possible to their new business concepts until they are proven and easier to sell to top management.

Notably, none of the three identified groups displays a clear combination of threat and either novelty or commonality, and indeed the largest of the identified groups is found to emphasize opportunity rather than threat in the framing of the new business concepts. Overall, the results from the baseline framing approaches and the cluster analysis indicate that the intrapreneurs in the current sample do not adhere to what the literature on the subject has identified as the most effective framing combinations.[5]

Implications for Survival in the Host Corporation

While the extant literature suggests that certain combinations of framing should be more successful and prevalent than others, the success and survival of new business concepts is influenced by a large set of other explanatory variables, such as the overall qualifications of the intrapreneur, the nature of the business concept, the entrepreneurial orientation of the corporation, or overall environmental conditions and business cycles. Taking full account of these factors is beyond the theoretical and empirical scope of the present chapter, but exploratory analyses can still shed some preliminary light on how the observed framing approaches are connected to the survival of the new concepts within the host corporations.

Out of the 46 cases that were included in the cluster analysis, at the time of observation 27 had been terminated and 19 had been retained (although technically speaking, all retained new business concepts remained at risk to be terminated). Life-table analyses connecting the three identified framing approaches to the survival of the new business concepts in the host organizations show no significant survival implications (Figure 6.1), whether in the short or long term. If anything, members of the passive groups face better survival chances than members of the active-strategic and active-optimistic groups, but again there are no significant differences in survival

---

[5] Further analyses were performed to examine the sensitivity of the results to the three-cluster solution. The two-cluster solution collapsed the active-strategic and active-optimistic groups, keeping them separate from the passive group. The four-cluster solution kept the active-strategic and passive groups intact, but split the active-optimistic group into two sub-groups. While these two sub-groups differed in their emphasis on individual criterion variables, relative values or directions of differences vis-à-vis the active-strategic and passive groups remained unchanged. There was one exception, however, as one of the two sub-groups displayed a significantly higher emphasis on commonality than the other.

rates across the three groups and any observable differences appear to disappear over time.[6]

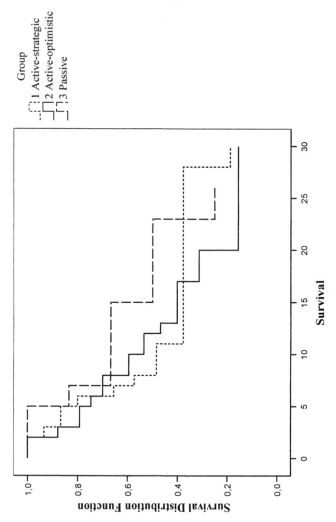

Figure 6.1 Survival of new business concepts, life-table analysis

---

[6] As in the case of the effect on the development of the new business concepts, the same fundamental results are obtained when applying a two- or four-cluster solution. For alternative analyses using perceived development times as the dependent variable, see Appendix C.

DISCUSSION

Framing Approaches

The results concerning the baseline framing of new business concepts among the respondents are at odds with what the existing literature considers to be the most effective framing approaches. One would expect that if the intrapreneur manages to convince other organizational members that the new business concept is a necessary response to an emerging threat (Dutton & Jackson, 1987; Jackson & Dutton, 1988), the chances of getting attention and support for the new concept would increase. Yet, the intrapreneurs in the sample indicate that they predominantly present their new business concepts as responses to a new market opportunity, and also that they frame their concepts as an opportunity to increase profits (rather than counteract a decline in profits).

One logical interpretation of the results is that most intrapreneurs see it as most natural to sell new business concepts as opportunities, perhaps because intrapreneurs are expected to pursue new opportunities and create the future rather than reactively respond to imminent threats. A related explanation would be that the respondents for various reasons did not care to frame their new concepts in any explicitly strategic way. As explained by one of the respondents during the pre-survey interviews:

'One can sell projects like used cars. But if one does so then it becomes difficult to sell a project a second time. It is best to use mostly facts mixed with the right amount of advertisement.'

Given the need for fitting new business concepts into the existing operations, practices, and norms and beliefs of the corporation (Dutton & Ashford, 1993; Dutton & Duncan, 1987; Dutton et al., 2001; Lounsbury & Glynn, 2001), downplaying rather than emphasizing the degree of novelty would appear to be the preferred and most commonly observed framing approach. Yet, the intrapreneurs in the sample do the opposite – they emphasize the degree of novelty associated with the new business concepts and are reluctant to associate their concepts with prior successful projects in the company. One potential explanation for this would be that practically all of the respondents were engineers, a group for which the development of new and different solutions is part of the professional identity. Most of the respondents also held or had held formal positions in R&D departments, where the preference for novelty may be particularly high compared to other parts of the organization. Another explanation for the reluctance to connect the new business concepts to historical precedents would be that associating the concepts with prior projects in the company could revive the political struggles associated with these projects; when the positions of other and potentially influential organizational members targeted for persuasion are unknown, intrapreneurs may find it sensible to adopt cautionary approaches.

The cluster analysis provides a more fine-grained analysis of framing approaches adopted by the sample intrapreneurs, although it must be re-emphasized that cluster solutions are sensitive to judgmental decisions concerning the number of clusters and criterion variables. The analysis reveals three specific groups of intrapreneurs in terms of their framing approaches, which can be mapped onto the theoretically derived expectations about the most effective combinations of framing categories. According to the established literature, a majority of the respondents would be expected to use a combination of threat on the one hand and either novelty or commonality on the other. To a large extent, however, the cluster analysis confirmed the fundamental tendencies revealed in the baseline results – the expected combination of the threat and novelty or commonality categories is typically not adopted.

The comparatively balanced emphasis on threat and opportunity in the active-strategic group deserves particular mention, because theoretically threat and opportunities are opposing rather than complementary possibilities. The basic interpretation of framing in this group is that its members use a differentiated framing approach, in which messages are framed differently according to the particular situation and receiver. An interview quote from one of the surveyed intrapreneurs may serve as an illustration:

'It is all about adapting to the flavor of the day. Sometimes one tries to emphasize the new business opportunities the project has to offer, or one tries to demonstrate how the project can support and improve the existing core business areas. At other times one tries to emphasize possible threats from competitors, like saying that other competitors have already started to invest in this technology and we run the danger of lagging behind.'

Such observations illustrate the malleability of framing, but while the active-strategic group tends towards the strategic use of framing, different-tiated framing approaches is not a prominent feature of the active-optimistic and passive groups.

Antecedents to framing.
These somewhat unexpected results pose the question whether intrapreneurs are uninformed about cognitive biases among top managers, or whether they simply frame their new business concepts in ways that reflect their 'true' or objective nature. One possible explanation for the observed framing approaches would be that the new business concepts differ in their funda-

mental qualities, which then translates straight into the intrapreneurs' framing approaches.

Exploring the strength of association between some objective qualities of the new business concepts and the adopted framing approaches can shed some preliminary light on the issue. Specifically, the data allow for a comparison between the actual threat experienced by the respective organizations and the adoption of threat-emphasizing framing approaches, and between the actual novelty introduced by the new concepts and any novelty-emphasizing approaches.

In two of the survey questions, the respondents were asked about the extent to which the development of the new concept 'took place under strong pressure from competing companies' and the extent to which 'competition from other companies with similar ideas has been hard' (both equivalent to a competitive threat). Answers to the first question were found to correlate positively and significantly with the respondents' inclination to frame their concepts as responses to threats against the company ($p<.01$). For the second question, however, the correlation was slightly negative and not significant. In other words, if the actual environmental threat to the company was small, the respondents refrained from presenting their new concepts as responses to external threats and vice versa, but this only applied in a general sense and not when considering competition in the realm of the specific new business concepts.

A set of introductory survey questions also asked about how the respondents rated the degree of novelty of the new business concepts in relation to the solutions that currently dominated the market. Drawing upon Schumpeter's (1934) categorization of innovations, respondents were asked to indicate whether the new business concepts 'introduced an entirely new product or service', 'introduced an entirely new way of manufacturing', 'introduced an entirely new organizational form', 'opened up an entirely new geographical market', 'opened up an entirely new customer segment', or 'utilized entirely new components or inputs'. All questions were answered on a 7-point scale, ranging from 1 (totally disagree) to 7 (totally agree), and the average score used as an overall indicator of the concept's degree of novelty.

The results show a positive but non-significant correlation between the underlying nature of the new business concepts and the actual framing approaches adopted by the intrapreneurs, suggesting that objectively novel business concepts also tend to be framed as novel but not in any systematic way. In combination with the results concerning the threat category, this suggests that there are considerable degrees of freedom for intrapreneurs to select preferred framing approaches, but the chosen approaches generally run contrary to what is identified as the most effective approach in the established literature.

Implications for Survival in the Host Corporation

In the absence of a model that incorporates a set of additional variables that may explain the survival of new business concepts in the host corporations, analyses of the relationship between the framing approaches of the identified clusters and survival remain exploratory. There are no signs that any of the three identified framing approaches produces significantly better chances of survival for the associated new business concepts, which can probably in part be explained by the relatively high intra-group heterogeneity of the identified clusters.[7] If framing approaches have direct effect on the survival of new business concepts, it then seems that the effect may be restricted to smaller and extreme sub-groups of intrapreneurs or involve other framing categories than those identified in the present chapter.

Of course, the absence of clear-cut effects on survival can also be explained by the inability of the intrapreneurs in the current sample to adopt the theoretically or normatively most effective framing approaches, especially those combining a clear emphasis on threat and either novelty or commonality. While it is possible to single out a handful of such cases in the present sample, the numbers are too small to allow for any meaningful cross-group comparisons and statistical tests. It must also be emphasized that the present data do not allow for the analysis of more subtle aspects of framing behavior and especially intertemporal variations in communication displayed by strategically skilled intrapreneurs. In sum, however, the current results suggest the absence of a simple connection between framing approaches and the success of new business concepts in established corporations.

Limitations and Critical Evaluation of the Findings

Several important limitations to the empirical investigations must be kept in mind. First, it can be noted that respondents did not necessarily perceive of threats, opportunities, novelty, and commonality in the opposing ways indicated by theory and prior empirical work. Specifically, the analysis of correlations between the criterion variables shows that the framing of new business concepts as a response to a threat to the company is weakly but positively correlated with framing in terms of opportunity (Table 6.3).

Although a negative correlation was expected, these results may conceal that in a large number of cases individual intrapreneurs have maintained one

---

[7] The inconclusiveness of the results is further supported by simple analyses of the performance implications of individual framing dimensions, where in Cox regressions neither threat, opportunity, novelty, or commonality emphases were found to have a direct, significant effect on the survival of new business concepts.

baseline approach to the framing of the new business concepts, for example typically emphasizing opportunities rather than threats, but consciously or unconsciously adapted and altered communication according to the specific context and organizational position of the receiver. In such cases, respondents would be able to report framing attempts that involve both threat and opportunity.

Additionally, Table 6.3 shows that the framing of new concepts as responses to threats against the company correlates positively and significantly with the framing of concepts in terms of their capacity to counteract declining profits, but even more so with opportunity. This could mean that many of the respondents do not necessarily associate the threat and opportunity categories with distinct attributes. Novelty is only weakly correlated with an emphasis on similarity with prior successful projects in the company, but in this case the weak association may reflect the difference between novelty in a general and company-specific sense. Taken together, these observations suggest that respondents may have had quite varied or even unclear perceptions of what constitutes threats and opportunities. At the same time, the very nature of framing, especially if seen from a strategic perspective, does not necessarily preclude mixed communication according to specific circumstances and the assumed priorities of the receiver.

Correlations among criterion variables

	Variables	1	2	3	4	5	6
1.	Threat						
2.	Counteract decline	.34*					
3.	Opportunity	.14	.45**				
4.	Increase profit	.14	.42**	.71**			
5.	Novelty	-.10	.11	.38**	.28		
6.	Similarity emphasis	-.18	-.17	-.07	.10	.02	

Notes:
Includes cases for which information across all criterion variables was available; n = 46.
** Correlation significant at the .01 level. * Correlation significant at the .05 level.

Table 6.3 Correlations among criterion variables

Second, we are very much aware of the basic measures that have been employed. The basic approach to measurement may be weighed against the insights that can be gained into a still incompletely documented phenomenon, and further studies may explore how more fine-grained measurement and an enlarged set of framing categories and attributes yield other results.

Third, the results from the cluster analysis are sensitive to judgmental decisions about statistical methods and identification of cluster solutions (Aldenderfer & Blashfield, 1984). While the results presented in this chapter provide an illustration of what appear to be *de facto* differences in framing approaches across groups of intrapreneurs, the exact specification of these groups and the nature of differences depend on the criterion variables and the model choices that have been made. It is also noticeable that variation in the individual criterion variables is high, suggesting that these groups that have been identified include individual cases which diverge quite significantly in terms of their selective emphasis on either threat, opportunity, novelty, or commonality. The framing approaches that have been identified in the present chapter therefore represent but a starting point for further and more fine-grained taxonomical work.

Finally, the sample is restricted to new business concepts in established Swedish firms, and the sampling technique that was used prevents any claims that a representative and unbiased sample has been obtained. Yet, it may be re-emphasized that the pragmatic approach towards sampling and data collection has been dictated by the general problems of conducting research on the nature and fate of new business concepts. In the absence of publicly available and systematic information about new business concepts in established corporations, flexible and opportunistic approaches are virtually a necessity for conducting large-sample surveys in this area.

SUMMARY AND CONCLUSIONS

The main purpose of this chapter has been to empirically explore how intrapreneurs go about framing new business concepts in established corporations. The findings suggest the existence of a baseline approach to framing in which intrapreneurs emphasize the opportunity and novelty associated with their new business concepts. In comparison, framing new concepts as a response to threats to the company or something that resembles prior successful projects within the corporation, tends to be used more sparingly. Given this baseline tendency, the chapter identifies three specific framing approaches among the surveyed intrapreneurs, labeled active-strategic, active-optimistic, and passive. An exploratory investigation of how the three framing approaches influence the survival of new business concepts in the host corporations did not reveal any significant direct effects.

Two main conclusions follow from the analyses. The first is that the surveyed intrapreneurs do not frame their new business concepts in ways the extant literature has identified as the most effective or successful. To the extent existing expectations about the most effective framing approaches are correct, it then follows that in general intrapreneurs could become more reflective and skilled in terms of how they frame new business concepts within their host organizations. Yet, given that we still know relatively little about the nature and implications of framing new business concepts in established corporations, offering more specific practical advice remains a task for future research to accomplish.

The second conclusion concerns the absence of a direct and simple relationship between framing and the success of new business concepts in established corporations. To the extent there is a direct relationship between framing approaches and the survival of new business concepts, the empirical results suggest that the quest for successful approaches must consider alternative forms of framing and more subtle relationships. Specifically, the effectiveness of framing approaches could depend on how they interact with contextual factors, or how intrapreneurs consciously or intuitively make intertemporal adjustments to framing when promoting their new concepts. These intertemporal adjustments have not been captured by the present chapter.

While the chapter offers some initial empirical insights into the framing of new business concepts in established corporations, its exploratory nature leaves a number of questions unanswered and open for future research. Validating and perhaps more likely, amending the three identified groups of intrapreneurs and their specific framing approaches by using larger and cross-country samples, is one obvious research avenue. This taxonomical work should also consider more fine-grained measurement and/or consider alternative framing categories and attributes. Future research may also explore the antecedents of framing approaches in more detail. Specific questions include how framing approaches depend on the characteristics of the intrapreneur, for example his or her professional background or general and firm-specific experience, and to what extent framing is an intuitive or conscious activity.

A second but comparatively difficult undertaking is to further explore the performance and survival implications of different framing approaches. More targeted research may address whether there is a trade-off in attracting attention to a new business concept and getting support for its implement-tation, or how intertemporal variations in framing may influence the development and survival of new business concepts. Additional questions concern how the effect of framing might depend on interaction with other variables and circumstances, and if some framing approaches more effective than others under certain organizational and environmental conditions. In all of these efforts, difficulties in accurately measuring the performance of new, ambiguous, and still evolving concepts are likely to persist, and survival times may prove the most useful and objective measure to employ.

Overall, there appear to be ample opportunities to further explore the nature and survival implications of framing new business concepts in established corporations, and more fine-grained investigations would undoubtedly address an important aspect of the life and growth of organizations. Ultimately, these efforts should be able to generate more fine-tuned theory and guidance for the practicing intrapreneur.

Appendix 6.A

In the first phase of the sampling process, which started in 2000, e-mails were sent to previous participants of Executive Education programs at the Stockholm School of Economics, many of whom had engineering backgrounds and were personally known by members of the research team. In a mailing of 131 letters, the contacted people were asked to identify 'products that have been introduced recently and represent something significantly new in terms of technology or functionality', adding that the products should 'not predominantly be improvements of existing products'. They were explicitly asked to think also about projects which had been either discontinued or had become spin-offs.

The mailing resulted in a total of 83 responses. In 36 cases, the contacted people suggested one or several specific concepts for further investigation, in the majority of cases (75 per cent) connected to their own organizations. 31 of the contacted people stated that they did not know of any concepts that matched the description, sometimes adding that they would continue holding a lookout for possible observations or suggesting names of other people in their organization who would possess the relevant knowledge. In addition, four leads were given to people who should be generally knowledgeable about the existence of products that matched the selection criteria (these people were associated with investment companies and engineering labor unions). 16 of the mails were returned as undeliverable.

A number of the identified concepts were not pursued further. For example, some concepts had been introduced through independent entrepreneurial efforts (i.e. they were not introduced within already established corporations), while others had been acquired from outside sources or represented close imitations of already existing technical solutions. In an additional number of cases, the prospective respondents were working for foreign-based firms, which because of the need for personal interviews were associated with prohibitive costs in terms of data collection. In total, the first phase of the sampling process generated 16 observations that became part of the final sample.

To expand on the number of observations, a second phase of the sampling process started with contacting the Royal Swedish Academy of Engineering Sciences (IVA). This organization maintains an extensive network of contacts with engineers, scientists, and senior executives throughout the Swedish business community. Discussion resulted in the establishment of a list of more than 50 members, representing 35 companies who were perceived as particularly suited for the identification of the aspired type of concepts and innovations.

A total of 47 people on the list from the Royal Swedish Academy of Engineering Sciences were contacted, starting in June 2002. In almost all cases, the people contacted referred to one or several other members of their current or past organizations, typically with engineering background and working within or with close contacts with formal research and development departments. In total, this second phase of the research process added 35 observations to the final sample.

In addition to the formalized search for observations to be included in the sample, observations were continuously sought and identified through searches of the Swedish business press, personal contacts of the members of the research team, and a range of occasional and unplanned encounters. Identified inventors or project figureheads were contacted over the phone and it was verified whether the identified concepts fulfilled the sampling criteria. These less formalized contacts generated 43 observations in the final sample, 20 of which were generated from one contact which provided access to the internal venturing department at one single company, and 15 that were the result of searches of secondary data sources.

As key informants were typically identified through personal referrals, there were very few dropouts after confirmed participation. Three confirmed respondents eventually declined participation, whereas an additional three respondents were contacted and met for an interview, yet never completed the survey. Data collection ended in October 2003, comprising 88 usable questionnaires and observations. Questions concerned with framing were introduced during the second phase of the sampling process, resulting in 49 observations that are used in the present chapter.

Appendix 6.B

In the process of data collection, the research team began each interview session with a short description of the ongoing research. The introduction was made in very general terms, and great care was taken not to let respondents know about any theoretical relationships or hypotheses that were being tested. The discussion then turned to some of the background variables and history of the new business concept, including its time of establishment and current stage of development. This part of the data collection process lasted from about 40 minutes up to 1.5 hours in some cases, and provided valuable insights into the history of the new business concept and any particular features associated with it. In addition, the introductory conversation was seen as important to aid recall among the respondents, ultimately turning their attention to the questionnaire that concerned detailed information about the new business concept and its relationship to the host organization.

After the introduction, respondents were asked to complete a five-page questionnaire. The design of the questionnaire drew upon the literature on survey design (Converse & Presser, 1986; Peterson, 2000) and initial discussions with two persons knowledgeable about the corporate venturing process. After completing the questionnaire with additional questions that were identified as relevant through the interviews, the preliminary question-naire was then pre-tested on: (a) researchers knowledgeable about the construction of questionnaires, and (b) two company representatives. The pre-testing resulted in further improvements to the general design and identified a set of questions that needed clarification and re-formulation.

Before filling out the questionnaire, respondents were reminded that the information concerned the new business concept in relationship to its host organization, and it was also stressed that each question came with a 'don't know' option. When filling out of the questionnaire, which on average took about 20-25 minutes, respondents followed the guidelines of the question-naires and worked on their own. Very occasionally, the research team would be asked to clarify individual questions, and answers were then given in a neutral way. Generally, there were no visible signs of fatigue among the respondents as they approached the final parts of the questionnaire.

Because the great majority of the questionnaires were filled out in the presence of one or two members of the research team, and prior contacts had confirmed the willingness of specific individuals to respond to the questionnaire, it is known that the collected data indeed reflected the per-ceptions of targeted respondents. There are no reasons to believe that any of the questionnaires were passed on to people who might have been less knowledgeable about the nature and development of the new business concepts.

Appendix 6.C

Additional analyses employed the intrapreneurs' self-reported estimates of development times, which correspond to satisfaction scores (Covin & Slevin, 1989; Venkatraman, 1990) and measures that capture the firm's ability to meet internal milestones on schedule (Thornhill & Amit, 2000). Two specific questions asked whether: (1) 'The market introduction of the new business concepts has gone faster than expected', and (2) 'The new business concept has developed better than expected'. Both questions employed a 7-point scale, ranging from 1 (totally disagree) to 7 (totally agree).

Question (from 1 'totally disagree' to 7 'totally agree')	Cluster		
	1	**2**	**3**
	(n=15) 'Active-strategic'	**(n=25)** 'Active-optimistic'	**(n=6)** 'Passive'
The market introduction of the new concept has gone faster than expected	3.27 (2.28)	2.76 (1.74)	2.00 (1.26)
The new concept has developed better than your expectations	3.73 (1.67)	4.32 (1.82)	3.33 (1.97)

Table 6.C1 Performance implications, raw score means (standard deviations within parentheses)

The results indicate that new business concepts promoted by intrapreneurs in the active-strategic group and the active-optimistic group were introduced faster on the market and developed better than those promoted by the passive group (assuming similar initial expectations and aspirations among the responding intrapreneurs). This is in line with expectations from the extant literature, suggesting that active framing of new business concepts speeds up implementation and development processes, but none of the observed differences across clusters are statistically significant.

REFERENCES

Ahuja, G., Lampert, C.M., 2001. Entrepreneurship in the large corporation: A longitudinal study of how established firms create breakthrough inventions. *Strategic Management Journal*, 22: 521-543.

Aldenderfer, M.S., Blashfield, R.K., 1984. Cluster analysis. Sage University Papers Series on Quantitative Applications in the Social sciences, 07-044. Beverly Hills, London, and New Delhi: Sage Publications.

Antoncic, B., Hisrich, R.D., 2003. Clarifying the intrapreneurship concept. *Journal of Small Business and Enterprise Development*, 10 (1): 7-24.

Bagozzi, R.P., Yi, Y., Phillips, L.W., 1991. Assessing construct validity in organizational research. *Administrative Science Quarterly*, 36: 421-458.

Benford, R.D., Snow, D.A., 2000. Framing processes and social movements: An overview and assessment. *Annual Review of Sociology*, 26: 611-639.

Biggadike, R., 1979. The risky business of diversification. *Harvard Business Review*, May/June: 103-111.

Block, Z., 1982. Can corporate venturing succeed? *Journal of Business Strategy*, 3 (2): 21-33.

Burgelman, R.A., 1983. A process model of internal corporate venturing in the diversified major firm. *Administrative Science Quarterly*, 28: 223-244.

Burgelman, R.A., 1991. Intraorganizational ecology of strategy making and organizational adaptation: Theory and field research. *Organization Science*, 2 (3): 239-262.

Chattopadhyay, P., Glick, W.H., Huber, G.P., 2001. Organizational actions in response to threats and opportunities. *Academy of Management Journal*, 44 (5): 937-955.

Converse, J.M., Presser, S., 1986. *Survey questions: Handcrafting the standardized questionnaire*. Sage University Paper Series on Quantitative Applications in the Social Sciences, 07-063. Beverly Hills: Sage Publications.

Covin, J.G., Slevin, D.P., 1989. Strategic management of small firms in hostile and benign environments. *Strategic Management Journal*, 10 (1): 75-87.

Daft, R.L., Weick, K.E., 1984. Toward a model of organizations as interpretation systems. *Academy of Management Review*, 9: 284-295.

Day, D.L., 1994. Raising radicals: Different processes for championing innovative corporate ventures. *Organization Science*, 5 (2): 148-172.

Doz, Y.L., Olk, P.M., Smith-Ring, P., 2000. Formation processes of R&D consortia: Which path to take? Where does it lead? *Strategic Management Journal*, 21: 239-266.

Dougherty, D., Hardy, C., 1996. Sustained product-innovation in large, mature organizations: Overcoming innovation-to-organization problems. *Academy of Management Journal*, 39 (5): 1120-1153.

Dutton, J.E., Ashford, S.J., 1993. Selling issues to top management. *Academy of Management Review*, 18 (3): 397-428.

Dutton, J.E., Duncan, R.B., 1987. The creation of momentum for change through the process of strategic issue diagnosis. *Strategic Management Journal*, 83 (3): 279-295.

Dutton, J.E., Jackson, S.E., 1987. Categorizing strategic issues: Links to organizational action. *Academy of Management Review*, 12 (1): 76-90.

Dutton, J.E., Ashford, S.J., O'Neill, R.M., Lawrence, K.A., 2001. Moves that matter: Issue selling and organizational change. *Academy of Management Journal*, 44: 716-736.

Fiol, M., 1994. Consensus, diversity, and learning in organizations. *Organization Science*, 5 (3): 403-420.

Galbraith, J.R., 1982. Designing the innovating organization. *Organizational Dynamics*, Winter: 5-25.

George, E., Chattopadhyay, P., Sitkin, S.B., Barden, J., 2006. Cognitive underpinnings of institutional persistence and change: A framing perspective. *Academy of Management Review*, 31 (2): 347-365.

Gilbert, C.G., 2005. Unbundling the structure of inertia: Resource versus routine rigidity. *Academy of Management Journal*, 48 (5): 741-763.

Golden, B.R., 1992. The past is the past – or is it? The use of retrospective accounts as indicators of past strategy. *Academy of Management Journal*, 35: 848-860.

Guth, W.D., Ginsberg, A., 1990. Guest editors' introduction: Corporate entrepreneurship. *Strategic Management Journal*, 11 (Special Issue): 5-15.

Hadaway, C.K., 1989. Identifying American apostates: A cluster analysis. *Journal for the Scientific Study of Religion*, 28 (2): 201-215.

Hair, J.F., Babin, B., Money, A.H., Samouel, P., 2003. *Essentials of Business Research Methods*. John Wiley & Sons.

Hamel, G., Prahalad, C.K., 1994. *Competing for the future*. Harvard Business School Press.

Hargadon, A.B., Douglas, Y., 2002. When innovations meet institutions: Edison and the design of the electric light. *Administrative Science Quarterly*, 46: 476-501.

Howell, J.M., Higgins, C.A., 1990. Champions of technological innovation. *Administrative Science Quarterly*, 35 (2): 317-341.

Huber, G.P., 1991. Organizational learning: The contributing processes and the literatures. *Organization Science*, 2 (1): 88-115.

Jackson, S.E., Dutton, J.E., 1988. Discerning threats and opportunities. *Administrative Science Quarterly*, 33: 370-387.

Kazanjian, R.K., Drazin, R., 1987. Implementing internal diversification: Contingency factors for organizational design choice. *Academy of Management Review*, 12 (2): 342-354.

Ketchen, D.J., Shook, C.L., 1996. The application of cluster analysis in strategic management research: An analysis and critique. *Strategic Management Journal*, 17 (6): 441-458.

Kiesler, S., Sproull, L., 1982. Managerial response to changing environments: Perspectives on problem sensing from social cognition. *Administrative Science Quarterly*, 27 (4): 548-570.

Kumar, N., Stern, L.W., Anderson, J.A., 1993. Conducting inter-organizational research using key informants. *Academy of Management Journal*, 36: 1633-1651.

Lounsbury, M., Glynn, M.A., 2001. Cultural entrepreneurship: Stories, legitimacy, and the acquisition of resources. *Strategic Management Journal*, 22: 545-564.

Lovas, B., Ghoshal, S., 2000. Strategy as guided evolution. *Strategic Management Journal*, 21: 875-896.

MacMillan, I.C., Block, Z., Narasimha, P.N., 1986. Corporate venturing: Alternatives, obstacles, and experience effects. *Journal of Business Venturing*, 1: 177-191.

McGrath, R.G., Venkataraman, S., MacMillan, I.C., 1994. The advantage chain: Antecedents to rents from internal corporate ventures. *Journal of Business Venturing*, 9: 351-369.

Milliken, F.J., 1990. Perceiving and interpreting environmental change: An examination of college administrators' interpretation of changing demographics. *Academy of Management Journal*, 33 (1): 42-63.

Nutt, P.C., 1998. Framing strategic decisions. *Organization Science*, 9 (2): 195-216.

Parker, W.D., 1997. An empirical typology of perfectionism in academically talented children. *American Educational Research Journal*, 34 (3): 545-562.

Peterson, R.A., 2000. *Constructing Effective Questionnaires*. Thousand Oaks: Sage Publications.

Piderit, S.K., 2000. Rethinking resistance and recognizing ambivalence: A multidimensional view of attitudes toward an organizational change. *Academy of Management Review*, 25 (4): 783-794.

Pinchot, G., 1985. *Intrapreneuring: Why you Don't Have to Leave the Corporation to Become an Entrepreneur*. New York, NY: Harper & Row.

Podsakoff, P.M., Organ, D.W., 1986. Self-reports in organizational research: Problems and prospects. *Journal of Management*, 12: 531-544.

Podsakoff, P.M., MacKenzie, S.B., Lee, J.-Y., 2003. Common method biases in behavioral research: A critical review of the literature and recommended remedies. *Journal of Applied Psychology*, 88 (5): 879-903.

Schumpeter, J.A., 1934. *The Theory of Economic Development*. Cambridge, MA: Harvard University Press.

Stopford, J.M., Baden-Fuller, C.W.F., 1994. Creating corporate entrepreneurship. *Strategic Management Journal*, 15 (7): 521-536.

Sykes, H.B., Block, Z., 1989. Corporate venturing obstacles: Sources and solutions. *Journal of Business Venturing*, 4: 159-167.

Thornhill, S., Amit, R., 2000. A dynamic perspective of internal fit in corporate venturing. *Journal of Business Venturing*, 16: 25-50.

Tsai, W.M.-H., MacMillan, I.C., Low, M.B., 1991. Effects on strategy and environment on corporate venture success in industrial markets. *Journal of Business Venturing*, 6: 9-28.

Tyre, M.J., Hauptman, O., 1992. Effectiveness of organizational responses to technological change in the production process. *Organization Science*, 3 (3): 301-320.

Venkatraman, N., 1990. Performance implications of strategic coalignment: A methodological perspective. *Journal of Management Studies*, 27 (1): 19-41.

Zahra, S.A., 1991. Predictors and financial outcomes of corporate entrepreneurship: An exploratory study. *Journal of Business Venturing*, 6 (4): 259-258.

Zahra, S.A., Covin, J.G., 1995. Contextual influences on the corporate entrepreneurship-performance relationship: A longitudinal analysis. *Journal of Business Venturing*, 10 (1): 43-58.

7. Refueling or Running Dry: Entrepreneurs' Energetic Resources and the Start-Up Process

Anders Landberg

INTRODUCTION

Venture creation is not a linear process towards the realization of an idea, but is instead fraught with goal-disruptive processes and events (Baum & Locke, 2004; Greene, Unpublished paper; Landberg, Forthcoming; MacMillan, 1983; Terpstra & Olson, 1993). Entrepreneurs need to cope with these goal-disruptions and when trying to explain what is needed of an entrepreneur, people often refer to the importance of drive and energy[1]. Drive can be likened to motivation, which has been extensively studied in entrepreneurship research (see for example Baum et al., 2004; Delmar, 1996; Raphael, Kenneth, Charlene, & John, 2001; Stephen & Melvin, 2006). Energy, on the other hand, has thus far been largely ignored[2]. Research has instead focused on matters such as passion and perseverance. It has, for example, been proposed that start-up survival and success is enhanced if entrepreneurs dislike giving in and passionately hold on to their goals (Cardon, Zietsma, Saparito, Matherne, & Davis, 2005) or if they have the tenacity or perseverance to overcome obstacles (Baum et al., 2004). Passion has been put forth as a driver that entrepreneurs use when facing uncertainty and resource shortages (Timmons, 1999) and it has even been said that it is 'perhaps the most observed phenomenon of the entrepreneurial process' (Smilor, 1997: 342).

---

[1] This was found in a survey of Swedish media: magazines, newspapers and the Internet.

[2] There are very few references to energy in entrepreneurship research. The two that I have found relate it to social energy in maintaining strong or weak ties (Podolny and Baron, 1997) which is an entirely different definition from the one used here and in the psychology research referred to, and to the energy level of entrepreneurs which is used to point to individual differences (Bird, 1992). Bird's use of energy is close to the one used here, however she never extends her discussion of the concept in any detail.

In most entrepreneurial start-up processes, an entrepreneur's passion or perseverance will be put to the test through hardships. The dynamics of such instances arguably have critical importance for whether the entrepreneur will continue. However, passion or perseverance themselves cannot explain the dynamics. Returning to energy, *energetic resources* – defined as the energy available in individuals to deal with stress and effort to cope – have been found to intensify negative emotions and fatigue as a result of goal-disruptive events (Zohar, Tzischinski, & Epstein, 2003). The concept of energy offers an avenue to deepen our understanding of how entrepreneurs endure over time to realize their venture ideas and cope in adverse environments.

During favorable conditions, energetic resources are ample and of no concern to the entrepreneur, but as soon as conditions become less favorable, energetic resources are likely to become important. In a theoretical scenario we can see that if behavior cannot proceed as planned, additional effort must be invested by the individual in mental problem solving and decision-making. This additional effort will begin to tax on the amount of energy available to the entrepreneur and will, if demand for energy is greater than its supply, become a reason for termination. What is intriguing and complicating here is that it is not only an entrepreneur's coping efforts that tax on energy supplies, but also what is happening to him or her in a wider perspective. In other words both mental effort and stress[3] will influence how rapidly energetic resources are being depleted[4].

The purpose of this chapter is to explore the influence of energetic resources on entrepreneurs during the start-up process. This is done by studying instances where energetic resource levels restrict or enhance goal performance. Such instances arise where goal-disruptive processes or events threaten the realization of the entrepreneurial idea. Examples of such instances are where novice entrepreneurs[5] with limited personal resources perceive resistance from stakeholders to their fledgling ventures, such as when family dislikes an entrepreneur's involvement in a start-up or a venture capitalist restricting access to capital for a start-up (Landberg, Forthcoming).

---

[3] Selye (1974; 1976) distinguishes between eustress and dystress. He equals stress with arousal and claims that a certain amount of arousal is good (eustress), while too much is bad (dystress). This implies that a deviation from an optimal level of arousal is negative to an individual. The problem however is to define an optimal level of arousal. With the approach taken in this chapter it is the dystress that is studied, that which requires effort and taxing of energetic resources.

[4] This paragraph was written using Kahneman's (1973) capacity model of attention as a basis for developing an entrepreneurial scenario involving energy.

[5] 'Novice' refers to entrepreneurs starting their first new venture. This means that they have no previous experience of entrepreneurship on which to base their actions and perceptions of stakeholders. It also means that they have not established any prior relations with actors in the creation of new ventures.

The concept of energetic resources is discussed in relation to cognitive appraisal theory (Folkman, Lazarus, Dunkelschetter, Delongis, & Gruen, 1986; Lazarus, 1999; Lazarus, 2001), behavioral economics (Schonpflug, 1986b, 1986a; Schonpflug & Battman, 1988) and specific studies of energetic resources (see for example Gaillard, 2001; Hockey, 1997; Hockey, Gaillard, & Coles, 1986; Wright & Brehm, 1989).

This chapter discusses how limited amounts of energetic resources diverts entrepreneurs' attention from their key activities aimed at venture creation to coping with goal-disruptions, both private and professional, how coping with goal-disruptions affect venture creation attempts as energetic resources are limited, and how failure to overcome goal-disruptions eventually leads to drained energetic resources and failure to carry out key tasks.

Next a theoretical model is built and then applied to the empirical material in order to further our understanding of energy from an entrepreneurial perspective. Finally the results are discussed and concluded.

THEORETICAL FRAMEWORK

The thought of energy as a limited resource influencing behavior has existed for a number of years (Duffy, 1962; Freeman, 1948). Explorations of its behavioral and physiological aspects began with studies such as those by Pribram and McGuiness (1975) who studied how the coordination of arousal[6] and activation constitutes a demanding activity requiring energy and centering on the hippocampus. Lately, researchers have started looking into how the energetics construct in terms of efforts such as activation, arousal, stress, fatigue and resources can be added to models of behavior (Hockey et al., 1986).

Regarding the applicability of the concept of energetic resources, it has been proposed that it provides a framework for, amongst other things, fatigue, individual differences in adjustment and coping, specifically with regards to work related demands (Hockey, 1997). The use of energetic resources has been proposed to be 'as a generic term encompassing all mechanisms that energizes and regulates the organism and directly or indirectly influence psychological processing' (Gaillard, 2001: 625). To understand the characteristics of energetic resources one can think of why they are applied and the results of such action. Energetic resources are activated in an effort to protect performance under stress and the result is behavioral and physiological costs (Hockey, 1997). This effort to protect performance is difficult to maintain

---

[6] 'to rouse or stimulate to action or to physiological readiness for activity' (Merriam-Webster, 2006).

(Kahneman, 1973) because conflicts likely crop up between emotional goals of up-keeping personal well-being and desired affective states (Hockey, 1997).

An underlying concept when studying energetic resources by taking Hockey's perspective (1997) is emotions. Stress, emotion and coping have been suggested to have a part-whole relationship with emotion as the superior conceptual unit (Lazarus, 1999). As will be discussed further on in this chapter, emotions or the risk of emotions influences how energetic resources develop and how entrepreneurs cope. What influences emotions in turn is the person/environment relationship (Lazarus, 1993).

A model of the process where energetic resources are applied can be generically depicted as in Figure 7.1. It starts with a stimulus, and as the focus of this study is on stressful situations, in this study stimulus is goal-disruptive. This event is appraised in two steps where a disruptive event could be evaluated as threatening or challenging (Lazarus, 1999).

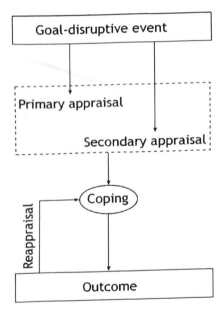

Figure 7.1 Application of energetic resources – a theoretical model

Appraisal next leads to an activation response which is regulated according to available energetic resources. Depending on how the situation is appraised and on available resources, various coping strategies are applied. These strategies are moderated by issues such as effort, motivation, and context-dependent factors. The result of coping on the goal-disruptive event causes a reappraisal which affects arousal and energy mobilization in the sense that it is increased, sustained or decreased. Depending on the energetic resources available to mobilize, performance risk being degraded if the outcome of coping strategies is not positively appraised. In the following sections, the model in figure 7.1 is discussed in more detail, forming the framework for the empirical study of energetic resources in the entrepreneurial process.

Appraisal of Goal-disruptive Events

Cognitive appraisal theory states that emotions arise from individual's appraisal of events based on their relevance to the individuals. Specifically, appraisal affects emotions, through a loss of vital energetic resources (Lazarus, 2001). This is problematic in the sense that a loss of resources needed to pursue a goal will become a threat to the achievement of that goal and result in negative emotion. The intensity of emotional reaction is further moderated by the desirability of the goal and the effect of environmental change on the estimated probability of achieving it on time (Lazarus, 1990; 1999).

Appraisal consists of primary appraisal, the process of evaluating whether an event is worthy of attention and mobilization of energetic resources, and secondary appraisal, focusing on the options for coping, what can be done. As far as timing is concerned, primary and secondary appraisal happen simultaneously and are part of the same process, but with different foci (Lazarus, 1999). In order to understand their dynamics and importance in the activation of energetic resources, the two types of appraisal are discussed separately in the following two sections.

Primary appraisal

The type of goal that is of interest here is the task-level goal, which involves immediate goals relating to performance (Kluger & DeNisi, 1996). The disrupted goal's relevance to overall performance, the degree of incongruence resulting from the disruption and the entrepreneur's personal reasons for pursuing the idea influence how the goal-disruptive event is evaluated (Lazarus, 1991).

Stress-levels caused by the event depends on how entrepreneurs perceive its significance to their values, beliefs, goal commitment and situational intentions (Lazarus, 1990, 1999). It has been found that initial stimulus evokes an evaluative reflex which seems to occur before higher-order cognitive appraisal. A negative evaluation is interpreted as a threat (Duckworth, Bargh, Garcia, & Chaiken, 2002) but as evaluations are individual, the same situation could be interpreted as a challenge (Lazarus, 1999) depending on such individual factors as self-efficacy (Bandura, 1997) and constructive thinking (Epstein & Meier, 1989). In an entrepreneurial context, threat implies that something is about to take place that might harm an entrepreneur's venture idea where the entrepreneur feels less confident of successful coping. A challenge on the other hand is something that the entrepreneur feels confident to be able to cope with (Lazarus, 1993). Whether an event is interpreted as a threat or a challenge, in both cases it signals that something risks the achievement of a task-level goal and is a wake-up call that 'something is amiss'.

Secondary appraisal

Secondary appraisal relates to the options an individual has for coping – what can be done about a stressful situation appraised as a threat or a challenge. Emotions play a part in this and entrepreneurs base their secondary appraisal on blame or credit for the disruptive event, coping potential and future expectations (Lazarus, 1999). Energetic resources come to play through goal-disruptive processes or events and thus blame is likely to be the first choice. Coping potential is whether an entrepreneur believes that a goal-disruption can be successfully overcome or not. Future expectations have negative or positive outcomes.

The amount of available energy when meeting an affective event also influences appraisal through both an emotional reaction and fatigue. Energy available is influenced both by the amount and the character of workload immediately before the event. With an already decreased level, negative emotions will be stronger than with a higher level of initial energy (Zohar et al., 2003). In addition, incremental loss of resources plays a role as cognitive appraisal proposes that a lesser possibility of successful coping poses an even larger threat (Hobfoll, 2001; Lazarus, 1991).

Coping with Goal-disruptive Events

To understand the process in which energetic resources become critical, two states of being can exemplify the dynamics involved. Our optimal state is one where our energetic resources are balanced with the activities we do and want to do. Mechanisms continuously regulate our body so that it is in an optimal state, energy-wise, to perform tasks and process information. This optimal state is a necessity for us to efficiently process as well as determine the available capacity to perform a certain task. Under these normal state conditions, we do not need to worry about regulating energetic resources and adapting. It is only in states described by stress, fatigue and strong emotions that energetic resources become an issue to us and we start regulating and directing it to uphold selected performance goals. Such a state happens when behavior is disrupted and cannot proceed as planned.

Regulating input of energetic resources

The behavioral economics model states that individuals are forced to invest additional resources in mental problem solving and decision making when behavior is disrupted and cannot proceed as planned. As energetic resources are limited, quickly consumed and require far more time to replenish than to consume, the effort invested into problem solving and decision making must be regulated. This implies that individuals must engage in coping based on a process aimed at gaining the most from the costs invested in challenging situations (Schonpflug, 1986b, 1986a; Schonpflug et al., 1988).

The management of energetic resources in disruptive events thus becomes critical and is carried out by mobilizing mental effort and is actively used by individuals to maintain performance stability in demanding situations. In other words, increasing task goal commitment will decrease the relevance of other personal and biological goals (Hockey, 1997).

As energy is a limited and critical resource for self-regulated action, depleting it most likely leads to negative emotions in instances where such action is required (Hobfoll, 2001). This also connects to the behavioral economics theory as energy expenditure and recovery balance in stressful situations influences the intensity of emotional reactions (Schonpflug, 1986b; Schonpflug et al., 1988).

Coping strategies and moderating variables

Coping is defined as 'cognitive and behavioural efforts to manage specific external and/or internal demands that are appraised as taxing or exceeding the resources of the person' (Lazarus & Folkman, 1984: 141). In short it is 'the effort to manage psychological stress' (Lazarus, 1999: 111), where appraisal decides how individuals cope. Accordingly, people respond differently to events depending on how the significance of these events is appraised (Lazarus, 1990; 1999).

There are two general coping strategies: problem-focused and emotion-focused. Problem-focused is used when a person believes that a stressor can be overcome. It involves strategies such as taking action to deal with the stressor, seeking instrumental support, and planning (Lazarus, 1999). Facing issues perceived as potentially goal-disruptive, this would mean that entrepreneurs would exert mental effort to mobilize extra energy in order to maintain performance at a certain level, a 'try harder' approach (Gaillard, 2001). This approach can only be upheld for a limited time as it brings with it high physiological and psychological costs. Examples of situations demanding mental effort are: sleep loss or fatigue, which leads to non-optimal energetic state; emotions continuously demand attention and thus upset the energetic state; an attention challenging task through varying input-output relations or strong demands on working memory; a complex task context forcing the division of attention between different tasks; and a learning situation involving the acquisition of new skills.

An emotion-focused strategy is used when a person does not believe that the stressful condition can be changed and aims at decreasing the experience of negative emotions. Strategies involved are suppression, restraint, seeking emotional support, acceptance, denial and disengagement. The result of emotion-focused coping is a change in individuals' interpretation of circumstances, for example giving up a sought after goal or the denial of a certain threat (Lazarus, 1999). Resorting to an emotion-focused strategy is risky as intense emotions take 'control precedence', meaning that they continuously require attention, which in turn decrease the available capacity for task relevant information processing and action (Gaillard, 2001).

This shows the importance of regulating energetic resources, especially under time pressure or threatening situations, in order to uphold an efficient task performance. This is difficult though as it is subjectively aversive and costly, it risks conflicting with personal goals of well-being or having a positive approach to other people. Availability of energetic resources on demand is a critical emotional factor as affective events require effort investments to cope with the disruptions (Zohar et al., 2003).

As stress and emotions arise, coping becomes a dual process where individuals cope with emotions in relation to internal aspects of the self, at the same time as they cope with stress and emotions in relation to social self, roles and relations (Martinovski & Marsella, 2005). When stress and emotions take precedent, fatigue is the result. Fatigue can be characterized as the mind and body's response to resource reductions resulting from carrying out mental tasks where there is a risk of performance failure in relation to task goals. It is affected both by the work that has been done and is being done, as well as work that will have to be done in the future – expectations of what is to come (Gaillard, 2001).

Reappraisal

When reappraising the situation, two aspects are important. The first is the discrepancy between task goal and actual situation, in other words the effect of the applied effort or coping strategy. The second is the rate of progress in terms of discrepancy reduction, for an entrepreneur this means how fast a disruption is overcome and if it is overcome. Research has shown that positive or negative mood is directly affected by this progress (Carver & Scheier, 1990). Even a change in the rate of progress influences mood, meaning that goal-disruptions likely result in negative mood as it has a negative impact on the rate of progress towards a focal goal (Zohar, 1999).

So if a goal-disruption is overcome after exerting effort in coping, things move on, but energetic resources are diminished. Entrepreneurs are thus more sensitive to new goal-disruptions after recently having overcome one. Resources available are decreased leaving less leeway for attention to multiple tasks. To deal with this problem, rest is needed which requires time.

If a goal-disruption is not overcome, the process of appraisal-coping-reappraisal will again take place, but this time with even less energetic resources at hand. Hence energetic resources are even further taxed when the cost of continued coping outweighs the benefit of overcoming and coping itself becomes a source of stress (Schonpflug et al., 1988).

Concluding the Theoretical Overview

In the theoretical overview I have argued that goal-disruptive processes or events, which are integrated aspects of new venture creation, bring energetic resources into focus. Goal-disruption forces entrepreneurs to appraise their efforts, significance to their plans and abilities to cope and overcome it. In the stress that comes from this, their energetic resources are used when they attempt to cope. The consequence to their venture creation efforts is that their planned or intended actions are halted as they instead have to focus attention on coping with the goal-disruption.

Gradually, as energetic resources are diminished, even more effort is required to pursue goals. This becomes problematic as energetic resources are limited, quickly consumed, takes time to replenish, and need regular replenishment. Moreover the actual lowered level of energetic resources in itself leads to additionally taxed levels. Entrepreneurs hence risk ending up in a potentially negative spiral that could lead to the final demise of a start-up attempt.

In the next section the research design is presented, followed by the empirical study of the dynamics of energetic resources.

RESEARCH DESIGN

The results presented in this chapter are based on four cases studies, each covering approximately 1½ years. The study takes an open-ended explorative approach, enabling the capturing of events as they unfold (Van de Ven & Engleman, 2004). A critical incident technique (Flanagan, 1954) is used to build an incident for each perceived goal-disruption. This choice of method was deemed as the most appropriate method as prior to the study, it was unclear how entrepreneurs' energetic resources influenced the entrepreneurial process (Perren & Ram, 2004).

The study began by selecting entrepreneurs who were very early in the venture creation process. They had not yet registered a firm, got funding, registered patents, hired staff or generated sales. In addition they had no earlier experience of entrepreneurship, and no personal financial means. This strategy of deliberately (Patton, 1990) selecting cases at the extreme aimed at increasing chances of the entrepreneurs' need for coping with goal-disruption, decreasing their means of coping, and increasing potential social dramas around coping and goal-disruption (Pettigrew, 1990). This would increase stress and the need for energetic resources.

Selection of entrepreneurs was also based on the would-be entrepreneurs' intentions. Only those with clear intentions to realize their ideas were selected to make sure that they would actually make efforts to overcome goal-disruptions (Gatewood, Shaver, & Gartner, 1995). Gestation was chosen as the focus period of the study because it was understudied and had implications for the growing new venture (Reynolds, Carter, Gartner, & Greene, 2004). It also served to delimit the study.

University business labs were used as channels to find the entrepreneurs. In this manner five[7] entrepreneurs were picked out of a sample of 25 on which encompassing case studies were built longitudinally through interviews (Eisenhardt, 1989; Yin, 1994). Each entrepreneur was interviewed approximately once every four to eight weeks for approximately one to one and a half years, totaling 34 interviews. The length of time for the study might seem like a short time, but in the life of a new venture, and particularly the gestation of it, it is a considerable time (Gersick, 1994). Before the case studies began, and to delimit the study, a number of criteria were set up to guide when the gathering of data would end. There were four criteria: when the ideas were developed to the point where sales began; if the venture creation attempts were cancelled; if progress stopped and effort appeared low; or if an empirical saturation of data was attained. The actual decision to stop data gathering supported the notion the given research period is a considerable time at the start of a new venture. Two of the entrepreneurs decided to abandon their creation attempts, one had come to a point where the idea was launched to customers, and one had reached a situation where development had come to an almost stand still.

Interviews focused on understanding the nature of relationships as the entrepreneurs perceived them, which is necessary in order to understand social and organizational behavior embedded in relationships (Granovetter, 1985). Interviews had thematic foci on how the entrepreneurs used their

---

[7] The fifth case was abandoned after three interviews due to access difficulties associated with finding interview times and willingness on behalf of the entrepreneur to freely share information with the researcher.

relations to build their ventures, who the critical stakeholders were, how they perceived stakeholders' responses to their ventures, how they perceived the development of their ventures, what their own actions, perceptions and feelings were in the face of perceived goal-disruptions, and how they mobilized their energetic resources in efforts to cope with goal-disruptions.

To improve the means of analyzing such a large amount of empirical data I used the software NVIVO[8], which is specifically developed to explore and analyze this type of data. In NVIVO I coded the data by building nodes for themes and actors and used these nodes to explore patterns and build models. The nodes were then given specific attributes which I used to explore dimensions and connections within the data.

The manner in which I did this in NVIVO was that all passages in the transcribed text discussing for example a certain supplier of an entrepreneur was marked and in that way made into a node with the name of that supplier. This made it possible to open that specific node and have all the information about that supplier gathered in one place.

Coding the material was an iterative process and I went over the material several times adding new nodes. In some instances this led to certain passages having more than five nodes overlapping such as multiple stakeholders, different entrepreneurial circumstances/characteristics, and goal-disruptions.

To make sense of the coded material, I did what Miles and Huberman call displaying the data (1994) by sorting it according to three questions: what were the key events and decisions in each case, how did they come about and why did they come about. In addition to this method of making sense of the material, I also contextualized the data with the aim to understand it as a whole. The way I did this was to build maps and matrixes which helped me grasp the big picture and how things related in the cases (Maxwell, 1996).

After having used NVIVO to build patterns of how the ventures evolved with a focus on disruptive events, mini-cases were written about each such instance. In total 24 instances of goal-disruptions were identified and those were then used to further understand the dynamics of effort exertion involving energetic resources. From these 24 instances, 20 energetic resources episodes were identified each spanning over more than one instance of goal-disruption. Those energetic resources span multiple instances of goal-disruption and is consistent with previous research of work-related performance episodes where affective states influencing performance spans multiple episodes (Beal, Weiss, Barros, & MacDermid, 2005).

In developing the energetic resources construct for the entrepreneurial process, most of the research drawn upon has primarily used subjective

---

[8] For more information about NVIVO, see http://www.qsrinternational.com

reports of affective states to measure effort. Much of this research is cross-sectional analyses of demand and outcome variables or experiments. Although research methods differ considerably, it has been shown that results produced from laboratory studies do not differ from those generated from field studies and the findings from one can thus be used in another (Locke, 1986).

In order to develop and explore theory, concepts and dynamics of energetic resources further, there has been a call for longitudinal studies (Hockey, 1997). Examples of such studies now exist with longitudinal surveys (see for example Zohar et al., 2003). In addition, the individual has been proposed to be a key methodological issue when studying stressful processes and consequent coping. The reasoning behind this is that coping depends on context and must change over time and between stressful situations to have the chance of being successful (Lazarus, 1993). Taken together this supports the current study both in terms of links with earlier research and the choice of method – qualitatively and longitudinally following individual entrepreneurs across a number of critical incidents. In this aspect the current study differs from earlier research on the concept of energy and can contribute to a broader conceptual development of the concept as the study is set in a naturalistic setting.

CASE STUDIES

The study consists of four encompassing case studies; all cases follow the entrepreneurs' very first actions to realize their products or services, primarily the gestation of the idea and the early infancy of the venture. All of the entrepreneurs are novices with no prior entrepreneurial experience. None have any personal financial means to invest in developing the idea. While attempting to realize their ventures, two of them spend time in a university business lab, while two instead take an extensive start-up course. Their ages range from the early 20s to the early 40s and they either have an MSc in business or in engineering. Both women live with their boyfriends and the men are married and have young children. Nina and Susanne are enrolled at university while attempting to realize their venture ideas, Eric is initially unemployed, then gets a full-time job and Jonas works as a university teacher. For all of them, their studies, work or unemployment initially gives them an income which enables them to survive while working with their ideas.

Entre-preneur	Idea	Conception of idea	Registered firm	Study began	Study ended	Female/male	Time spent
Nina	Cosmetics	2004-01	2004-09	2004-06	2005-06	Female	Full
Eric	Game	2003-01	2004-03	2004-01	2005-06	Male	Part
Susanne	Horses	2003-10	2004	2004-03	2005-03	Female	Full
Jonas	Internet	2003-06	2003	2004-01	2005-03	Male	Part

Table 7.1 Case studies

A brief introduction to each of the four cases:

Nina begins thinking about her venture idea in the winter of 2004. The idea comes to her when she writes her Master's thesis in Business Administration about beauty products for men. She realizes that the cosmetics industry in Sweden is almost exclusively focused on women, while men are only catered for as a sub-group of cosmetics for women. She reads a text by a professor in economic history about the cosmetics industry's development in the 20th century which discusses how the industry and media together created a demand for the products. Prior to this, the market for cosmetics was very limited but as demand was created it grew rapidly. It dawns on her that male-only cosmetics could offer similar potential today as history shows for the female cosmetics. She realizes that male-only cosmetics stores exists solely as small web-based ones and the opportunity she sees is to open a male-only cosmetics store in the form of a physical location as well as a web based one.

Being an ardent soccer fan, **Eric** is annoyed each time he misses a match with his favorite team, especially if he is away from a TV. He begins thinking about if this could somehow be dealt with, if one could watch soccer games live on low bandwidth cell phones. In the spring of 2003 he becomes unemployed and decides to use his time to try and realize his idea, so he starts developing a service broadcasting real movements of the ball while simulating players' movements using low bandwidth.

Susanne loves her horse, but one of its greatest joys is to roll itself in the mud. Each time this happens she has a lot of work to clean it. She figures that there has to be a better way to clean horses than those on the market. Her father is a hobby inventor and there are many inventors in her family and among the friends of her family with a number of patents among them. Susanne also describes herself as inventive, saying that 'I have always had a lot of ideas'. Together with her father she ponders the problem of cleaning horses and in the autumn of 2003, she comes up with an idea to make a special type of brush.

Jonas is a lecturer at a technical college in Stockholm and in many of his courses, students carry out assignments of varying length and difficulty. As a part of what his department could offer students, he nurtures an idea where students can develop their own venture ideas as a part of course assignments. In the middle of 2003 Jonas comes up with an idea of his own – a service which would offer anyone with a mobile phone to produce and sell ring signals for mobile phones over the Internet.

THE INFLUENCE OF ENERGETIC RESOURCES ON NEW VENTURE CREATION

During the study, all entrepreneurs faced the problem of diminishing energetic resources, but not all goal-disruptions meant that the entrepreneurs had to use their energetic resources. There were 24 observed goal-disruptions and in 20 of those, the entrepreneurs' energetic resources played an important role. Moreover, energetic resources brought some of the goal-disruptions together in the sense that diminished energetic resources lead to additional goal-disruptions.

This section will discuss the empirical findings of the role of energetic resources in an entrepreneurial context. The structure follows the theoretical model (see Figure 7.1), beginning with appraisal, then coping and finally outcome.

Before turning to appraisal, a few words about the goal-disruptions observed. Each entrepreneur met a number of instances as goal-disruptions where each of them represents a goal that was deemed more or less critical to the entrepreneur's plans for how to realize the venture idea. In the following, the theoretical model (see Figure 7.1) is used to present and discuss the empirical findings and the influence of energetic resources on the venture creation process.

Appraisal

Jonas has a set of goals which are important to him, his work, his family and his venture idea. The order of priority between these puts the venture idea below the other two. In spring 2004 he foresees that by autumn his time allocation will shift even more towards his family. He fears that his creation attempts might fail, that time will not be enough and says that 'it might even be good if it fails'.

Eric experiences similar things in respect to multiple goals where there is a pull in different directions for attention from the various goals. This works until some shift occurs, in Jonas' case where his time allocation changes and in Eric's case where he gets a new job that prohibits him from spending time on personal venture ideas. At this point, their venture creation efforts change from ease to mental struggles of how they are to exert their efforts and which goals to focus on.

What furthermore influences the entrepreneurs' perceptions of the goal-disruptions is how severe those appear in respect to their believed prospects of realizing their ideas. Nina for example depends on funding to set her strategy in motion as it involves setting up a store in Stockholm which is costly. She has no personal means to put into her venture and so turns to external funding. However her application for funding is rejected by a Swedish government funding agency because of what she feels is her handling officer's ignorance. Feeling that she has no possibility to realize her idea without funding, she is angry and sad. She describes the officer as 'a lady in her 50s who does not even live in Stockholm and who does not have any idea about what it looks like here [in Stockholm]'.

This is also a pattern that appears through the entrepreneurs' appraisals of goal-disruptions. The more important and the less control they feel they have over the situation, the more emotional their reactions are. However, externalizing the cause of the goal-disruption, like Nina does, is not the only strategy. Eric, for example is cut off from testing his idea at the Swedish Soccer League by the Swedish Football Association. Without the possibility to test he is unable to develop his idea, and there is little he can do about the situation. Instead of blaming the association he links this to his early actions in starting up, where he took help from a friend of his with a website that he later finds out supports international betting companies. This in turn makes the association terminate his testing as they depend on the Svenska Spel for funding and they do not want any competition on the Swedish market. This insight helps him see an opportunity for the future where he believes he can negotiate a deal with the association.

In a similar vein, the belief of the entrepreneurs that they will be able to deal with a goal-disruption influences how much effort they exert. Eric who also needs funding to hire programmers and buy hardware finds out that he needs a business plan when approaching any funding agency. This business plan is something that he fails to write. He states that "it is hard to do a marketing analysis for the venture... in a business plan it must show that we have a clear grasp of the situation... that we have checked what the market wants... there should not be any question marks... it should be like fill in the blanks and give us the money... but our plan... it is like lame... a little bit lie 'this is nice'. Again and again he returns to this throughout the study, and again and again he says that he does not have the skills needed to write a business plan. Even though he never produces a business plan, the thought of what a business plan could offer him is constantly on his mind, simultaneously with the feeling of inadequacy. This is a permanent source of stress to him.

Susanne has a problem when her prototype does not work as she had hoped and she must develop it further. She realizes that she does not want to be an inventor but only an entrepreneur that takes inventions to the market. As problems arise with the prototype she worries that it will take a long time to bring it to the market and she questions whether she wants to put in the time needed for this. She also needs to patent it in order to start talking about it to people without having to worry that someone might steal her idea. Getting a loan also takes time.

Coping

Jonas expected that his time would not be enough to cope with what would come. He does nothing active to cope, only waits and works with what he can at the moment. As it turns out, initially this is not a problem as the situation of the venture idea changes so that his time is no longer the bottleneck. The real problem turns out to be the student programmers whose student projects end, meaning that they have to work in their spare time. To Jonas this is almost a relief as he can continue as before with the same priorities and without feeling that it affects the venture as its pace has already been decreased by other sources.

The way in which Eric deals with his new employer who prohibits his work on the venture idea is to ignore his employer's demands. Yet his employer must not suspect anything. So each time Eric needs to work with his venture he must sneak away and come up with excuses. He elicits his wife in this, but without telling her exactly what it is that he will do. Eventually she finds out and he is forced to deal with her anger also. He is now beginning to feel 'stretched out' over multiple activities and this he says is tiring. Eric's wife was initially supportive of his venture idea, but as it is pitted against his employment she becomes worried as she sees it as important with a steady income. As he tries to balance his work, his venture and his family, he is forced to repeatedly negotiate with his wife about why he should spend any time at all on his venture. While she questions his time spent on the venture idea, Eric himself grapples with the image of himself as gender equal to his wife, taking equal responsibility at home. He faces lot of difficulties in motivating others and himself about why he should put effort into the venture.

Where Jonas chooses a laissez-faire approach, Eric chooses a more direct one to deal with the goal-disruption. In both cases, the goal-disruption poses great difficulties to them as it arises from their priorities in relation to multiple goals where their venture ideas are one. Jonas sticks to his laissez-faire strategy while Eric gradually becomes more disillusioned and starts questioning himself and his choices.

Nina's initial response to her loan application being rejected was anger and despair. She thinks of giving up, but calls her best friends first for some emotional support. This helps regain her energy and she calls the handling officer to try and convince her. It does not work though and she begins thinking about how to change her strategy given that she is not getting any loans for the store.

Although Nina responds emotionally to the rejection and the prospect that she is unable to realize her venture idea, her coping strategy is non-emotional. She herself gives credit to her friends whom she called. She says that in situations like this, her friends are there to support her unconditionally and that gives her the energy she needs to move on and be proactive. On more than one occasion of goal-disruptions, she does this; calls her friends for emotional support to help her gain energy to continue coping.

Susanne aspires to a high pace in her venture creation efforts, and wants to see quick results. However as she tries to develop the prototype, looking for people who can help her, she realizes that it will never be quick. She feels frustrated and does not really see a way to deal with this. Instead she starts looking for other alternatives to realize her entrepreneurial aspirations.

Outcome
As time goes by, Jonas does not increase the priorities of his venture creation activities and although his programmers were the bottleneck, he does not bring in the effort to take the last step towards finalizing the venture idea. From the onset of his idea, he worked few hours and prioritized other aspects of his life above his venture idea. This was a continuous source of worry for him and without prioritizing his venture he never focused his effort on it. After approximately 1½ years spent developing the service, his venturing efforts faded to zero. With the laissez-faire approach that Jonas took, he did not bring enough energy into the idea to move it forward. For himself consistently during the period of study the venture was something that took up his limited time, but as it came far down on his list, he had to make room for it to do anything at all. He was never happy about this, and even expressed that he rather he did not have any venture at all. In itself the venture thus appeared to be a goal-disruption to the rest of his life.

Eric, who actively tried to cope up and who always saw his venture idea as the most precious goal to achieve did manage to spend time on his venture and to develop the platform. However what he saw as the constant battle between what his heart wanted, the venture idea, and what he should do, his family and his employment, took a toll on his stamina. As problems mounted with the soccer association and also as his partner did not do what he had committed to, Eric found it increasingly more difficult to do everything himself and still fulfill his other commitments. Towards summer 2005 he finally concludes that his venture creation attempts have ceased to exist, and that it is a relief to him.

This is also an example of how goal-disruptions link into each other through the decreasing level of energetic resources. Eric's internal and external pressure to uphold his multiple goals, particularly the non-venture ones, demanded his effort. With lowered levels he had to cope with the testing being disrupted and develop the service to convince the soccer association to allow him to continue testing. Although he was successful in this and was offered a national soccer match for testing, he could not muster the effort needed to actually do the testing. Instead he gradually gave up on the idea.

Nina who faced disruptions that threatened her whole idea and had few possibilities to cope with, took a day to mourn and be angry and use her friends to recover her energy. She then changed her strategy for how to do business based on her funding situation. Instead of directly doing both a physical store and a web shop she decided to initially only focus on a web shop.

She gives credit to her friends for helping her change focus and overcome the difficulties and her disappointment. This also helped her move on and prevented lowered energetic resources that could have spilled over into her next tasks.

Susanne stumbled upon a solution to her problematic prototype when she was looking for people to help her. One person suggested that she should license it. The problem for her is that she cannot license it until it is developed. Instead she found another person who was setting up a venture focusing on licensing as a business idea. This was a new prospect to her and one she felt had more to offer than her own venture idea. As the problems with her prototype continued she now focused more of her effort on the new idea. This in turn meant that she had less time and effort to put into the brush.

Looking back at the beginning of Susanne's venture creation efforts, her idea to develop the brush appealed to her as long as she believed she could keep a high pace and quickly develop the brush to market. As soon as problems arose she began questioning her own basis for venture creation and the two did not synchronize. This is a somewhat different aspect compared with the other cases. It shows how entrepreneurs' intentions must synchronize with what they aspire to do. If this is not the case, as with Susanne, their energetic resources will quickly become lowered and there is not much available for coping with disruptions.

DISCUSSION

In the empirical presentation above, I showed how the studied entrepreneurs appraise and cope with goal-disruptions, as well as the outcomes of this on their venture creation activities.

The presented empirical episodes, where energetic resources come to play indicate that the perceptions of goal disruptions are influenced by the goals and their relevance to the realization of their ideas. How the entrepreneurs appraise goal-disruptions would thus according to theory impact the entire process. Interpreting it as a threat would bring negative stress, more likely to incapacitate action and generate negative emotions, while interpreting it as a challenge would have the opposite effect. Nina's appraisal, for example, is closer to threat and Eric's to challenge. However when looking at how the episodes unfold, Nina overcomes the disruption through help from her friends and a change in strategy. Eric on the other hand ends up in a downward spiral where his energetic resources eventually runs out and he gives up on his venture idea. So the manner in which a disruption is appraised does not have a path-dependent impact on what is to come. Nina uses her friends to help her refill her energetic resources and thus musters the extra effort needed to cope despite her bleak prospects of success and is an example of how entrepreneurs use their social assets to energize themselves and thus function as an external source of energetic resources. Eric's energetic resources are at such a low point that his 'victories' in venture creation does not help lift his energetic resources levels enough to bring in the extra effort for the final steps.

In all the cases presented above, the entrepreneurs' appraise goal-disruptions as severe to the prospects of realizing their venture ideas. As such, relevance influences the stress entrepreneurs feel in respect to disruptions. The coping potential appraised by the entrepreneurs differed between them and later also influenced how they coped and the outcome.

Jonas believes that a problem will arise and that it will be caused by his priorities, but he cannot see how he can change his priorities. Nina cannot foresee any opportunities in the future, based on her initial strategy. Eric is abruptly cut off from testing his service but believes that he will be able to change this to his own advantage. Susanne realizes when facing a disruption that her intentions differ from what she originally thought. Although she believes she will be able to overcome the problems with product development, her emotions are affected and she starts losing interest in her venture idea.

Appraisals of goal disruptions thus begin to tax on the entrepreneurs' energetic resources and they choose coping strategies, either problem- or emotion-oriented.

Jonas takes an emotion-focused coping strategy. He believes he will face disruptions and indeed he does. To cope, he wishes to fail so that there will be no problems, a little like closing his eyes and hoping it will disappear. He takes no active initiatives but waits and hopes that it will somehow solve itself. Nina initially responds emotionally, but her coping is from the beginning problem-focused aiming at overcoming the disruption. Eric's and Susanne's strategies are also problem-focused. These problem-focused strategies have been the attention of earlier entrepreneurship research of coping. Eric's discussions with the soccer association to give him a chance is a case of persuasion (Dees & Starr, 1992). Nina's attempt to make her handling officer change her mind and support her application is a case of co-optation by using others for persuasion (Gargiulo, 1993; Starr & MacMillan, 1990). Susanne's relations with her stakeholders aiming at gaining knowledge and funding which she needs for product development is a case of acting *as if* she was trustworthy and with the required structure (Starr et al., 1990). The problem-focused approaches taken by the entrepreneurs were adaptive to the chosen coping strategies, and were changed when the entrepreneurs did not believe that they produce the desired results.

Coping efforts are important for the influence of energetic resources, the point where emotions arise or are kept at bay. Eric depicts what happens when emotions take 'control precedence' as Gaillard has pointed out (2001). He believes that it is important to fulfill one's obligations and he sets high demands on himself. This eventually puts him in a situation where he has three major contexts in his life to live up to, his private and professional spheres as well as his venture idea. As long as his venture idea works smoothly without incidents everything is fine, but when disruptions arise, he feels that his life gets complicated. Then on top of that, there are problems at work, and at home they take on a major project renovating their house.

Initially he attempts to cope with all aspects, but over time his energetic resources are reduced and eventually his problem-focused strategy for coping turns into an emotion-focused one. Now other parts of his life take precedence and eventually the venture idea itself becomes a goal-disruption to fulfilling his other life goals. As less and less energetic resources become available his appraisal of new disruptions is also affected. Eric is able to cope for shorter period of time, investing heavy in extra effort. But over time he is forced to regulate his energetic resources to cope with the other aspects of his life. This validates energetic resources as a limited resource that needs regulation and replenishment, and in Eric's case it means decreasing the amount of overall goals in his life.

Nina responds differently to similar situations that Eric faces. She regulates her energetic resources by focusing more effort on coping and by implicitly decreasing her attention to other aspects of her life. At the same time as she actively regulates her use of energetic resources she uses strategies to energize herself. Through this she avoids the emotional consequence of depleted energetic resources.

This shows how important it is for entrepreneurs to have energetic resources available on demand as argued in the theoretical framework. Increasing levels of stress and decreasing levels of energetic resources go hand in hand, and emotions arise as an effect of this. When emotions take over, theory and empirical findings indicate that overcoming goal disruptions becomes difficult as other aspects of an entrepreneur's life take over and become more important to the existing channel and decrease energetic resources towards it.

The cases show that entrepreneurs' entire life-situations come to play in how they evaluate and cope with a certain goal disruption. Mobilizing mental effort to maintain performance stability in demanding situations incurs costs to the entrepreneurs' lives. The more severe the goal disruptions, the more effort is needed and the greater the costs. Eric for example states again and again that his relationship with his wife is characterized by equality, that he takes responsibility for his sons and his home. With a view of the importance of such responsibility, it is likely to generate conflicting demands with other goals in times of decreasing energetic resources, and this is is what happens and what eventually leads to his decision to abandon his venture creation efforts.

In addition to entrepreneurs' entire life situations, the importance of regulating emotions, especially under time pressure or threatening situations in order to uphold an efficient task performance is a key issue.

Another aspect of decreasing energetic resources and the need for exerting mental effort is the arrival of moodiness and fatigue. Jonas and Eric keep their mood in check but gradually grow tired of coping with disruptions and balancing their lives. Susanne on the other hand becomes irritated and less interested in her venture idea.

Increasing despair and fatigue is a result and a signal of decreased energetic resources and it also heralds those negative side-effects to an entrepreneur's start-up attempts. As Jonas' and Eric's weariness grow, they have to invest more and more effort into coping, and the episodes show how they finally have no more energy to continue this negative spiral. In addition to this, the fact that it happens, in itself makes them feel even more stressed with pressure to be all they want to be at home, at work and with their venture ideas. Ultimately this begins to influence their perceptions of the disruptions they meet. As they appraise their situations as becoming more and more difficult to handle, what they earlier perceived as disruptions possible to overcome, turn into something impossible. This feeds back into the system and additionally increases stress levels and emotional reactions. In a similar manner Susanne is stuck in a negative spiral.

With Nina's successful regulation of energetic resources and energizing approach, she avoids much of the negative side-effects. What she has to do is to try harder and increase the amount of effort she puts into realizing her idea. As she overcomes goal-disruptions, she stops the negative spiral risking increased stress and perceptions of goal-disruption.

It is thus possible to explain the puzzling result of the entrepreneurs' initial perception of goal-disruptions as a threat or a challenge and their ability to cope or not. Theory would predict that a challenge approach would be more likely to result in successful coping. As the episodes show, this was not the result because Nina with a threat approach was the one coping while Eric did not. A challenge approach is apparently not a sufficient requirement for successful coping and the episodes show why. Nina persisted through a combination of energizing and self-regulation of how she spent her energetic resources. Energizing was achieved externally through her friends as has been discussed, and it was also achieved through self-monitoring. Self-monitoring meant that Nina continuously reframed her approach to the goal-disruptions she perceived and was able to constructively cope[9].

As discussed earlier the empirical study shows that the influence of energetic resources on an individual's attention, behavior and emotions is moderated by the perceived seriousness of a goal-disruptive event – the appraised ability to cope with the situation, the actual result from coping, and the perceived time it will take to cope, as well as the time it has taken to cope up to a certain point.

Concluding the discussion, I will bring in an alternative way of viewing venture creation and the effect this has on the influence of energetic resources. In this chapter, plans and goals run like a red thread, but such a view is challenged by Sarasvathy who proposes that venture creation is characterrized by effectuation (Sarasvathy, 2001). This implies that entrepreneurs do not plan but instead build their ventures through a creative process where they constantly adjust and adapt. However, the entrepreneurs followed in this study, all made plans and set goals which they attempted to attain. This came out in their rhetoric and their actions. When they met disruptions, they used various coping strategies to overcome it. Their choices of strategies were influenced by issues such as their perceptions of the situation and their beliefs in their capacities to cope. Choices and coping were also influenced by the

---

[9] Research has found that avoidance coping, being the opposite of a problem-focused approach devising constructive strategies to overcome goal-disruptions, is more uncommon in people with high internal strategies (Ingledew, Hardy, and Cooper, 1997) resulting in constructive thinking (Katz and Epstein, 1991).

amount of available energetic resources. Eric's energetic resources were gradually taxed by his various commitments and eventually he had no more energy to realize his venture idea, even though he had the possibility to do so. If we ignore the entrepreneurs' own view of what venture creation is and what it entails and assume that they are guided by a perspective of effectuation where the belief that plans are met becomes paradoxical, then what are the implications of energetic resources on the creative process? Without plans and goals, entrepreneurs adapt and cope with what they meet. In the case of Eric for example this would mean that he constantly tries to adapt his venture to the situation he is in while at the same time doing the same in the other aspects of his life. With a perspective of effectuation, energetic resources would thus influence him in a similar way as he still has to exert effort to cope and that effort is limited and must be refilled when drained. However if plans and goals are seen as a non-issue then it becomes difficult to talk about disruptions and thus about coping. This is not necessary though as this study is based on the perceptions of the studied entrepreneurs who clearly express the ever present reality of plans, goals and disruptions in their venture efforts.

CONCLUSIONS

The purpose of this chapter was to explore the influence of energetic resources on entrepreneurs during the start-up process. This was done by studying instances where energetic resources levels restrict or enhance goal performance in the face of goal-disruptions, which threaten the realization of the entrepreneurial idea. This new knowledge deepens our understanding of the entrepreneurial processes, particularly the early stages where knowledge is lacking (Aldrich, 1999; Reynolds et al., 2004). For very early ventures, still far from showing positive performance in any traditional business aspect, the empirical study indicates that entrepreneurs' energetic resources influence whether they are able to continue overcoming goal-disruptions and stay in business or not.

The two main findings from this study are (1) that perceived goal-disruptions force entrepreneurs to prioritize between all life-goals as a consequence of decreasing energetic resources, and (2) that entrepreneurs can energize themselves, thus offering a way to off-set the consequences of decreasing energetic resources.

Concerning the first finding, each entrepreneur has a different amount of energetic resources, perceive the importance of an instance of goal-disruptions differently, and perceive his or her ability to cope differently. The perception of importance and ability to cope are linked since disruptions which can easily be overcome pose little threat, while those which are perceived as impossible to overcome could have terminable consequences to an emerging venture. The former only slightly taps the energetic resources while the latter drains it quickly. This study shows that entrepreneurs' commitment[10], coping skills[11], cognitive control[12] and self-efficacy are related to the initial amounts of available energetic resources and also moderates the speed with which it is decreased when facing goal-disruptive events.

The importance of the second finding to the creation of new ventures was shown in the differences in creation attempts between all four entrepreneurs. Nina was the only one who was able to energize herself and continuously overcome the disruptions she met, while Eric gradually lost more and more energetic resources without being able to refill what he lost, eventually terminating in order to uphold his other life-goals. Jonas also had a similar development and Susanne lost interest and could not uphold her energetic resources. Nina is an example of a positive energetic resources spiral and the other three of a negative energetic resources spiral. Entrepreneurs' social assets have an important role in energizing through emotional support primarily from friends in times of hardship. The importance of emotional support from friends has been discussed in entrepreneurship research for a considerable time (see for example Bird, 1989; Jianwen & Harold, 2005; Nelson, 1989), but its use as an energizing strategy and its importance for the survival of emerging new ventures has not previously been acknowledged. In addition to this, an awareness of the need for regulation of energetic resources and the monitoring of this process seems to enable entrepreneurs to move to and stay in a positive spiral.

To entrepreneurship research, in general, the study shows that energetic resources are important, since it enables inclusion of the influence of world outside the start-up activities, which this study shows needs to be taken into consideration. The study points to direct link between entrepreneurs' whole life situation and their perceptions and responses to goal-disruptive events pertaining to their creation attempts.

To practitioners, this need to look at the whole life situation is also important, particularly to stakeholders supporting an entrepreneur's start-up attempts. From a perspective of energetic resources, it is not enough to only focus on the start-up process. All aspects of an entrepreneur's life need to be taken into account to make the most from a support effort. Connected to this is also a support for coaching activities. There are dynamics in relation to

---

[10] Commitment, coping skills, and cognitive control have been positively linked to executives' ability to handle high amounts of stress without becoming ill (Kobasa, 1979). The observations from this study indicate that these concepts in a similar vein allow entrepreneurs to handle more stress without being forced to decrease energetic resources.

[11] See footnote 9.

[12] See footnote 9.

energetic resources, which can both facilitate regulation and help keep energetic resources levels at a more even high. Coaching could help developping these aspects, and as with self-monitoring can help to refill entrepreneurs' energetic resources.

The study suggests that further research is needed into the implications of entrepreneurs' perceptions of disruptions as a threat or a challenge and the implications this has on the model of entrepreneurs' energetic resources and venture creation. The contribution of such research could help further explain why owners make certain choices in respect to their ventures (Gimeno, Folta et al. 1997), and the development of new ventures over time, particularly the early phases (Bruderl and Schussler 1990; Fichman and Levinthal 1991). Energetic resources could thus aid in bridging our knowledge gap between seeing the results of entrepreneurial activity and understanding how new businesses come into existence (Reynolds et al., 2004). In addition to this the study indicates that future research should explore the influence of energetic resources on entrepreneurs' decisions to cease creation attempts.

With the empirical data of this study based on novice entrepreneurs only, it does not compare novice with serial entrepreneurs. However, studies of mental workload indicate that such comparison could be important as mental workload acts as a 'go-between' between task difficulty, skill-level of the individual and observed performance (Moray, 1979). As such it seems to support previous studies of entrepreneurs pointing to experience as a key factor to success (Baron & Markman, 2000; Bruderl, Preisendorfer, & Ziegler, 1992; Shepherd, Douglas, & Shanley, 2000; Wennberg, Forthcoming). According to this, entrepreneurs with previous experience can potentially deal with relatively more difficult tasks without adversely affecting performance than novice entrepreneurs. When using the concept of energetic resources this conclusion becomes less certain according to the study. As individuals during limited periods of time can 'try harder' by incurring additional costs to energetic resources in order to maintain performance levels (Hockey et al., 1986). However this study also points to experience as being an issue with positive effects on energetic resources. Future research should explore this and untangle the dynamics of energetic resources and its effects on novice versus serial entrepreneurs.

REFERENCES

Aldrich, H. E. 1999. *Organizations Evolving*. London, Thousands Oak, New Delhi: SAGE Publications.

Bandura, A. 1997. *Self-efficacy: The exercise of control*. New York: Freeman.

Baron, R. A. & Markman, G. D. 2000. Beyond social capital: How social skills can enhance entrepreneurs' success. *Academy of Management Executive*, 14(1): 106-116.

Baum, J. R. & Locke, E. A. 2004. The relationship of entrepreneurial traits, skills, and motivation to subsequent venture growth. *Journal of Applied Psychology*, 89(4): 587-598.

Beal, D. J., Weiss, H. M., Barros, E., & MacDermid, S. M. 2005. An Episodic Process Model of Affective Influences on Performance. *Journal of Applied Psychology*, 90(6): 1054-1068.

Bird, B. J. 1989. *Entrepreneurial behavior*. Glenview, Ill.: Scott, Foresman.

Bird, B.J. 1992. The Operation of Intentions in Time: The Emergence of the New Venture. *Entrepreneurship: Theory & Practice*, 17(1):11-20.

Bruderl, J. and Schussler, R. 1990. Organizational Mortality: The Liabilities of Newness and Adolescence. *Administrative Science Quarterly*, Vol. 35, 1990.

Bruderl, J., Preisendorfer, P., & Ziegler, R. 1992. Survival Chances of Newly Founded Business Organizations. *American Sociological Review*, 57(2): 227-242.

Cardon, M. S., Zietsma, C., Saparito, P., Matherne, B. P., & Davis, C. 2005. A tale of passion: New insights into entrepreneurship from a parenthood metaphor. *Journal of Business Venturing*, 20(1): 23-45.

Carver, C. S. & Scheier, M. F. 1990. Origins and functions of positive and negative affect: A control-process view. *Psychological Review*, 97: 19-35.

Dees, G. J. & Starr, J. A. 1992. Entrepreneurship through an ethical lens: Dilemmas and issues for research and practise. In D. L. Sexton & J. D. Kasarda (Eds.), *The State of the Art of Entrepreneurship*. Boston: PWS-Kent.

Delmar, F. 1996. *Entrepreneurial behavior and business performance*. Stockholm School of Economics, Stockholm.

Duckworth, K. L., Bargh, J. A., Garcia, M., & Chaiken, S. 2002. The Automatic Evaluation of Novel Stimuli. *Psychological Science*, 13(6): 513-519.

Duffy, E. 1962. *Activation and behavior*. New York: Wiley.

Eisenhardt, K. M. 1989. Building theories from case study research. *Academy of Management Review*, 14(4): 532-550.

Epstein, S. & Meier, P. 1989. Constructive thinking: A broad coping variable with specific components. *Journal of Personality and Social Psychology*, 57: 332-350.

Fichman, M. & Levinthal, D.A. 1991. Honeymoons and the Liability of Adolescense - a New Perspective on Duration Dependence in Social and Organizational Relationships, *Academy of Management Review,* 16(2):442-468

Flanagan, J. C. 1954. The critical incident technique. *Psychological Bulletin*, 51(4): 327-358.

Folkman, S., Lazarus, R. S., Dunkelschetter, C., Delongis, A., & Gruen, R. J. 1986. Dynamics of a Stressful Encounter - Cognitive Appraisal, Coping, and Encounter Outcomes. *Journal of Personality and Social Psychology*, 50(5): 992-1003.

Freeman, G. L. V. 1948. *The energetics of human behavior*. Ithaca: Cornell Univ. Press.

Gaillard, A. W. K. 2001. Stress, workload and fatigue as three biobehavioral states: A general overview. In P. A. Hancock & P. A. Desmond (Eds.), *Stress, workload and fatigue*: 623-640. Mahwah, N.J.: Erlbaum.

Gargiulo, M. 1993. Two-step leverage: Managing constraint in organisational politics. *Administrative Science Quarterly*, 38: 1-19.

Gatewood, E. J., Shaver, K. G., & Gartner, W. B. 1995. A Longitudinal-Study of Cognitive-Factors Influencing Start-up Behaviors and Success at Venture Creation. *Journal of Business Venturing*, 10(5): 371-391.

Gersick, C. J. G. 1994. Pacing strategic change: The case of a new venture. *Academy of Management Journal*, 37(1): 9-45.

Gimeno, J., Folta, Timothy B., Cooper, Arnold C. and Carolyn Y. Woo, 1997. Survival of the Fittest? Entrepreneurial Human Capital and the Persistence of Underperforming. *Administrative Science Quarterly*, Vol. 42, No. 4 (Dec, 1997), pp. 750-783.

Granovetter, M. S. 1985. Economic action and social structure: The problem of embeddedness. *American Journal of Sociology*, 91(3): 481-510.

Greene, P. G. Unpublished paper. Dimensions of perceived entrepreneurial obstacles: Rutgers University.

Hobfoll, S. E. 2001. The Influence of Culture, Community, and the Nested Self in the Stress Process: Advancing Conservation of Resources Theory. *Applied Psychology*, 50(3): 337-421.

Hockey, G. R. J., Gaillard, A. W. K., & Coles, M. G. H. (Eds.). 1986. *Energetics and human information processing*. Dordrecht: Nijhoff in coop. with NATO scientific affairs division.

Hockey, G. R. J. 1997. Compensatory control in the regulation of human performance under stress and high workload: A cognitive-energetical framework. *Biological Psychology*, 45(1-3): 73-93.

Ingledew, D. K., Hardy, L., & Cooper, C. L. 1997. Do resources bolster coping and does coping buffer stress? An organizational study with longitudinal aspect and control for negative affectivity. . *Journal of Occupational Health Psychology*, 2(2): 118-133.

Jianwen, L. & Harold, W. 2005. Roles of Social Capital in Venture Creation: Key Dimensions and Research Implications*. *Journal of Small Business Management*, 43(4): 345.

Kahneman, D. 1973. *Attention and effort*. Englewood Cliffs, N.J.: Prentice-Hall.

Katz, L. & Epstein, S. 1991. Constructive thinking and coping with laboratory-induced stress. *Journal of Personality and Social Psychology*, 61(5): 789-800.

Kluger, A. N. & DeNisi, A. 1996. The effects of feedback interventions on performance: A historical review, a meta-analysis, and a preliminary feedback intervention theory. *Psychological Bulletin*, 119: 254-284.

Kobasa, S. C. 1979. Stressful life events, personality, and health: An inquiry into hardiness. *Journal of Personality and Social Psychology*, 37(1): 1-11.

Landberg, A. Forthcoming. *Resistance to new venture creation*. Stockholm School of Economics, Stockholm.

Lazarus, R. S. & Folkman, S. 1984. *Stress, appraisal, and coping*. New York: Springer.

Lazarus, R. S. 1990. Theory-Based Stress Measurement. *Psychological Inquiry*, 1(1): 3.

Lazarus, R. S. 1991. *Emotion and adaptation*. New York: Oxford Univ. Press.

Lazarus, R. S. 1993. From psychological stress to the emotions: A history of changing outlooks. *Annual Review of Psychology*, 44(1): 1.

Lazarus, R. S. 1999. *Stress and emotion : a new synthesis*. New York: Springer.

Lazarus, R. S. 2001. Conservation of resources theory (COR): Little more than words masquerading as a new theory. *Applied Psychology*, 50(3): 370-408.

Locke, E. A. 1986. *Generalizing from laboratory to field settings : research findings from industrialorganizational psychology, organizational behavior, and human resource management*. Lexington: D.C. Heath and Co.

MacMillan, I. C. 1983. The politics of new venture management. *Harvard Business Review*(November-December): 8-16.

Martinovski, B. & Marsella, S. 2005. *Theory of mind and coping in discourse*. Paper presented at the Artificial Intelligence and the Simulation of Behavior, AISB.

Maxwell, J. A. 1996. *Qualitative research design : an interactive approach.* Thousand Oaks, Calif.: Sage.

Merriam-Webster; Merriam Webster Online; http://www.m-w.com/cgi-bin/dictionary.

Miles, M. B. & Huberman, A. M. 1994. *Qualitative data analysis : an expanded sourcebook* (2. ed.). Thousand Oaks, Calif.: Sage.

Moray, N. 1979. *Mental workload : its theory and measurement : proceedings of the NATO symposium on theory and measurement of mental workload, held at Mati, Greece, Aug. 30 - Sept. 6, 1977.* New York: Plenum P.

Nelson, G. W. 1989. Factors Of Friendship: Relevance Of Significant Others To F. *Entrepreneurship Theory and Practice*, 13(4): 7.

Patton, M. Q. 1990. *Qualitative evaluation and research methods* (2. ed.). Newbury Park, Calif. ; London: Sage.

Perren, L. & Ram, M. 2004. Case-study method in small business and entrepreneurial research - Mapping boundaries and perspectives. *International Small Business Journal*, 22(1): 83-101.

Pettigrew, A. M. 1990. Longitudinal Field Research on Change: Theory and Practice. *Organization Science*, 1(3, Special Issue: Longitudinal Field Research Methods for Studying Processes of Organizational Change): 267-292.

Podolny, J., M. & Baron, J., N. 1997. Resources and relationships: Social networks and mobility in the workplace. *American Sociological Review*, 62(5): 673.

Pribram, K. H. & McGuiness, D. 1975. Arousal, activation, and effort in the control of attention. *Psychological Review*, 82(2): 116-149.

Raphael, A., Kenneth, R. M., Charlene, Z., & John, M. O. 2001. Does money matter?: Wealth attainment as the motive for initiating growth-oriented ventures. *Journal of Business Venturing*, 16(2): 119.

Reynolds, P. D., Carter, N. M., Gartner, W. B., & Greene, P. G. 2004. The Prevalence of Nascent Entrepreneurs in the United States: Evidence from the Panel Study of Entrepreneurial Dynamics. *Small Business Economics*, 23: 263-284.

Sarasvathy, S., D.2001. Causation and effectuation: Toward a theoretical shift from economic inevitability to entrepreneurial contingency. *Academy of Management, The Academy of Management Review*, 26(2):243.

Schonpflug, W. 1986a. Effort regulation and individual differences in effort expenditure. In G. R. J. Hockey (Ed.), *Energetics and human information processing : proceedings of the NATO advanced research workshop on Adaption to stress and task demands ..., Les Arcs, France, 23-28 August, 1985*: xv, 450. Dordrecht: Nijhoff in coop. with NATO scientific affairs division.

Schonpflug, W. 1986b. Behavior economics as an approach to stress theory. In R. Trumbull & M. H. Appley (Eds.), *Dynamics of stress : physiological, psychological and social perspectives*: xvii, 342. New York: Plenum.

Schonpflug, W. & Battman, W. 1988. *The costs and benefits of coping*. Chichester: Wiley.

Selye, H. 1974. *Stress without distress*. Philadelphia: Lippincott Williams & Wilkins.

Selye, H. 1976. *The stress of life* ([2.] rev. ed.). New York: McGraw-Hill.

Shepherd, D. A., Douglas, E. J., & Shanley, M. 2000. New venture survival: Ignorance, external shocks, and risk reduction strategies. *Journal of Business Venturing*, 15(5-6): 393-410.

Smilor, R. W. 1997. Entrepreneurship - Reflections on a subversive activity. *Journal of Business Venturing*, 12(5): 341-346.

Starr, J. A. & MacMillan, I. C. 1990. Resource Cooptation via Social Contracting: Resource Acquisition Strategies for New Ventures. *Strategic Management Journal*, 11: 79-92.

Stephen, C. & Melvin, W. 2006. Entrepreneurial Intention: Triggers and Barriers to New Venture Creations in Singapore. *Singapore Management Review*, 28(2): 47.

Terpstra, D. E. & Olson, P. D. 1993. Entrepreneurial start-up and growth: A classification of problems. *Entrepreneurship Theory and Practice*, 17(3): 5-19.

Timmons, J. A. 1999. *New venture creation : entrepreneurship for the 21st century* (5th ed.). Boston: Irwin/McGraw-Hill.

Van de Ven, A. H. & Engleman, R. M. 2004. Event- and outcome-driven explanations of entrepreneurship. *Journal of Business Venturing*, 19(3): 343-358.

Wennberg, K. (2009) Entrepreneurial Human Capital: A Real Options Perspective. In C. Holmquist & J. Wiklund (Eds.), *Entrepreneurship and the Creation of Small Firms* (pp. 35-63). Cheltenham, UK and Northampton, MA, USA: Edward Elgar.

Wright, R. A. & Brehm, J. W. 1989. Energization and goal attractiveness. In L. A. Pervin (Ed.), *Goal concepts in personality and social psychology*: 169-210. Hillsdale, N.J.: Lawrence Erlbaum Associates.

Yin, R. K. 1994. *Case study research : design and methods* (2. ed.). Thousand Oaks, CA: Sage.

Zohar, D. 1999. When things go wrong: The effect of daily work hassles on effort, exertion and negative mood. *Journal of Occupational and Organizational Psychology*, 72: 265.

Zohar, D., Tzischinski, O., & Epstein, R. 2003. Effects of energy availability on immediate and delayed emotional reactions to work events. *Journal of Applied Psychology*, 88(6): 1082-1093.

8. International Entrepreneurship and the Theory of Effectuation

Svante Andersson

INTRODUCTION

Because of lower trade barriers, increased competition and rapid techno-logical development more and more SMEs start their international operations during the first year of their operation or at least soon after their establish-ment and a great share of their total sales is from foreign markets.

These types of firms have been given several names; usually they are called born global firms or international new ventures. The most common concept is born global, and this is the concept that will be used in this chapter (Rialp, Rialp & Knight, 2005). These developments with more new firms growing internationally from inception or early on have created the new research area international entrepreneurship. A review of international re-search in this field is done by Rialp et al (2005) and also there are studies done in Sweden (Andersson & Wictor, 2003; Bengtsson, 2004; Sharma & Blomstermo, 2003). Sweden is, as a small country, very dependent on inter-national business. Many Swedish companies have been successful on the international market. Large organizations such as Volvo, Saab, Scania, Ericsson, H&M, Electrolux and IKEA are just some of the Swedish firms that are dependent on international business to succeed. Not only the large and old Swedish organizations are dependent on international markets, but also some small young firms are growing fast abroad. Hopefully some of the Swedish born globals will become large and successful multinationals in the future. However, earlier research on Swedish SMEs has shown that born globals are still a rather uncommon phenomenon in Sweden (Andersson & Wictor, 2003). More research is needed to better understand why some SMEs are growing rapidly internationally and others are not. Although the area has been researched for some time there is still a need for theories and concepts that can be used to better understand and explain born globals (Autio, 2005). An important finding that many researchers in this area have pointed out is that internationalization and entrepreneurship are similar processes and that theory from the entrepreneurship area can enhance the understanding of firms' internationalization (Andersson, 2000). Following that suggestion, the theory of effectuation that treats decision-making in an entrepreneurial context (Sarasvathy, 2001) will be used to analyze the phenomenon of born globals. The aim of this chapter is to enhance the understanding of a born global firm's early internationalization process and decision to internationalize by using effectuation theory.

First in this chapter a theoretical background of the research area, international entrepreneurship is presented. Thereafter follows a discussion on two different ways of decision-making, causation and effectuation. Causation models go from many alternatives to one goal while effectuation models start with one set of alternatives that can end in many different ways. In this chapter these two ways of decision-making are discussed in connection with the decision to internationalize. An explorative case study is used to illustrate decision-making processes in born globals. Effectuation theory is used to analyze a born global firm and it is concluded that effectuation theory gives new insights in the born global phenomenon.

INTERNATIONAL ENTREPRENEURSHIP

The development from a small national to a multinational firm has been an area of great research interest and one of the most important models in this field is the so-called Uppsala Model, which was developed by Johanson and Vahlne (1977, 1990). The model defines internationalisation as a process of increasing experiential knowledge (Penrose, 1959). The discussion is focused on development over time and the main themes are the firms' behaviour when it comes to different establishment sequences in terms of markets and entry modes. Markets are entered with successively greater psychic distance. Psychic distance is defined as the factors preventing or disturbing the flow of information between firm and market. Examples of such factors are differentces in language, culture, political systems, level of education, level of industrial development, etc. (Johanson and Wiedersheim-Paul, 1975). The firm's international behaviour in a single market is a consequence of a successively greater organizational learning and commitment. As the firm learns about the market it commits more resources and goes through different steps, which can be described as follows (Johanson and Wiedersheim-Paul, 1975:
- no regular export activities
- export via independent representatives
- export through sales subsidiaries
- manufacturing subsidiaries

The theoretical point of departure of the field of international entrepreneurship is a criticism of the Uppsala internationalisation model and other similar models for being deterministic (Bell, 1995; Reid, 1981; Turnbull, 1987). If the firms are developed in accordance with the models, individuals will have no strategic choices. However, later studies have shown that entrepreneurs can choose to internationalize in different directions (Andersson, 2000). Some firms internationalize rapidly and became global within a short time period after their inception (e. g. Knight & Cavusgil, 1996; Madsen & Servais, 1997). The new internationalizing firms also show a variety of entry modes decisions, which are not in accordance with the step-wise pattern that is discussed above (Andersson, Gabrielsson & Wictor, 2006).

The definition of International Entrepreneurship has developed over time. Wright and Ricks (1994) highlighted it as an emerging research arena defining it as a 'comparison of entrepreneurial behaviour in multiple countries and cultures' and 'organizational behaviour that extends across national borders and is entrepreneurial'. In this setting we will focus on the second view that centres around organizational behaviour across national borders. Here McDougall and Oviatt's (2000) definition got a great influence

'International entrepreneurship is a combination of innovative, proactive, and risk-seeking behaviour that crosses national borders and is intended to create value in organizations'. (McDougall and Oviatt, 2000)

The definition is still developing. The McDougall and Oviatt (2000) definition has its origin in the management literature (e.g. Covin and Slevin, 1989; Miller, 1983) and focuses on the behaviour at the firm level. Firms that are innovative, proactive and take risks are defined as having an entrepreneurial orientation. There is a discussion on how many and which dimensions to include in the entrepreneurial orientation concept (Lumpkin & Dess, 1996). As in entrepreneurship literature, there has also been a discussion in international entrepreneurship regarding the entrepreneurship concept. Oviatt & McDougall (2005) expanded their discussion from earlier by including Shane and Venkataraman's definition on entrepreneurship.

'Examination of how, by whom, and with what effects opportunities to create future goods and services are discovered, evaluated, and exploited'. (Shane and Venkataraman, 2000, p. 218)

The emphasis is that entrepreneurship has two parts: a) opportunities and b) individuals who want to take advantage of these opportunities. Oviatt and McDougall (2005) agree to these observations and see this definition as useful to deviate from the general emphasis on the firm level, entrepreneurial orientations and the many dimensions that are important for definitional purpose. Here the individual entrepreneurs are more focused upon. Some scholars have criticized Shane & Venkataraman's definition because it depicts opportunities as objective phenomena. Oviatt & McDougall agree with this criticism and include Weick's (1995) concept of enactment to emphasize that opportunities are not only in the environment but different entrepreneurs interpret the environment differently and may see opportunities where others do not. Following the above discussion, Oviatt & McDougall (2005) end with the following definition:

International entrepreneurship is the discovery, enactment, evaluation and exploitation of opportunities – across national borders – to create goods and services. (Oviatt and McDougall, 2005, p. 540)

The above definition can be used on different levels (organizations, groups, and individuals). However it relates to the view on entrepreneurship that not only focuses on start-ups but also on entrepreneurial behaviour later on in a firm development (Zahra, Ireland & Hitt, 2000). Also it is built on a view that focus on entrepreneur's ability to interpret the environment differrently, which makes the entrepreneur a central actor to understand firm's development. This definition is also in line with Sarasvathy's (2001) concepts of causation and effectuation that will be discussed in next section.

THE PROCESS OF CAUSATION AND EFFECTUATION

Causation models go from many alternatives to one goal while effectuation models start with one set of alternatives that can end in many different ways. Sarasvathy (2001) exemplifies a causation process as the one described in main-stream text-books in marketing (Kotler, 2003). The logic in these books is that firms should start with analyses of the firm and its environment, and after that create a plan for the firm that is implemented and controlled. The same logic is also used in international and global marketing textbooks (e.g. Doole & Lowe, 2004). The process starts with an analysis of the firm and its international environment. Markets are chosen after an analysis of different markets and different foreign market entry methods are evaluated. Thereafter different market strategies are implemented on different markets. Firms can choose a standardized marketing strategy for all markets (to gain economies of scale) or adapt to different markets (to be able to meet local differences in demand).

Effectuation processes do not go towards one goal. Instead it starts from a given set of means, i.e. on the individual level: Who someone is (traits, tastes, and abilities) what someone knows (knowledge corridors) and whom someone knows (social networks). These questions acknowledge the importance of the individuals in firms' international development (Andersson, 2000) and correspond to the resource based theory of the firm and its physical, human and organizational resources (Barney, 1991). The effectuation theory also points out the importance of networks (Coviello, 2006).

Sarasvathy (2001) argues that while causation processes are more effective in static environments where the future is possible to predict, effectuation processes are regarded more effective when the future is unpredictable. The logic of effectuation is particularly useful in areas where human action is the most important factor shaping the future (Sarasvathy, 2001). In a new firm that is aiming for international markets right from its inception, the environment is hard to predict and the founding entrepreneur is decisive for the firm's development. That is, effectuation logic ought to be applicable in that setting. This discussion is in line with Andersson (2004) who points out different internationalization theories as applicable in static and unpredictable environments. Next, the effectuation theory will be compared with the previous research on international entrepreneurship.

INTERNATIONAL ENTREPRENEURSHIP AND THE THEORY OF EFFECTUATION

The decision to internationalize is a very important strategic decision for a small new firm. However, this decision is not focused upon in literature on internationalization. Benito & Gripsrud (1992) categorized the two dominant schools in internationalization in one process and one economic school. In neither of these schools is the decision to internationalize in focus. More recently a new strand of research has emerged treating the inception and early phases of firms' internationalization, 'international entrepreneurship'. In this strand of research some have focused on firms that internationalize early on after inception. Here the discussion on the firm's start-up and the influence of entrepreneurs has been more intense. To understand the behavior of these firms, concepts and theories have been borrowed from strategic management and entrepreneurship, for instance Knight and Cavusgil (2004) use the resource based view. Other scholars have focused on the entrepreneur and his/her behavior and treats. As in the case of entrepreneurship research (Gartner, 1988), the findings in international entrepreneurship are mixed (Andersson et al, 2004) and there seem to be many different types of entrepreneurs that create born globals. Another fruitful strand of research has focused on networks and born globals (Coviello, 2006). A characteristic of an early internationalizing firm is that they act in new markets that are hard to predict. That is, these firms act in environments where effectuation theory ought to be effective (Sarasvathy, 2001). The advantage with the effectuation theory is that it treats the individual level, the firm level and the environment/ networks with a process perspective. It combines some of the earlier findings on international new ventures and puts them in a more cohesive structure.

Oviatt & McDougall (1994) showed that earlier theories used in international business were not enough to explain the phenomenon of international new ventures. They suggested that entrepreneurship theory and the resource-based view of the firm should be fruitful. These theoretical ideas have been used widely in studies of international new ventures. In the entrepreneurship area the entrepreneurial orientation construct has often been used (Covin & Slevin, 1989). A lack with this type of research is that it is often used in cross-sectional studies and has problem to catch the process involving the development of international new ventures.

The advantage with Sarasvathy's effectuation theory is that it explicitly treats the individual and the firm level. The theory also connects to earlier theories regarding decision making that seem fruitful to understand early processes in international new ventures. Sarasvarthy builds on a school that challenges the assumption of preexistent goals (March, 1991). Decision-making processes are much more complicated than described in traditional text-books (Kotler, 2003). Decisions are made in interactions with others, both inside and outside the own organization. The decision-making process is not an optimization process but rather a process to find a satisfactory solution with many partners involved (Cyert & March, 1963). A consequence of the March discussion is that a linear planning approach is not a good description of decision-making in most firms. This was further developed when scholars of management started to criticize the conceptual understanding of management for being far away from actual managerial practice (Mintzberg, 1973). That stream of research revealed that the classical way to describe managerial work as consisting of activities such as 'planning', 'organizing', 'coordinating', and 'controlling', does not fit the behaviour of individual managers (Hales, 1986). A frequent and often proposed generic finding in previous research on what managers do is that managerial work is characterrized by brevity, variety, and discontinuity (Mintzberg, 1973; Florén, 2006). In Mintzberg's (1994) further research he pointed out the importance of action and synthesis instead of analysis and prediction in decision-making processes.

Sarasvarthy also refers to Weick in her discussion on effectuation. Weick (1979) argues that an organization's environment does not directly affect the organization. Decision makers interpret the organizations' environments and due to earlier experience have developed different cognitive schemas and come up with different interpretations and decisions. Weick's discussion is in line with the cognitive perspective (Sadler-Smith, 2004). In this perspective the focus is on how firms' decision-makers conceptualize information and how this impact decision-making. Decision makers shape their environment through enactment and sense-making. (Rasmussen, Madsen & Evangelista, 2001). In the context of international entrepreneurship, this will lead to the importance to study and get information of the entrepreneurs' activities before they start the born global company. During that period the entrepreneurs create mindsets (cognitive schemata) that make them see international opportunities, where most others do not find them. By including the theoretical points of departure in the effectuation theory, an analysis of a born global firm will be carried out. The following four principles of effectuation, pointed out by Sarasvathy (2001, p. 252), will be used.

1. Affordable loss rather than expected returns.
2. Strategic alliances rather than competitive analysis.
3. Exploitation of contingencies rather than exploitation of pre-existing knowledge.
4. Controlling an unpredictable future rather than predicting an uncertain one.

METHOD

The method in this study is inspired by the critical method described by Alvesson & Deetz (2000). A main point in their discussion is to use empirical findings as arguments for intelligent and interesting interpretations and not as a test if a theory is true or not. In this chapter effectuation is seen as an alternative perspective compared with the dominant paradigm in former literature (causation). This new interpretation of the internationalization decision gives new insights that will increase the understanding of the phenomenon of international new ventures. According to Alvesson & Deetz (2000), it is not possible to study something without theory and all writing is construction. A fruitful way to expand the knowledge of a research area is to study it from different perspectives. Alvesson and Deetz (2000) discuss this matter in connection with management research and the same reasoning can be applied to international business.

This study relies on theoretical rather than random sampling of cases (Eisenhardt, 1989), as the aim of the study is to expand and develop theories and not to make inference about a population on the basis of empirical findings (Yin, 2003). Based on the born global definition used of Andersson & Wictor (2003), a pool of potential companies was identified. From that pool, one specific case was chosen to get more detailed information about and hence achieve a deeper understanding of the decision making processes.

Alfa is a company with a product that consists of a system of cable entries and seals, which is based on a multidiameter technology in rubber that is protected by patents. The company has a market channel strategy built on joint ventures and franchising contracts. All their sales are made through distributors and manufacturers, and they never make any sales directly to end-users. Already from inception, the whole world was regarded as the market for Alfa and the company entered approximately 10 markets per year during their inital years. Alfa was chosen as it was considered the company that, by all criteria, fulfilled our definition of a born global company (Andersson & Wictor, 2003), A company that has achieved a foreign sales volume of at least 25% within three years of its inception and that seeks to derive significant competitive advantage from the use of resources and the sales of outputs in multiple countries.

Both historical records and personal interviews have been collected and used as sources. The study started with data from secondary sources within the company. Annual reports and other written documents were requested and provided. This information was completed with newspaper articles and information from publicly available databases. From these sources, relevant background information such as revenues, income, employment etc. as well as more qualitative information like important historic events and major strategic decisions could be collected for the company,. However, the secondary data was not enough to gain a satisfactory understanding of the companies' international development. Therefore, in the next stage of the data collection process the companies were contacted to get first-hand information from the individuals working within the companies. Key informants with experience from critical internationalization decisions were identified. Secondary data was used as a base to discuss internationalization with the key informants. A semi-structured interview guide was used, and all interviews were taped. The main reason for using a semi-structured approach was to ensure that the discussion was driven by what the respondents felt was important in order to stay as close as possible to their lived experience. The key informants were thus allowed to tell their stories freely and discuss how the international development of the companies has developed over time. This method has been used in earlier studies of small company internationalization by Crick and Jones (2000). Our interviews started in 2000 and the company has been followed up during several years. The founder and first CEO were interviewed as well as the two subsequent CEOs. Based on the information collected, case descriptions of the international development in the company were written. The interviewees were given the opportunity to read and comment on these descriptions. To preserve confidentiality, the name of the company is fictitious.

THE ALFA CASE

Alfa was founded by four colleagues from a company where they were employed in different positions. The four colleagues saw more opportunities than the owner did and therefore started their own business, Alfa, in 1990. Alfa's business is based on Multidiameter technology, protected by patent. Alfa's products consist of a system of cable entries and seals, based on the Multidiameter technology. Besides this, they also offer custom-made systems.

The entrepreneur who was dominant in the start-up of Alfa has a long experience of international business from his former work for a company in the same industry. Right from inception the whole world was regarded as the market for Alfa.

Alfa entered approximately 10 markets per year, and in 2001 they were present in 80 nations. The main early expansion strategy was to work via independent distributors. This was an obvious strategy for breaking into many markets despite a lack of resources. In recent years they also established seven subsidiaries. Sometimes these subsidiaries are regional offices, like the one in Madrid, which also serves Latin-America, and the one in Dubai which serves the Middle East.

The Founder and First CEO

There were four people who started the company. However, there was one very dominant person among them, who was the principal leader. As he put it himself:

'There can only be one captain on the ship.' (The founder and CEO in Alfa.)

The founder had a long experience of international business from his former work as CEO of a company in the same industry. He had both industry and international experience. In school he was more practically than theoretically oriented and he had no academic education.

'I was not motivated in school. My best subject was drawing. What I like with business is to create something new, see opportunities and act.' (The founder and CEO in Alfa.)

Already from inception, the whole world was regarded as the market for the founder. This global mindset was important for the firms' development.

Company Resources

Although the product is important for Alfa's development, it is from the marketing side that the CEO has been the most innovative. Alfa builds on production, yet does not describe itself as a company in the rubber product industry. Instead, Alfa considers itself as a knowledge-based company. They try to out source non-strategic production, thus the production department is rather small. However, in contrast they have a large marketing department. They are very active when it comes to international activities. The CEO tries to recruit people with international experience to key positions in the organisation, to overcome language and cultural differences. Alfa recruited employees that lived in Sweden but have a background in China, Syria and Chile. After a couple of years in Sweden they moved to their former home countries to develop Alfas activities.

'The recruiting of people from different cultural backgrounds was a deliberate strategy to develop our international business.' (The founder and CEO in Alfa.)

Networks

The founder's local and international networks proved important for Alfa's early development, especially during the first few years when it was vital in terms of a good position in the local network vis-à-vis local bankers who were required to finance the early development. In his former position as CEO the founder had built an international network, which was important for Alfa's international development. To grow internationally, Alfa had the ambition to grow through network partners (contacted distributors) and not by subsidiaries. By this strategy Alfa, in a resource lean way, could expand very fast on many international markets.

THE THEORY OF EFFECTUATION AND ALFA'S DECISION TO INTERNATIONALIZE

Sarasvathy's (2001, p. 252) four principles of the theory of effectuation will here be compared with Alfa's early internationalizing and decision to internationalize.

Affordable Loss Rather than Expected Returns

Alfa started with a vision that the whole world should be the market. This vision was a tool to open the eyes for members in the company. It was also a sign to actors inside and outside of the company that the firms aimed for international growth and not for short-term profit.

The company's growth was financed by the founder's financial resources, the company's profits, bank loans and a loan from ALMI (a government organization supporting new firms). The founders aimed for a long-term growth and wanted to keep control of the company. They did not want to include financiers such as venture capitalists that might want to sell the companies after a couple of years to get return on their investments. Going public was not considered as the founders thought that it would lead to a stronger focus on short-term profits. The objective of Alfa was to grow fast internationally and they used all available resources to achieve that goal.

Strategic Alliances Rather than Competitive Analysis

The founder's local and international networks were important for Alfa's early development, especially during the first few years when it was vital in terms of gaining a good position in the local network vis-à-vis local bankers who were required to finance the early development. In his former position as CEO in a firm in the same industry as Alfa, the founder had built an international network, which was important for Alfa's international development.

To be able to grow internationally, as fast as 10 markets per year, Alfa preferred not to start its own subsidiaries internationally. Instead they worked with independent distributors. However, in important markets where they could not find any suitable alliances they started sales subsidiaries. The goal was to sell them preferably by management buyouts, so they did not lock financial resources in own subsidiaries. Markets were chosen primarily where they found distributors with whom they could create a strategic alliance

Exploration of Contingencies Rather than Exploitation of Pre Existing Knowledge

Products were just one part of Alfa's competitive advantage. The main part of their competitive edge was how they developed their relations with customers. Although the product is important for Alfa's development, it is on the marketing side that the founder has been most innovative. Alfa produces rubber products, yet does not describe itself as a company in the rubber product industry. Instead, Alfa considers itself as a knowledge-based company. They try to out source non-strategic production, thus the production department is rather small. However, in contrast they have a large marketing department and are very active when it comes to international activities.

In the first year Alfa focused on the off-shore segment. After a couple of years that segment was saturated and sales did not grow as fast. However, the management broadened their vision and entered other segments such as electronic and constructing industries. This segment has totally different ways of selling the product.

The CEO explained the period of slower growth of the company as a consequence of the CEO's interpretation of business opportunities and not as 'real' environmental circumstances.

'We thought the product was only applicable in a few industries, however this was just a barrier in our minds. We did not think of all other possibilities that were feasible in other industries.' (CEO, Alfa)

To be able to see these opportunities, the management in Alfa needs to change their cognitive mindset and learn a new way. The founder recruited young ambitious personnel with a background from different cultures. He explored these personnel's knowledge about foreign markets and used their knowledge instead of formal market research.

Controlling an Unpredictable Future Rather than Predicting an Uncertain One

The entrepreneur in the international new venture did not follow the industry recipes (Grinyer & Spender, 1979) in the rubber industry. Most producers of rubber are suppliers to other industries such as the car industry and build their competitive edge on cost (a large part of the rubber industry in western Europe and North America has been located to developing countries due to lower costs). The entrepreneur in Alfa saw the company as a knowledge company and not a rubber company. He defined a new way of doing business in the sector and found a niche where he could develop a competitive advantage. Instead of relying on formal market research he used resources within the company to decide which market Alfa should enter and used a market entry strategy that has shown to be successful in other markets.

CONCLUSION

The effectuation theory gives new insights in analyzing the creation of born globals. It is important to point out that the examples from the study have been made to illustrate effectuation logic. Internationalization in born globals is a very complex process that include both causation and effectuation logic. However focus is on effectuation logic and therefore, for theoretical clarity we have focused on these examples in the analysis (Read & Sarasvathy, 2005). The case used in this chapter illustrates how effectuation logic fits with the early development in a born global firm. Firstly, it explicitly treats both the individual level and the firm level. Secondly, it also includes a process perspective that better describes the firm's development than earlier theories used to analyze firms' internationalization.

The effectuation theory put the entrepreneur in focus. The entrepreneur is regarded as an effectuater, that is: 'an imaginative actor who seizes contingent opportunities and exploits any and all means at hand to fulfill a plurality of current and future aspirations, many of which are shaped and created through

the very process of economic decision making and are not given a priority'
(Sarasvathy, 2001).

In line with earlier research on entrepreneurship (Gartner, 1988), we
maintain that the entrepreneurs in born globals are not regarded as special
type of individuals when it comes to who they are. We believe that a more
fruitful way to understand born globals is to study how the firms are
developing and compare this with the behavior of the entrepreneurs in the
born global firms. They are individuals with cognitive limitations, influenced
by their earlier experiences. These individuals have developed heuristics and
inductive logics that lead to the decision that their firms should expand
internationally.

These logics could explain the international behavior in the born global
firms. Contrary to the earlier research on internationalization, born globals
enter many markets in a short time and market choice is not controlled by
cultural differences and psychic distance (Johanson & Vahlne, 1990). Market
choices in a born global firm are better understood by using effectuation
logic, i.e., the effectuater uses his own and his company's resources and
networks and takes advantage of opportunities when they are created or
observed (Weick, 1979). This was also shown in a study where small firms in
established industries followed more of causation strategies, while firms in
emergent industries used effectuation strategies (Boter & Holmquist, 1996).

Market entry modes decisions could also be understood by using an
effectuation logic. Born globals are using different and multiple modes of
entry (Andersson, Gabrielsson & Wictor, 2006). These choices are decided
by a logic that is used on most markets, however the entrepreneur can step
away from this logic if he finds the opportunity on the market interesting
enough.

The effectuation logic also gives new insights to international entrepreneurship literature. Earlier research has found that born globals are expanding
fast internationally and explained that this was a consequence of a planned
niche strategy (Oviatt & McDougall. 1994; Knight and Cavusgil, 1996). The
effectuation logic used in this study show a development that is controlled by
a growth vision and that the entrepreneurs are able to see opportunities that
are not in line with a plan. These findings are in line with Spence & Crick
(2006) who found both planned and emergent strategies in high–tech SMEs
internationalization.

Future research should include the effectuation theory when doing
research on born globals. Especially interesting is to try and catch the process
of internationalization and include the pre start phase that is important to
understand the further development. Both qualitative and quantitative longitudinal approaches are recommended to catch the process view. Observational
studies should be especially useful to find out what decison-makers actually

do in the different phases (Mintzberg, 1973). In this study the very early phases in a firm's international development is treated. Earlier research has pointed out that causation logic should be more useful in later stages of a firm's development (Read & Sarasvathy, 2005). In future research it would be interesting to explore how a company can deal with the challenges that arise when the company grow and if it is possible to change a firm's behavior from effectuation logic to causation logic. A comparison between the behaviors of decison-makers in different stages of the processes ought to give useful implications both for theory and practitioners. Internationalization should also be studied in different context such as different industries to explore if effectuation or causation reasoning is more applicable in different industrial contexts.

The author is grateful for financial support from the Knowledge Foundation (KK-stiftelsen).

REFERENCES

Alvesson, M. & Deetz, S. 2000. *Doing Critical Management Research.* London: Sage Publications.

Andersson, S. 2000. Internationalization of the firm from an entrepreneurial perspective. *International Studies of Management & Organization,* 30 (1): 63-92.

Andersson, S. 2004. Internationalization in different industrial contexts. *Journal of Business Venturing,* 19: 851-875.

Andersson, S., Gabrielsson. J & Wictor, I. 2004.. International activities in small firms. Examining factors influencing the internationalization and export growth of small firms. *Canadian Journal of Administrative Science.* 21 (1): 22-34

Andersson, S., Gabrielsson. J & Wictor, I. 2006. Born Globals' Market Channel Strategies. *International Journal of Globalisation and Small Business.* 1 (4): 356-373.

Andersson, S. and Wictor, I . 2003. Innovative internationalisation in new firms – Born Globals the Swedish case. *Journal of International Entrepreneurship,* 1(3): 249-276.

Autio, E. 2005. Creative tension: the significance of Ben Oviatt's and Patricia McDougalls's article 'toward a theory of international new ventures'. *Journal of International Business Studies,* 36:9-19.

Autio, E, Sapienza, H. J and Almeida, J. G. 2000. Effects of age at entry, knowledge intensity, and imitability on international growth. *Academy of Management Journal,* 43(5): 909-924.

Barney, J. 1991 Firm Resources and Sustained Competitive Advantage. *Journal of Management,* 17 (1): 99-120.

Benito, G. R. G, & Gripsrud, G. 1992. The expansion of Foreign Direct Investment: Disrete rational location Choices or a Cultural learning Process? *Journal of International Business Studies,* 23(3):461-476.

Bengtsson, L. 2004. Explaining born globals: an organisational learning perspective on the internationalisation process. *International Journal of Globalisation and Small Business,* 1 (1):28–41.

Bell, J. 1995. The internationalisation of small computer software firms: A further challenge to 'stage' theories. *European Journal of Marketing.* 29 (8):60-75.

Boter, H. & Holmquist, C. 1996. Industry Characteristics and Internationalization Processes in Small Firms. *Journal of Business Venturing,* 11(6):471-487.

Coviello, N. E. 2006. The Network dynamics of international new ventures. *Journal of International Business Studies,* 37:713-731.

Covin, J.G. & Slevin, D.P. 1989. Strategic management of small firms in hostile and benign environments. *Strategic Management Journal*, 10(1): 75-87.

Crick, D. and Jones M. V. 2000. Small High-Technology Firms and International High-Technology Markets *Journal of International Marketing*, 8(2):63-85.

Cyert, R.M. & March J.G. 1963. *A behavioral theory of the firm*. Englewoods Cliffs, NJ: Prentice-Hall.

Doole, I. and Lowe, R. (2004). *International Marketing Strategy*. Thomson Learning, London.

Eisenhardt, K. M. 1989. Building Theories from Case Study Research. *Academy of Mangement Review* 14.(4):532-550.

Florén, H., 2006. Managerial work in small firms – Summarizing what we know and sketching a research agenda. *International Journal of Entrepreneurial Behaviour & Research*, 12(4): 272-288.

Gartner, W. B. 1988. 'Who is an entrepreneur?' is the wrong question. *American Journal of Small Business,* 12 (4): 11-32.

Grinyer, P.H. & Spender, J.-C. 1979. Recipes, crises and adoption in mature industries. *International Studies of Management and Organization* (9): 113-133.

Hales, C. P. 1986. What Do Managers Do? A critical examination of the evidence. *Journal of Management Studies,* 23(1): 88-115.

Johanson, J. and Vahlne, J.-E. 1977. The Internationalization Process of the Firm - A model of Knowledge Development and Increasing Foreign Market Commitments. *Journal of International Business Studies,* 8: 23-32.

Johanson, J. & Vahlne, J.-E. (1990). The mechanism of internationalization. *International Marketing Review*, 7 (4): 11-24.

Johanson, J. & Wiedersheim-Paul, F. (1975). The Internationalization of the firm: Four Swedish cases. *Journal of Management Studies*, 12 (3): 305-322.

Knight, G. A. and Cavusgil, S. T. 1996. The Born Global Firm: A challenge to traditional internationalization theory. *Advances in International Marketing*, 8: 11-26.

Knight, G. A. and Cavusgil, S. T., (2004). Innovation, organizational capabilities, and the born global firm. *Journal of International Business Studies*, 35:124-141.

Kotler, P. 2003. *Marketing Management*, Englewood Cliffs, N.J: Prentice-Hall

Madsen, T. K. and Servais, P. 1997. The Internationalization of Born Globals: an Evolutionary Process? *International Business Review*, 6:561-583.

Lumpkin, G.T. and G.G. Dess, 1996. Clarifying the Entrepreneurial Orientation Construct and Linking it to Performance. *Academy of Management Review* 21(1): 135-172.

March, J. G. 1991. Exploration and exploitation in organizational learning. *Organization Science*, 2:71-87.

Madsen, T. K. and Servais, P. 1997. The Internationalization of Born Globals: an Evolutionary Process? *International Business Review*, 6:561-583.

McDougall, P.P. & Oviatt, B.M. 2000. International entrepreneurship: The intersection of two research paths. *Academy of Management Journal. 43*: 902–908.

Miller, D., 1983. The Correlates of Entrepreneurship in Three Types of Firms', *Management Science* 29(7): 770-791.

Mintzberg, H. 1973. The Nature of Managerial Work. New York: Harper & Row.

Mintzberg, H. 1994. Rounding Out the Managers Job. *Sloan Management Review,* 36(1):11-26.

Nummela, N. Saarenketo, S. & Puumalainen, K. 2004. A Global Mindset – A Prerequisite for Successful Internationalization. *Canadian Journal of Administrative Sciences,* 21(1): 51-63.

Oviatt, B. M. and McDougall, P. P. 1994. Toward a theory of international new ventures. *Journal of International Business Studies,* 24: 45-64.

Oviatt, B. M. and McDougall, P. P., 2005. Defining International Entrepreneurship and Modeling the Speed of Internationalization. *Entrepreneurship Theory and Practice.* 29 (5): 537–554.

Porter, M. E. 1985. *Competitive Advantage: creating and Sustaining Superior Performance.* New York: Free Press.

Penrose, E.T. 1959. *The Theory of the Growth of the Firm,* Oxford: Basil Blackwell.

Rasmussen, E., Madsen, T.K. & Evangelista, F. 2001. The founding of the Born Global Company in Denmark and Australia: Sensemaking and networking. *Asia Pacific Journal of Marketing and Logistics,* 13 (3): 75-107.

Read, S. & Sarasvathy, S. D. 2005. Knowing what to do and doing what you know: effectuation as a form of entrepreneurial expertise. *The Journal of Private Equity,* 9(1): 45-62.

Reid, S.D. (1981). The decision maker and export entry and expansion. *Journal of International Business Studies,* 12 (2), 101-112.

Rialp, A, Rialp, J. & Knight G. A. 2005. The phenomenon of early internationalizing firms: what do we know after a decade (1993-2003) of scientific inquiry?, *International Business Review,* 14:147-166

Sadler-Smith, E. 2004. Cognitive Style and the Management of Small and Medium-Sized Enterprises. *Organization Studies*, 25(2):155-181.

Sarasvathy, S. D. 2001. Causation and effectuation: toward a theoretical shift from economic inevitability to entrepreneurial contingency. *Academy of Management Review,* 26(2): 243-263.

Sharma, D. D., & Blomstermo, A. 2003. The internationalization process of born globals: A network view. *International Business Review*, 12: 739–753.

Shane, S. & Venkataraman, S. (2000). The promise of entrepreneurship as a field of research. *Academy of Management Review. 25*: 217–226.

Spence, & Crick, D. 2006. A comparative investigation into the internationalisation of Canadian and UK high-tech SMEs. *International Marketing Review,* 23 (5): 524-548.

Turnbull, P.W. (1987), 'A Challenge to the Stages Theory of the Internationalization Process,' in *Managing Export Entry and Expansion*, P.J. Rosson and S.D. Reid, eds. New York: Praeger, 21-40.

Weick, K.E. 1979. *The Social Psychology of Organizing*. Reading, MA: Addison-Wesley.

Weick, K.E. 1995. *Sensemaking in organization*s. Thousand Oaks, CA: Sage Publications.

Wright, R.W., & Ricks, D.A., Trends in International Business Research: Twenty-Five Years Later, *Journal of International Business Studies,* Vol. 25, No. 4 (4th Qtr., 1994), pp. 687-701.

Yin, R.K. 2003. *Case Study Research - Design and Methods.* Newbury Park: Sage.

Zahra, S.A., Ireland, R.D., & Hitt, M.A. 2000. International expansion by new venture firms: International diversity, mode of market entry, technological learning and performance. *Academy of Management Journal, 43*: 925–950.

9. Learning from Swedish Entrepreneurship Research

Carin Holmquist and Johan Wiklund

In this chapter we discuss what can be learnt from Swedish entrepreneurship research, as presented in this book but also from a wider context. In Chapter 1 we pointed to the specific characteristics of Swedish entrepreneurship research:

(a) continued attention to quality of empirical work and extensive empirical work, generally leading to high quality research;
(b) a multitude of approaches to studying entrepreneurship, many of which are novel, and could be inspiring for others;
(c) a great concern for the relevance and practical implications of the research; and
(d) a global outlook, quickly integrating research from the US, Europe and elsewhere.

The contributions of this book bear witness to all of these traits. The extensive empirical work is evident in all chapters and there is a multitude of empirical approaches to the phenomenon ranging from ethnographic case studies to panel studies of large populations relying on government statistics. All chapters are also concerned with relevance and practical implications. The global outlook is visible in the sense that authors are well linked to mainstream global research – but also to specific niches appropriate for the research questions at hand.

As demonstrated, Swedish research on start-up and growth is multi-faceted. This variation in disciplinary background, in choice of theories, in methods etc might lead to a scattered picture but on the other hand the object of study – start-up and growth of entrepreneurial ventures – is in itself multi-faceted. For a comprehensive understanding of the phenomena studied, it is essential to allow a variety of perspectives and methods that collectively grasp the complexities at hand.

This openness, we argue, is the hallmark of Swedish research – an openness with its roots in the focus on practical problems and relevance rather than on theoretical schools and methods. Theory and method, in this tradition, are viewed as tools to help understand and/or change empirical phenomena – and not as goals in themselves. The openness is the reason for the variety of theories and methods and also for the acceptance of different scholarly approaches in the Swedish research community – a tolerance which over the years has led to fruitful cross-pollination between different theoretical and methodological schools. Information and communication among entrepreneurship researchers is enhanced by this embrace of approaches. Yet, over time most researchers tend to specialize and position themselves – in terms of object and level of study.

Swedish entrepreneurship research in general, and research on start-up and growth in particular, may on the surface present a scattered image because of the variety in questions, theories and methods. The common denominator is, as pointed out, the focus on empirical problems.

The empirical context is the starting point for the remainder of this chapter. We will discuss how to interpret important trends and themes on the basis of the research presented in this book. Of course we will also use our own experience, our ideas and visions for the future in the discussion. We admit it is not an easy task to identify and discuss themes and trends, especially since we ourselves are part of the Swedish tradition of tolerance and variety.

THEMES

In order to analyze the contribution of this book and to position it within entrepreneurship research more generally, we use the interrogative pronouns: what, why, how, who, where, and when to each of the chapters included. By using these pronouns, we should provide an extensive description of the nature of the chapters.

What refers to the phenomenon studied. *Why* addresses the research question and intended contribution. What motivated the study in the first place? *How* denotes research design and how the study was carried out, *Who* refers to unit of analysis. *Where* refers to the geographical area where the study was carried out. *When*, finally, addresses the temporal aspect of the study and whether data were collected at one or many points of time.

Our responses to these questions are provided in Table 9.1.

Although the chapters included in this book are vastly different, we can see that the answers to the questions what, why, how, who, where, and when actually provides some noticeable similarities that are worthy of further commentary. The chapters are all 'traditionally' Swedish in the sense that they have a strong empirical focus. That is, examining the 'why' dimension of the table, which denotes the research question asked and thus reflects the intended contribution and the motivation of the study, it is evident that research questions and main intended contributions are empirical in all studies; the studies are designed with the primary purpose of filling some empirical void, while theoretical advancement is a secondary consideration.

	What	Why	How	Who	Where	When
Svensson	Commercialization of patents	To describe and analyze the mode chosen for commercialization of patents and which implications this choice has on commercialization performance	Survey and government data	Patent holders	Sweden	Repeated cross-section
Wennberg	Entry into and exit from self-employment	To highlight the distinction between how entrepreneurial human capital affects entrepreneurial entry, performance and continuation	Government data	All Swedes	Sweden	Panel
Saarinen & Ylinenpää	Start-up and early growth processes	Different strategies during the start-up process and their consequences	Interview-based case studies	University spin-offs and non-spin-offs	Luleå	Longitudinal cases
Wiklund, Delmar & Hellerstedt	Entry into self-employment	The engagement in entrepreneurship by individuals with substantial human capital	Government data	Sweden's whole science and technology labor force	Sweden	Panel
Czernich & Zander	Strategies intrapreneurs use to receive internal support for corporate ventures	To generate systematic knowledge about how intrapreneurs make use of framing as part of their new business venture activities	Face-to-face interviews and surveys	Intrapreneurs	Sweden	Retrospective interviews and survey
Landberg	Nascent entrepreneurs' energy to cope with goal disruptive events	To explore the influence of energetic resources on entrepreneurs during the start-up process.	Interview-based case studies	Nascent entrepreneurs	Stockholm	Longitudinal cases
Andersson	decision making in a born global firm	To enhance the understanding of a born global firm's early internationalization process and decision to internationalize by using effectuation logic.	Interview-based case study	Born global firm	Sweden	Longitudinal case

Table 9.1 Chapter themes: summary

Turning to the data used for analysis, i.e., the 'How' dimension of the table, we again find that the studies included here do not reflect the field in general. Entrepreneurship research is dominated by survey research (Chandler & Lyon, 2001). Out of the seven studies reported in this book, two are indeed based on survey research, but these studies are complemented by face-to-face interviews in one case and secondary data in the other. It is particularly interesting to note that the two studies that rely solely on government data actually analyze all people in the country on the one hand and all individuals with a particular education. What is even more impressive is that these two studies construct panels and follow these individuals for extensive periods of time. It is difficult to imagine that such studies could be carried out in many other countries simply because data of such range and quality are very unusual.

The 'Who' dimension of the table refers to the sampled units of observation used to empirically inform the research question. It is noteworthy that all studies have gone through substantial effort to access units of observation that are appropriate given the research question. For example, Czernich and Zander used newspapers, magazines and personal contacts to find individuals who championed entrepreneurial projects within established companies and Svensson sifted through all Swedish patent applications during a single year to find the individuals that filed these applications. Such painstaking efforts to identify appropriate units of analysis are not the norm in the field. On the contrary, the majority of entrepreneurship research relies on units of analysis that are easy to sample and where sampling frames can be constructed relying on generally available data sources (Chandler & Lyon, 2001). The most common respondent in entrepreneurship research is the owner or founder of a small business or new venture.

Further, in a recent study Brush, Manilova and Edelman (2008) found that there is a general predominance for research on the firm level, with performance as the dependent variable. The chapters of this book are atypical in that respect since there is a strong focus on the individual, or rather on the relations between the individual (patent holder, entrepreneur, employee, or high-tech alumnae) and entrepreneurial ventures.

Examining the 'When' aspect of the table, i.e., the time-aspect of research design, it is apparent that all studies extend beyond examining entrepreneurship in a static cross-sectional manner. Virtually all reviews of the state-of-the art of entrepreneurship research reach the conclusion that more longitudinal research is needed (e.g., Chandler & Lyon, 2001: Davidsson, 2004). This is because entrepreneurship is fundamentally a process and in order to tap into the process nature of the phenomenon, studies are needed that examine changes over time. In this respect the Swedish research included does very well. All studies utilize data from more than one point of time.

WHERE IS THE FIELD MOVING?

Brush et al. (2008) note that there are different views on where our field should be moving. One is inspired by the normal science ideal, the 'brick-by-brick' tradition where science is viewed as a cumulative process. Researchers should build on each other, leading to knowledge constantly becoming more unified and homogeneous – or standardized. Another is the diversity view, the 'niche' tradition where researchers gather in smaller communities, each developing its own methods and theories because there is no theory of entrepreneurship that can account for the diversity of topics that are currently pursued by entrepreneurship scholars (Gartner, 2001). A third is the pragmatic view, the 'problems' tradition where the practical implications of the research for education, practitioners or policy makers is the primary consideration. In this tradition, the research question at hand leads the way and methods and theories are chosen to inform the question. Internationally, the normal science view seems to be gaining grounds, but as shown by Welter & Lasch (2008) and Hjorth (2008) other views are also present and developing.

Examining Swedish entrepreneurship research, we hold that it is gradually moving away from a strong tradition of the pragmatic view to encompass also the two other views – Sweden became more international in its outlook earlier than many other European countries and this has led to a situation where the normal science view is more common than in many other parts of Europe. Our impression is that the pragmatic view remains a very strong undercurrent in Swedish entrepreneurship research and that the adaptation to internationally dominant normal science view has not changed this pragmatism very much. This leads to a unique combination of relevant and rigorous research – a combination made possible by the unique access to high quality data in Sweden.

Texts advocating the normal science view tend to converge on two recommendations. The first is the need for theory driven research and the second is the need for longitudinal data that can deal with the dynamic and emerging nature of entrepreneurship. The field as such is definitely moving in a direction which is in line with these recommendations. The very extensive Panel Study of Entrepreneurial Dynamics (see Gartner, Shaver, Carter & Reynolds, 2004) is a good illustration of an initiative that uses longitudinal data to focus on one of the central issues of entrepreneurship research namely the nature of individuals' behaviors in the process of organizational emergence. Yet another theme is the need for relevance of research – that research addresses (empirically) relevant topics and questions.

The Swedish entrepreneurship research presented in this book relates to the calls for theory driven research and the use of longitudinal data in some distinct ways. First, Davidsson and Wiklund (2001) argue that in order to conduct theory driven research that addresses central issues in entrepreneurship, great care needs to be taken in terms of identifying, sampling, and analyzing suitable units of analysis. We would argue that this is an area where Swedish research has done extraordinarily well. Rather than settling for the kind of data that is easily available, researchers have sampled the units that are appropriate for the research questions asked. While such an approach makes it possible to conduct empirical research that is theory driven, it is interesting to note that the research carried out indeed is typically not theory driven. Suitable units of analysis is a necessary but not sufficient requirement for conducting theory driven research. Thus, Swedish entrepreneurship research has the potential for doing theory driven research but at the current state appear more concerned about the relevance and practical implications of the research.

Second, the call for longitudinal research has certainly been heeded by the Swedish researchers presented in this book and much of the research presented is of process nature. As such, the research presented here addresses and answers questions that would have been different should it have relied on cross-sectional research design.

WHAT CAN BE LEARNT?

From our discussion it should be clear that we think that much could be learnt from Swedish entrepreneurship research, but also that it can be further developed. For example, the very extensive empirical work that has been conducted should provide a wonderful basis for inductively generating relevant entrepreneurship theory. It would provide a relevant alternative to importing and testing theory which has been developed within other disciplines. Our advice for development of theory is not in conflict with a pragmatic view, rather the opposite since theories can help formulating and analyzing phenomena and problems better.

This said, we are quite proud to be part of the Swedish entrepreneurship research community since the quality and activity is very high. The pragmatic view has helped incorporate ideas, methods and theoretical strands, still adapting them to the Swedish context. During the recent decades Swedish entrepreneurship research has quickly embraced methodological rigor as requested by the international publishing research community. Today, all young researchers are well trained in quantitative as well as qualitative methods. Methodological rigor is enhanced by the access to high quality data Sweden, ranging from official statistics, to high survey response rates and willingness of companies and entrepreneurs to take part in case studies. As shown in this book, it is possible to combine the methodological rigor of the normal science view with the empirical relevance of the pragmatic view – this, we believe, is the best contribution of Swedish entrepreneurship research.

REFERENCES

Brush, C.G., Manolova, T.S. and Edelman, L.F (2008) Separated by a Common Language? Entrepreneurship Research Across the Atlantic. *Entrepreneurship Theory and Practice* (32)2: 249-266

Chandler, G.N. & Lyon, D.W. (2001). Issues of research design and construct measurement in entrepreneurship research: the past decade. *Entrepreneurship Theory and Practice,* 25(4): 101-113.

Davidsson, P. (2004). *Researching Entrepreneurship: International Studies in Entrepreneurship.* Boston: Springer Science

Davidsson P., & Wiklund, J. (2001). Levels of analysis in entrepreneurship research: Current research practices and suggestions for the future. *Entrepreneurship Theory and Practice,* 25(4): 81-99.

Gartner, W. (2001). Is there an elephant in entrepreneurship? Blind assumptions in theory development. *Entrepreneurship Theory and Practice,* 25(4): 27-39.

Gartner, W., K. Shaver, N. Carter, and P. Reynolds (Eds.) (2004). *Handbook of Entrepreneurial Dynamics. The Process of Business Creation,* Sage Publication Inc.

Hjorth, D. (2008). Nordic Entrepreneurship Research. *Entrepreneurship Theory and Practice* (32)2: 313- 338

Welter, F. and Lasch, F. (2008). Entrepreneurship Research in Europe: Taking Stock and Looking Forward. *Entrepreneurship Theory and Practice* (32)2 pp 241- 248

Index